Practices, techniques,
Technologies of Collaboration
— 2nd layer down from
the senior-team collaboration
— The key issues at the
senior level are the willingness
and ability to modify beliefs
that hinder collaboration. = see
Ch. 9, on leadership

THE CULTURE OF
COLLABORATION

MAXIMIZING TIME, TALENT AND TOOLS
TO CREATE VALUE IN THE GLOBAL ECONOMY

EVAN ROSEN

Red Ape Publishing
San Francisco

The publisher offers special quantity discounts on this book for premiums, sales promotions and corporate training. For more information, please contact:

Special Sales Department
Red Ape Publishing
1750 Montgomery St.
San Francisco, CA 94111

415-566-1777 tel
415-664-3653 fax
sales@redapepublishing.com

Book designed by Dottie Marsico
Cover designed by Calvin Chu

First Edition
Printed in the United States of America.
1 2 3 4 5 6 7 8 9 10   10 09 08 07

♾ Printed on acid-free paper.

Library of Congress Cataloging-in-Publication Data
Rosen, Evan.
    The culture of collaboration : maximizing time, talent and tools to create value
    in the global economy / by Evan Rosen.
        p.   cm.
    Includes bibliographical references and index.
    ISBN-13: 978-0-9774617-0-7 (hardcover : alk. paper)
    ISBN-10: 0-9774617-0-X (hardcover : alk. paper)
    1. Business networks. 2. Cooperativeness. 3. Interorganizational relations.
4. Group decision making. 5. Globalization--Economic aspects. I. Title.
HD69.S8R67 2007
658'.046--dc22   2006026299
                                                                CIP

To my parents,
Lois and Gerald Rosen

CONTENTS

PREFACE

Before the BMW X5 Sports Activity Vehicle rolled off the Spartan-burg, South Carolina production line in September of 1999, the automaker's standard time to market was sixty months. But this new vehicle had defied the standard. Thirty five months earlier, the X5 was nothing more than a concept. BMW had slashed time to market almost in half. What had changed?

The X5 was the first BMW vehicle completely developed and produced through telecooperation. BMW defined *telecooperation* as technology-supported collaboration and communication allowing globally-distributed teams to design and produce a product. Also, the automaker was moving from a "sequential" to a "parallel" devel-opment process in which the second phase of design begins before the first phase ends.

The changing economics of the automobile industry required faster concept-to-delivery, and BMW determined that telecoopera-tion was the best way to achieve that goal. The company wisely real-ized that the shift was about much more than tools and systems. BMW anticipated that telecooperation would change the nature of work and the culture of its organization. Therefore, savvy leaders developed ways to integrate telecooperation into every business unit, function, and partner organization.

During the last several hectic months before the X5 launch, BMW invited me to visit its design center in Munich. There a spark flew that ignited the idea for this book. BMW's experience was an early manifestation of a phenomenon that is now pervading organizations of all kinds. The phenomenon is the Culture of Collaboration.

Globalization has created opportunities to maximize time, talent and tools. Realizing these opportunities, however, requires a cultural shift. This book examines the role of culture in collaborating, provides a look inside leading enterprises in multiple industries that create value through the Culture of Collaboration, and offers a framework for making teams and organizations collaboration-friendly.

INTRODUCTION

Our collective culture, particularly in the United States, perpetuates the Myth of the Single Cowboy. This is the notion that one self-sufficient, rugged individual can achieve smashing success without help from anybody. Consider our preoccupation with celebrity. We turn athletes, chefs, politicians, surgeons, television hosts, entrepreneurs, corporate leaders and many others into stars. This tendency creates the impression that we accomplish great feats by ourselves.

In fact, a meal in an upscale restaurant is often the work of an executive chef, sous chef, line cooks, prep people, expeditors, servers and others. And without an anesthesiologist and nurses, a surgeon—not to mention the patient—would be in trouble. The world's best quarterback needs receivers, running backs and linemen. To save Gotham City, Batman needs Robin. And even the Lone Ranger needs his sidekick, Tonto.

Many organizations reinforce the Myth of the Single Cowboy by embracing a star culture. Such cultures reward people for competing with colleagues. The primary motivator often becomes fear rather than value creation. In these environments, getting ahead requires hoarding ideas and information. Why share knowledge with competitors? In such cultures, opportunities to maximize time, talent and tools die on the vine.

The Culture of Collaboration is about changing business models and organizational DNA. Collaborative organizations promote sharing over hoarding, trust over fear and community over isolation.

With these and other values, we can more easily replace linear, serial business models with concurrent, real-time approaches that are infinitely more compelling.

Rather than designing parts individually and assembling them into a product, we can design parts, products and manufacturing processes all at the same time. In service industries, it's a similar story. We can include people from multiple functions in developing services and processes. They can participate simultaneously, instead of passing instructions through levels and functions for others to implement.

The Culture of Collaboration also enables companies to participate in developing, assembling, delivering, and supporting products and services throughout the world. By creating a universe of globally-distributed business partners, organizations can operate as a single enterprise round-the-clock. They may utilize collaboration tools and common processes and systems to reduce barriers including geography and time zones. These partnering companies form the *global collaborative enterprise*, which we will discuss in chapter 10.

With the expectation of closing the distance gap, companies with operations in multiple countries may adopt the right processes, systems, strategies and tools to enable collaboration. In many cases, however, their efforts come up short. Collaboration may occur, but only sporadically. Something is missing.

Managers may blame the lack of collaboration on technological shortcomings. And, in fact, technology plays a role. In most cases, however, the overwhelming reason why collaboration eludes organizations involves culture. This book's fundamental premise is that maximizing time, talent and tools to create value requires the Culture of Collaboration.

> *Without a Culture of Collaboration, the best processes,*
> *systems, tools, and leadership strategies fall flat.*

Let's begin by examining the sweeping changes that are redefining work, business models, and organizations.

CHAPTER 1

CLIMATE SHIFT: EMBRACING RICH, REAL-TIME COLLABORATION

The script has changed.

No matter where we live or how we earn a living, we face a significant shift in our personal and professional lives—the transition to the Culture of Collaboration.

Let's face it. The shift is happening all around us. And it's impacting our work styles, our paychecks, our relationships and our habits. In short, the transition is changing our world. So understanding the implications is key to staying in the game and succeeding.

At work, information used to arrive in our in-baskets, later in our email in-boxes. We received instructions and passed them to others. Somebody else had to do their part before we could do ours. Then we tossed our work product to the next person so that they could fulfill their function. We were running relay races rather than creating and producing in concert with colleagues.

The in-box culture is dead. It's no longer acceptable to let work and requests for decisions languish in email. The quest for value creation has forced the deserialization of work. Simply put, we are curbing the pass-along approach. Receiving

The quest for value creation has forced the deserialization of work.

1

a document or spreadsheet, making notes, and sending it to somebody else for their comments slows decisions and complicates resolution. To solve problems and make decisions efficiently, we must often come together in real time rather than wait for the email, the file, or for somebody else's input.

This workplace trend parallels developments in how we get our news and information. Once upon a time, we waited for information. Each morning the newspaper arrived. Each evening, television networks and local stations broadcasted their newscasts at 5:30 or 6:00 p.m. Then news magazines summed up the news at the end of the week. The media fed us news on schedule rather than on demand.

Now, however, there is no reason to wait for information to reach us. We can get it whenever, wherever, and however we want it. Perhaps more importantly, we can interact with people about the information as we receive it. So rather than waiting for a filtered report regarding the disaster, the election or the scientific study, we can get primary-source information on demand and analyze the implications in real time with people who share our interests.

Likewise at work, as issues arise, we can collaborate in real time with people throughout the supply chain or decision chain regardless of their location. Deserialization is reaching beyond interaction, beyond decision making and is impacting how we develop and produce products and services. Real-time is the name of the game. In manufacturing, a key challenge is to transition from linear to concurrent design. This involves composing parts while simultaneously designing the product and the manufacturing processes. As we will discuss in chapter 10, this increasingly means leveraging multiple time zones to create twenty-four hour production.

Immediacy requires rich, interactive environments that bring together globally-dispersed collaborators. Together from anywhere we can design and build cars, planes, trains, ships, buildings, electronic components, animation, commercials, and countless other products and services. In short, we are increasingly interactive and decreasingly passive.

Not long ago, we were isolated. Living in rural areas often meant having minimal contact with urbanites. Also, there was a bigger divide between developing and developed countries. Residing in Karnataka state in India, for example, inhibited interaction with people in the states of Minnesota or Virginia in the United States. If we worked at headquarters, we rarely interacted with colleagues at regional offices. Our focus was more local than global. Isolation, however, is rapidly giving way to community; but this community knows no boundaries of time or space. We increasingly interact with people regardless of location.

> *Isolation is rapidly giving way to community, but this community knows no boundaries of time or space.*

When information flowed mostly in one direction, we often operated in command-and-control mode. We received and issued instructions with minimal input from others. As information increasingly moves in multiple directions, we are more often making decisions based on consensus rather than on shoot-from-the-hip whims of individuals.

A few decades ago, formality pervaded business. Men wore suits and ties, and women wore dresses to work. People communicated through letters written with stilted language, and they rarely addressed each other by first name. Office environment design reinforced hierarchy and discouraged interaction. However, we have moved through many stages of decreasing formality. Casual clothing pervades many workplaces. As office walls come down both literally and figuratively, workplace environments encourage sharing ideas rather than hoarding information.

But does the culture match the environment? The design of virtual environments including electronic collaborative spaces and tools makes exchanging thoughts easier. But does the culture accept the capabilities that virtual environments and tools provide? Frequently, culture—collective, regional, organizational, functional, and business unit—lags behind capabilities. Meantime, the pace of business demands real-time solutions and decisions. As the culture catches up with capabilities, interactions are increasingly spontaneous rather than scheduled. We are becoming less formal, less rigid and more flexible.

> *Frequently, culture—collective, regional, organizational, functional, and business unit—lags behind capabilities.*

Against this backdrop, people who were once disenfranchised because of their location, their background, their level, or their role are becoming empowered. When people move to a rural area for family reasons, they can still keep their jobs—even if they are a thousand miles from headquarters. Evolving organizational cultures that increasingly emphasize collaboration over control, coupled with the availability of broadband and collaborative tools, are enabling us to work from anywhere.

In another example of empowerment, factory workers who rarely participated in making product and process decisions now play a role. Factors that once limited their participation, including hierarchy, are becoming less relevant as organizations focus on creating value through collaboration. Broader input from more regions and multiple cultures means greater potential for better decisions and for creating value.

> Broader input from more regions and multiple cultures means greater potential for better decisions and for creating value.

FOUR KEY TRENDS

Four key trends are changing the business landscape and are fueling the demand for richer interactions within and among companies of all sizes. They are:

1. **Technological**: convergence of video, voice and data over Internet protocol (IP).

2. **Economic**: exploiting the best talent at the best price regardless of geography.

3. **Cultural**: the desire for instant feedback and the expectation of immediacy.

4. **Regulatory**: complying with scores of new federal, state and local laws plus treaties.

Each of these broader trends sparks many more specific ones, some that impact all businesses and others that pertain to specific industries—all of which are putting collaboration on the front burner. Let's discuss each trend.

Technological Trend: Convergence of Video, Voice and Data

Converged networking—the ability to carry data, voice and video over a single network—is changing how companies exchange information. Traditionally, companies have kept data, voice, and video separate. Driving the convergence is the lower cost of use and more flexible architecture of a single IP network. The convergence combined with broadband to homes, remote offices and wireless devices creates an environment in which people can collaborate and communicate more effectively regardless of geography.

The convergence also enables integration of collaborative capabilities with business applications. We can launch a voice, video or text exchange from a spreadsheet or from an enterprise resource planning (ERP) system. Also, organizations are integrating systems so that rather than having multiple purchasing systems, all business units use a single, integrated approach. Converged networking coupled with integrated systems creates a common platform so that business units, departments, and regional entities within organizations can easily share data and interact. This, in turn, enables enterprise-wide collaboration in that people in different "silos" within organizations who rarely interacted can now share information.

Economic Trend: Exploiting the best talent at the best price regardless of geography

People are rapidly becoming location-independent. It's no longer necessary to live in major metropolitan areas if we have skills and knowledge to create value. In fact, there's no need to reside in a developed country. Technology is rapidly leveling the playing field, and companies exploit the best talent regardless of location. This applies not only to relatively low-paid call center workers, but also to highly-skilled professionals and managers.

A "reverse brain drain" is drawing talented engineers educated in the United States back to India. Students in China seize opportunities at home rather than seeking employment abroad. Companies,

Location independence creates demand for collaboration, and collaboration fuels location independence by making distributed teams more viable.

in turn, gain the greatest value by recruiting from everywhere, rather than limiting the talent pool to a few regions. Location independence creates demand for collaboration, and collaboration fuels location independence by making distributed teams more viable.

Cultural Trend: The desire for instant feedback and the expectation of immediacy

Not since the Progressive Era early in the twentieth century has business focused so much on time. During that era, efficiency experts used time and motion studies to find the fastest way to perform each stage of production. Charlie Chaplin later satirized industry's maniacal focus on efficiency in *Modern Times* (1936), a quasi-silent movie often considered the last of the silent film genre. Today companies strive to shorten product development time, reduce response time, and deliver parts just in time.

Traditionally, business interactions were mostly scheduled. Making an appointment or scheduling a meeting or videoconference was the standard. Sending an email, fax, memo, letter or leaving voice mail gave colleagues, customers and business partners an opportunity to respond later. But the expectation of immediacy now requires that collaborators come together in spontaneous, real-time interactions. No appointment necessary.

> *The expectation of immediacy now requires that collaborators come together in spontaneous, real-time interactions. No appointment necessary.*

New possibilities always precede new expectations. In the United States, television networks used to run their news divisions at a loss. The pay-off was strictly in soft dollars in that people perceived that the three major networks—CBS, NBC and ABC—performed a public service. When the networks discovered that their news divisions *could* make money, the new expectation became news *must* make money. Therefore, the possibility created a new expectation.

To further illustrate this point about enabling expectations, let's think about eating habits. Before the 1960s in the United States, preparing and eating meals took time. As people increasingly settled in the suburbs and fast food franchising proliferated, getting a quick bite on the road became the norm. As the microwave oven took hold in kitchens, meals could be cooked in minutes rather than in hours. With these developments came the possibility, and therefore the cultural expectation, of satisfying hunger immediately. Similarly, information technology and broadband networks have created the possibility of immediacy in business. And our culture has embraced immediacy as a requirement. Spontaneous, rather than scheduled, interactions address this need.

Regulatory Trend: Complying with scores of new federal, state and local laws

As companies focus on time, governments slow them down with new regulation compliance issues. Obeying laws requires easy access to data and information. Therefore, compliance becomes a key motivator for companies to reduce and integrate myriad information systems, so that enterprises can function more efficiently and data can be found. As systems begin talking to each other, people using the systems begin interacting and new opportunities arise for them to collaborate.

Sarbanes-Oxley, designed to level the playing field for investors, impacts almost every major company. The Patriot Act, a terrorism security measure, impacts many industries. But there are many other new regulations and treaties that affect specific industries. We will discuss compliance in chapter 8.

THE COLLABORATION GAP

The technological trend of converged networks, the economic trend towards exploiting the best global talent, the cultural trend towards instant feedback and the expectation of immediacy, and the regulatory trend towards compliance have spotlighted collaboration. Globally-dispersed people must now collaborate to design, produce, sell and support products and services.

Globally-dispersed people must now collaborate to design, produce, sell and support products and services.

Vendors market a host of products as collaboration solutions, and business embraces *collaboration* as a buzz word. Meantime, these trends spark demand for a new generation of collaborative tools. However, a gap grows in many companies between the desire to collaborate, or perhaps the desire to appear collaborative, and the creation of value through collaboration.

To collaborate effectively, we must first understand our organizational and personal comfort zones. Control often defines the organizational comfort zone. Therefore, organizations *traditionally* favor:

- Chain-of-command decision-making over on-the-fly resolution.
- Scheduled encounters over ad hoc or spontaneous interaction
- The more manageable nature of email over the relative free-for-all of instant messaging

To stay in our personal comfort zones, we as individuals often embrace:

- Status quo over change
- Procrastination over resolution
- Hoarding over sharing information

To collaborate effectively, we must BREAK OUT of our organizational and individual comfort zones.

To collaborate effectively, we must BREAK OUT of our organizational and individual comfort zones. Changing our patterns requires a cultural shift that adopts collaboration into work styles and lifestyles. To make this happen, we must understand how culture impacts collaboration and vice versa. In the following pages, we will explore how maximizing time, talent and tools to create value requires a Culture of Collaboration.

WHAT IS COLLABORATION?

Collaboration sounds positive, but what does the word mean? According to Wikipedia, "collaboration refers abstractly to all processes wherein people work together." *The Oxford English Dictionary* defines *collaboration* as "united labour, co-operation; especially in literary, artistic, or scientific work." In *No More Teams!* (Currency Doubleday, 1995), Michael Schrage writes that "collaboration describes a process of value creation that our traditional structures of communication and teamwork can't achieve." Certainly, collaboration creates

AT The senior mgmt level, reflects the idea that no one person has all the answers greater value than do the traditional structures of communication and teamwork. Nevertheless, communication plays a significant role in collaboration.

The meaning of *collaboration* has evolved to reflect the death of distance and the participation of once-unlikely collaborators. *Collaboration* used to suggest shared creation by people in the same place in the same field with similar training—"especially in literary, artistic, or scientific work," as noted above. The implication is that collaboration occurs within these fields rather than across them.

We are conditioned to expect scientists to collaborate on experiments, writers to collaborate on books, and musicians to collaborate on songs rather than to expect a scientist and an artist to collaborate on a product. Increasingly, however, collaboration transcends hierarchy, education, field, function and location. We can define *collaboration* as:

> *Working together to create value while sharing virtual or physical space.*

THE TEN CULTURAL ELEMENTS OF COLLABORATION

There are ten cultural elements that are typically present when collaboration works. They are:

1. Trust
2. Sharing
3. Goals
4. Innovation
5. Environment
6. Collaborative Chaos
7. Constructive Confrontation
8. Communication
9. Community
10. Value

Trust: Developing Comfort with Colleagues

To exchange ideas and create something with others, we must develop trust. A fear among prospective collaborators is that their colleagues will steal their ideas and take credit for them. This concern is legitimate, particularly in competitive organizational cultures. Nevertheless we must get over our fears and develop trust if we are to collaborate effectively.

Ideas often get better as more people kick them around. So the idea that seems priceless is often just a start and needs collaborative input to become ready for prime time. So a "stolen" idea may actually be worth little until others contribute to its development. Running the risk that somebody else may co-opt our concepts can pay off individually and collectively by creating a better idea and greater value. We will explore the role of trust in collaborating in subsequent chapters.

Sharing: Letting Ideas Flow and Grow

It may sound basic, but collaboration requires sharing—and not everybody likes to share. Many people carefully guard their "stuff." These information hoarders like being the go-to guy or woman, forcing their colleagues to seek them out. They may believe that this approach makes them indispensable to their companies. The problem is that hoarding information prevents the free flow of ideas and therefore sabotages collaboration. Sharing what we know improves collective creation by an order of magnitude and therefore makes everybody more valuable.

Goals: Reading from the Same Script

Collaboration requires one or more common objectives or goals. Taking the time to agree on goals at the beginning of a collaborative project pays off exponentially by providing the impetus for shared creation. In contrast, embracing different goals creates conflict, breeds confusion, and short circuits collaboration. Common goals create clarity, encourage brainstorming, and spark innovation and collaboration.

Common goals create clarity, encourage brainstorming, and spark innovation and collaboration.

Innovation: Embracing New Approaches

The desire to innovate fuels collaboration. In turn, collaboration enhances innovation. After all, why collaborate just to maintain the status quo? The best collaboration produces new approaches. Therefore, creating value through collaboration requires real organizational commitment to generating fresh ideas and to innovating processes, products, and services. Clearly, *innovation* is a buzz word that is central to countless corporate initiatives. But there is a difference between talking the talk and walking the walk. Organizations, like humans, often cling to the familiar, so it's a constant struggle to ensure that we develop, recognize, polish and implement great, new ideas.

Environment: Physical and Virtual

The design of both physical space and virtual environments impacts innovation and collaboration. Walk around a company and you get an immediate sense of whether the environment encourages the free flow of ideas, collaboration, and communication.

Sometimes there is a disconnection between a company's commitment to openness and its physical environment.

Are there open spaces where people can congregate informally and talk over a beverage? Are most leaders sequestered on plush executive floors where people talk in hushed tones or do leaders work closer to their teams?

Sometimes there is a disconnection between a company's commitment to openness and its physical environment. Franklin Becker and Fritz Steele in their book *Workplace by Design* (Jossey-Bass Publishers, 1999) describe office environment as providing the "silent language of environmental cues." In effect, workplace environment is a company's body language. And if body language says something different than words, the message gets garbled. Leaders and corporate communicators may invite input and emphasize collaboration, but the environment must reinforce the message.

Because collaborators are often geographically-dispersed, virtual environment is as important as physical environment. How user-friendly are team sites and spaces? Can collaborators easily transition from asynchronous to synchronous interaction? Can collaborators easily reach one another for spontaneous interaction? If collaborators in different countries need to look one another in the eye, how can they do this virtually with the greatest degree of comfort? It is essential that virtual environments enhance collaboration rather than complicate it. The best virtual environments make collaboration at a distance more effective than collaboration across a table. In chapter 3, we will discuss physical and virtual environments.

Collaborative Chaos: Making Room for the Unexpected

> Collaborative chaos means the unstructured exchange of ideas to create value.

While all people and organizations require order, effective collaboration requires some degree of chaos. The word *chaos* often suggests anarchy or disorganization, but the meaning here is different. We can define *collaborative chaos* as the unstructured exchange of ideas to create value. While order encourages predictable results, *collaborative chaos* allows the unexpected to happen and generate rich returns.

The Hirzel Canning Company, which grows and cans tomatoes and specialty sauces near Toledo, Ohio, faces shrinking margins in an increasingly competitive business. The company's culture embraces collaboration internally and with business partners. Leaders expect thinking, input and analysis from every employee regardless of level. Many larger competitors have gained market share through innovative packaging such as plastic squeeze bottles for pizza sauce. Cross-functional collaborators brainstorm about how to compete with larger rivals. Keep the antiquated can or kick the can and replace equipment at considerable cost? Through collaborative chaos, a better solution emerges: create a resealable can.

An organizational culture that embraces collaborative chaos helps us recognize opportunity amid new business challenges and helps us find value in accidents and mistakes. In fact, some of the best "Eureka!" ideas happen by chance rather than through some formal process of idea development. Antibiotics, for exam-

> Some of the best "Eureka!" ideas happen by chance rather than through some formal process of idea development.

ple, were born out of chaos rather than order. While researching influenza, Alexander Fleming noticed that mold had invaded a culture plate of staphylococci and had created a bacteria-free circle around itself. Fleming called this mold penicillin.

The development of artificial sweeteners also happened by accident. In 1976, researchers at Tate & Lyle, a British sugar company, were collaborating with Professor Leslie Hough's laboratory at Queen Elizabeth College, now part of King's College in London. The goal of their research was to find ways of using sugar as a chemical intermediate. A foreign graduate student misread a request for a test of a chlorinated sugar as a request that he taste the substance—and *Voila*! The collaborators discovered an artificial sweetener called sucralose.

Another product developed serendipitously is Scotchgard. In 1953, a group headed by 3M's Patsy Sherman was developing a new kind of rubber resistant to airline fuel. A lab assistant spilled an experimental compound on her new sneaker. Later, Patsy Sherman and chemist Sam Smith noticed that the sneaker resisted soiling, and they recognized the commercial potential of the substance. They switched gears and focused on developing a revolutionary product that could repel oil and water from fabrics.

However, accidents and chance discoveries are just the beginning of collaborative chaos. To create value, cross-functional collaborators brainstorm to turn ideas into products and services. Therefore, we must enable the unstructured exchange of ideas. The Culture of Collaboration requires collaborative chaos.

Constructive Confrontation: Taking a Stand

Great collaboration requires exchanging viewpoints, and sometimes that means constructive confrontation! While many of us may tend towards going along or keeping the peace, the work product of collaborators suffers without voicing opinions. We can define constructive confrontation as expressing candor about ideas. The idea is to confront concepts rather than people. Focus group facilitators conducting market research almost always instruct participants to disagree with one another and challenge prevailing opinions. The facilitators encourage dissent so that they can derive a better, more accurate work product: their report about how the market is likely to receive a product or service.

Former Intel CEO Andy Grove has famously advocated constructive confrontation, which is ingrained in Intel's culture. The idea is to encourage debate so that participants will understand and wrestle with differing points of view. Ultimately, business issues come into clearer focus. In *Only the Paranoid Survive* (Currency Doubleday, 1996), Grove writes, "Debates are like the process through which a photographer sharpens the contrast when developing a print." Grove's point is that debate brings clarity, which management requires to make tough decisions at crucial times. Similarly, collaborators must confront each other so that they can hash out their differences and make their shared creation better.

Communication: Crucial to Shared Creation

Collaboration is inextricably linked with communication. Communication includes interpersonal and organizational. In the interpersonal realm, we should feel comfortable engaging one another. From an organizational perspective, channels of communication must remain open for collaboration to occur. Finding and connecting with people regardless of business unit or geography should be easy. Also, organizational culture should support reaching out across the company to engage potential collaborators.

Is it possible to collaborate without communicating? Collaboration without communication suggests designing a product, planning a budget, or editing a newsletter without exchanging thoughts, information or opinions. Indeed, collaborators must communicate!

Community: Sharing Interests and Goals

In many ways, the acid test for collaboration tools, environments, and approaches is whether they create a sense of community. Community is the sense of belonging we feel in our neighborhoods, in classrooms, in online chat groups, and in work teams. Shared interests and values define community. Without community, we often lack comfort and trust. Therefore, community must be present for effective collaboration to occur.

Value: The Culminating Element

The Ten Cultural Elements of Collaboration culminate in value. Collaboration without creating value is like driving without reaching a destination. We can measure value in many ways. Value is reducing cycle or product development time, creating a new market, solving problems faster, designing a more marketable product or service, or increasing sales. Collaborating to check out cool, new tools or to make the work day pass more quickly falls short. The primary reason we collaborate is to create value.

> *The primary reason we collaborate is to create value.*

A NEW CONSCIOUSNESS FOR COLLABORATION

Collaboration used to be a bad word. At times the word has suggested everything from colluding with competitors in restraint of trade and monopolizing industries to plotting against others. Collaboration owes its unfortunate legacy in part to World War II when the Allies used the word *collaborator* to describe anybody who helped the Nazis.

People who came of age during that era, while they may understand the current meaning of collaboration, nevertheless have lingering negative feelings about the concept. To them *collaboration* at worst may suggest spying for the competition and, considering more recent connotations, at best might mean an egalitarian view of business that challenges hierarchy and authority. The World War II generation has, with few exceptions, retired. Consequently, suspicion of collaboration has receded.

Positive feelings about collaboration in the workplace seem to have coincided with the increasing numbers of women in organizational leadership roles. Recently a Fortune 500 company asked me to coach its senior leadership team to communicate effectively. Before beginning the project, I met with a senior human resources executive and two of her direct reports—all of whom are women.

The idea was to have an off-the-record chat about the personalities involved and what I might be facing. In effect, HR wanted to give me its take on the senior leadership. "Our leaders are almost all men, and many of them rule this place with bravado!" the senior

HR executive exclaimed. "They need to move beyond command-and-control management." One of her colleagues commented, "There's just too much testosterone around here."

The desire for more collaborative leadership has ignited interest among HR people in 360-degree feedback and evaluations. In a 360 evaluation, a manager gets input on his or her performance from people who work above, below and alongside them in the organizational hierarchy. In some cases, business partners—including suppliers and customers—participate in a 360. Getting high ratings often requires that managers seek maximum input before making decisions. A manager who uses a command-and-control approach typically fairs poorly in 360 evaluations. The popularity of 360's has raised awareness about the value of collaborative leadership

Consciousness for collaboration is pervading business.

Today *collaboration* is a good word. CEO's use it in their state of the company speeches. HR people pepper presentations with the word. Public relations people put *collaboration* in news releases. Business and technology magazines publish countless articles about collaboration. Vendors market products as collaboration solutions.

While business embraces the word, many people who use it fail to collaborate! They may meet, talk, and exchange data and information but stop short of creating value. We will explore the nature of collaboration and collaborative culture in subsequent chapters. The important point here is that a consciousness for collaboration is pervading business. While it takes much more than using the word to deliver the benefits of collaboration, paying lip service paves the way for cultural acceptance.

Grappling with Globalization

The rise of the Internet and rapid advances in telecommunications are creating an infrastructure to link the world's economies. Since 148 countries ratified agreements creating The World Trade Organization in 1995, the WTO's agenda of open trade has shifted globalization into high gear. Large corporations and many smaller ones are conducting a broader array of business processes away from headquarters and often in multiple global regions.

Also, companies are increasingly organizing along business unit—rather than regional—lines. So a manager is more likely to lead a globally-dispersed group. Teams

> *Teams may lack cohesion without a Culture of Collaboration.*

are often comprised of members in multiple countries, speaking multiple languages, with various cultural backgrounds. In fact, within many large enterprises, it is the rare team that is confined to a single location. This environment creates advantages in that the team's work product reflects broader input and reach. The down side, however, is that teams may lack cohesion without a Culture of Collaboration.

The Price of Presenteeism

A friend of mine has worked in outside sales from a home office for years. She clearly has the education, ability and insight to lead teams and perhaps companies, but her desire to avoid the office and achieve life/work balance has prevented her from seeking management roles. The office environment drains her energy, because numerous distractions prevent her from achieving her objectives. These distractions include everything from non-productive meetings to becoming a sounding board for colleagues with personal problems. She can accomplish more for herself and for her employer by spending most of her work hours in her home office or at customer locations.

Telework, also called telecommuting, is now mainstream. And by 2010, JALA International forecasts over forty million teleworkers in the United States alone. The availability of broadband has made telework more viable. Meantime, companies that once believed working from home meant goofing off have updated their thinking. Some firms embrace the newer paradigm that results are more important than controlling employees. Many companies that once forbade or discouraged telework have launched programs allowing employees to work remotely, if not every day, at least one day a week.

Reinforcing the telework trend are statistics showing that making people show up can be expensive. Companies have long analyzed the cost of absenteeism. It turns out that presenteeism, the opposite of absenteeism, may hurt the bottom line more than absenteeism.

Presenteeism may hurt
the bottom line more than
absenteeism.

The Harvard Business Review estimates that presenteeism costs U.S. companies $150 billion per year. Presenteeism means coming in early and staying late, often in hopes of achieving job security.

The word can also mean being sick, exhausted, or distracted on the job. Distractions may include eldercare, childcare or other family issues. More companies are realizing that presenteeism impacts teams by hurting morale and slowing progress. To cash in on work/ life balance, organizations are increasingly permitting flexible work hours and telework. They're also encouraging new approaches to collaboration among dispersed teams. Before long, as we will discuss in chapter 4, words like *telework* and *telecommuting* may disappear from the lexicon and the concept of "flexible" work arrangements may fade as new collaboration approaches become commonplace.

Comfort with Being Virtual

At one time, being alone meant feeling isolated. We could reach for the telephone, but a friend with time to chat had to be available when we wanted to talk. Now we can be alone physically without feeling isolated. Consider the rise in chat rooms and online communities or the use of online dating. I know people who were never comfortable with face-to-face mating rituals who delight in discovering potential dates online.

Many people prefer connecting with others online who share their interests in bridge or astrology than talking with numerous people at health clubs, bars, art openings or cocktail parties in hopes of finding somebody with whom they have common ground. Many online gamers get more satisfaction playing with geographically-distant strangers from their terminals than they ever would playing with friends at a video arcade. In short, people feel comfortable being virtual. This trend fuels the growth of telework and home-based businesses.

Because being virtual feels right, people are more open to collaborating virtually. If you're already playing bridge or sharing life experiences with people you've never met, it's easier to plan a presentation, design a newsletter, or develop animation screen-to-screen with somebody you rarely see face-to-face. Of course, collaboration for

Online communities plant the seeds of collaboration.

work is higher stakes than collaboration for play. Nevertheless, online communities plant the seeds of collaboration. Being virtual creates a climate that feeds the Culture of Collaboration.

THE POWER OF PRESENCE

Reaching people is often a hit or miss process. If you want to connect with somebody, you may send email—or maybe an instant message—first. If there is no response, you may try calling his or her work number. Next, assuming you get voice mail, you might call a mobile phone. Depending on your relationship, you might even try a home or home office number. Of course, the person you are trying to reach may be sitting at his or her desk, engrossed in work, and unwilling to be disturbed. Since you are unaware that the person you are trying to reach is busy, you may keep trying the shotgun approach of trying to track him or her down.

What is Presence?

Finding people and determining whether they are available can waste time and energy. Often a gap exists between a collaborator's availability and the knowledge of whether they are available. Presence fills that gap. Microsoft defines presence as the ability of a person or device to communicate with others and to display levels of availability. Presence awareness is the knowledge of the person or device's presence.

Instant Messaging (IM) has introduced us to presence. IM lets us know whether a buddy or colleague is available for text chat. However, presence is spreading across applications, devices and modes of collaboration and communication. Developers are embedding presence into everything from word processing and spreadsheet software to specialized applications like programs insurance adjusters use to value claims. Any device—mobile phone, personal digital assistant (PDA), telephone, videoconference system—can become presence-enabled.

If we are working in a spreadsheet and we have questions regarding an item, we can connect directly from the application with a colleague who has answers. We can view a buddy or colleague list, see whether the appropriate colleague is available, and determine how they can be reached. Modes may include IM, voice, web conferencing, or videoconferencing.

If they are available, we can click on the icon indicating their presence status and connect in real time via any mutually acceptable mode. We can then work together in the spreadsheet. If a colleague is unavailable, we can determine whether somebody else who is available can answer the question. Or, through integration with a presence-enabled calendar program, make an appointment to connect with the colleague in real time.

Presence goes well beyond personal productivity software. Team sites, spaces or portals plus virtual workspaces provide presence icons for each team member. Collaborators can see who is available regardless of location or time zone. From the portal, we can connect in real time with available team members. There are many manifestations of presence. Say you're at a trade show, and you want to meet a colleague or business partner. Presence-enabled mobile devices can let us know whether the person is available, how they can be reached, and where and when we can find them.

We can also customize our preferences to restrict the list of colleagues who can gain immediate access to us. Developers are embedding presence into such enterprise applications as customer relationship management (CRM) and supply chain management. Also, presence-enabled gateways are linking legacy private branch exchanges (PBX) and the public switched telephone network (PSTN) with IP-oriented communications and collaboration.

User vs. Group Presence

There is a distinction between user presence and group presence. While user presence is about the individual, group presence refers to the availability of teams. Suppose you need to have a medical procedure and you want to determine whether your company's health plan covers it. You visit an employee benefits site on the company intranet, find material on the health plan, but are unable to find the answer you need.

From the plan document, you can determine the group presence of the employee benefits team. You may not know any individuals on the team. However, group presence will determine which team members can answer your question, their availability, and through which mode you can connect. You can then establish text chat, voice or video connection with an employee benefits specialist by clicking an icon in the intranet-based application.

Automated Presence

Presence automation means that devices behave intelligently based on user preferences. If you walk through your workplace, for example, your mobile phone may ring if somebody is trying to reach you. But the moment you sit down at your desk, your PC and your mobile phone sense the shift in your behavior and adjust accordingly. If somebody tries to reach you, email or IM may become the preferred mode rather than voice. So, your mobile phone would either no longer ring or would be less likely to ring, depending on your preferences.

While some interactions must be scheduled, there are many others that can occur more efficiently on the fly.

Presence enhances the Culture of Collaboration by encouraging spontaneous interaction.

Presence enhances the Culture of Collaboration by encouraging ad hoc or spontaneous interaction. While some interactions must be scheduled, there are many others that can occur more efficiently on the fly. This is particularly true among team members with tight deadlines. Instead of taking the time to arrange a meeting, phone call, or videoconference, presence allows available collaborators to connect spontaneously using modes that fit their preferences, tool capabilities, and the situation.

THE RISE OF RICH, REAL-TIME COLLABORATION

Technological, economic, cultural, and regulatory trends are creating organizational and individual desires to collaborate. Comfort with being virtual and discomfort with presenteeism compound that urge. The notion of presence plunges collaborative capabilities into applications and distributes those capabilities across multiple devices, so that collaboration fits work styles and lifestyles. Presence also makes it easier to find and reach one another when and how we wish to be contacted.

Rich, real-time collaboration suggests a more fulfilling experience and the use of rich media including real-time video interaction. The phrase describes the marriage of web conferencing and IM capabilities with real-time audio and video. Regardless of which tools and capabilities we choose for particular situations, collaboration is moving well beyond its *Oxford English Dictionary* definition of "united labour, co-operation; especially in literary, artistic, or scientific work" and its *Merriam-Webster Dictionary* definition of "to work jointly with others or together especially in an intellectual endeavor." These definitions smack of elitism and the latter one creates an image of gentlemen in tweed jackets smoking pipes while discussing literary criticism. Collaboration lets people with a variety of skills and talents in multiple fields and functions come together spontaneously to create value regardless of geography.

Rich, real-time collaboration lets people with a variety of skills and talents come together spontaneously and create value.

CHAPTER 2

THE CULTURE OF COLLABORATION

As a tornado approached southeast Minnesota on August 21, 1883, the Mayo Clinic's Culture of Collaboration was already taking shape. Curiosity propelled Drs. Will and Charles Mayo to hitch a horse to a buggy and start towards a slaughterhouse at supper time. The brothers wanted to obtain a sheep's head on which they could practice eye surgery. As the young doctors reached their destination, the sky grew darker. The butchers, having spotted a funnel cloud, were fleeing. The tornado that touched down in Rochester, Minnesota minutes later would determine the Mayo brothers' destiny.

As the brothers galloped home, they witnessed the wind sucking up buildings. A falling cook house cornice smashed the wheels and shafts of the buggy, according to some accounts. Their terrified horse fled, and the Mayos took shelter in a blacksmith's shop, embracing the wall until the storm subsided.

With thirty-seven people dead and more than two hundred injured in southeast Minnesota, The Sisters of St. Francis responded to fate, becoming de facto nurses. Turning their convent, a dance hall, and other public buildings into makeshift hospitals,

Courtesy of Mayo Clinic Archives

Figure 2.1   Doctors Will and Charles Mayo and their father, Dr. William Worrall Mayo, founded the Mayo Clinic on the principle of collaboration. "Individualism can no longer exist," insisted Dr. Will Mayo.

the nuns tended to the injured. Dr. William Worrall Mayo and his sons, Drs. Will and Charles who practiced with their father, worked closely with the nurses. After the temporary facilities closed, the Mother Superior raised the money to build a permanent hospital in Rochester and recruited Dr. William Worrall Mayo to lead the project (see figure 2.1).

The Mayos assembled a cross-functional team of doctors, laboratory experts, business people, and communications specialists.

The sisters and the Mayos would build the first general hospital in southeastern Minnesota. It would be no ordinary hospital, especially for the 1880s. The Mayos assembled a cross-functional team of doctors, laboratory experts, business people, and communications specialists. The team promoted a new approach to medicine called private group practice. "It has become necessary to develop medicine as a cooperative science; the clinician, the specialist, and the laboratory workers uniting for the good of the patient," insisted Dr. Will Mayo. "Individualism can no longer exist." (see figure 2.2) For the first decade, the brothers operated as a team, each doctor trading off as the other's first assistant.

The Mayo Clinic was founded on the principle of collaboration.

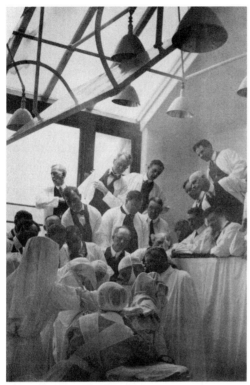

Figure 2.2 Medicine as a cooperative science. Collaborators perform surgery at St. Mary's Hospital, a Mayo Clinic affiliate, circa 1900.

Courtesy of Mayo Clinic Archives

Therefore, diagnosis and treatment at Mayo is different than at most other hospitals. If your home-town doctor finds something suspicious in an X-ray, he or she might send you to a surgeon, oncologist, radiologist or any number of specialists. These physicians may be in different buildings or towns, use different scheduling systems, and have their own bias. A surgeon may prefer to operate. A radiologist may prefer to radiate. An oncologist may prefer chemical treatment. There may be minimal interaction among doctors you consult for a particular problem.

If you present the same problem at the Mayo Clinic, a primary care or coordinating doctor immediately assembles a team to evaluate your condition. All Mayo doctors get a salary, so there is no profit motive to defend turfs. There is a common scheduling system so that you can see all the specialists to whom you are referred within a day or two. The doctors then huddle and discuss your condition until they have determined the best options or course of action. They are then available as a team to answer questions and alleviate concerns. Mayo calls this approach "integrated clinical practice."

If we define culture as the collective attitudes and behavior of a society, region, or organization, the Mayo Clinic certainly has a Culture of Collaboration. Mayo governs itself by consensus leadership. Rather than concentrating power in the hands of a CEO, Mayo spreads influence around the organization. The CEO, required by the bylaws to be a practicing doctor, serves a fixed term and then typically returns to full-time clinical work.

EXPORTING CULTURE

In the mid-1980s, Mayo leveraged its brand by opening clinics in Jacksonville, Florida and Scottsdale, Arizona. Suddenly, distance presented a problem. Jacksonville and Scottsdale were completely different environments from Rochester. Underground walkways connect all major hotels, clinics and office buildings in downtown Rochester so that people can avoid the impact of cold winters. Scottsdale and Jacksonville are sun spots with large retirement age populations. With the drastic differences in environment among its locations, how could Mayo export its organizational culture? Mayo turned to tools.

The culture paved the way for the tool, and the tool has extended the culture.

The earliest collaborative tool that Mayo implemented is a customized paging system still in use today. Anybody can dial five digits and page a colleague at any location. Wall-mounted phones are found throughout Mayo corridors. A paged colleague can hit #, dial their own number and be connected instantly with the person who paged them. The expectation is that any Mayo employee answers his or her pager immediately. One manager tells me that if he were to page Mayo's CEO, he would be talking with him within a few minutes. The culture paved the way for the tool, and the tool has extended the culture.

Shortly after the introduction of the paging system, Mayo's then CEO Dr. Robert Hattery realized that exporting Mayo's culture would require higher-impact interactions. Hattery believed that if employees in Jacksonville and Scottsdale could see their colleagues in Rochester, the team would feel more united—and Mayo would be in a better position to infuse its new locations with a culture encouraging integrated clinical practice and consensus leadership.

Therefore, Mayo implemented a satellite-based videoconferencing network. Hattery believed that the standard practice in many organizations of charging departments or business units for using videoconferencing would impede interaction at Mayo. Videoconferencing should be a utility like water and electricity, Hattery felt, and that any employee should be able to use the tool without any charge to his or her department. Video interaction is now part-and-parcel of Mayo's culture.

TOOLS AND CULTURE

Collaborative tools take hold more effectively in organizations with a Culture of Collaboration. However, culture is dynamic and evolves because of tools. Claude S. Fischer notes in his book *America Calling: A Social History of the Telephone to 1940* (University of California Press, 1994) that early in the last century, people wondered whether the telephone might prevent friends from visiting one another. In fact, the telephone ultimately did reduce face-to-face encounters. However, the telephone allowed people to interact more often and at a greater distance.

> Collaborative tools take hold more effectively in organizations with a Culture of Collaboration.

By the 1920s, the telephone forced organizational cultures to evolve. The new expectation in many companies was that people would make phone calls to arrange meetings. The immediacy of telephone contact increased the speed of business and improved efficiency by ensuring that people's schedules would jive before they attempted to meet.

> When new tools become available, there is often an expectation that they will democratize organizations and society.

When new collaboration and communication tools become available, there is often an expectation that they will democratize organizations and society. In a 1916 public relations announcement, according to Fischer, AT&T insists that "the telephone is essentially democratic." The tool, theoretically at least, gave people greater access to one another.

More recent tools including email have certainly had a democratizing impact on companies and the collective culture. If you send your company's CEO an email, you will generally get a response. Likewise at Mayo, the CEO returns his pages. The difference is that an email recipient responds on his or her schedule, while a page recipient often responds more immediately and on somebody else's schedule.

Often corporate cultures are slow to embrace new tools, particularly those that fundamentally change how people work.

Often corporate cultures are slow to embrace new tools, particularly those that fundamentally change how people work. Employees in such cultures embrace the status quo, cling to their comfort zones, and resist change. In 1995, a large financial services company struggled to achieve a return on its investment in videoconferencing. The company has a reputation for agility and strategic use of technology. Therefore, the lack of video use baffled the company's IT organization. The systems were gathering dust in conference rooms, because there was little consciousness for the medium. These were the days when IT organizations "deployed" tools whether or not users demanded them.

The company asked my colleagues and me to create a strategy that would increase video interactions. The culture circa 1995 was formal and hierarchical, and managers would think twice before initiating interaction with those who outranked them. Our research indicated that because of the culture, videoconferencing was too in-your-face and perhaps overly democratizing. Our strategy emphasized integrating videoconferencing into the culture rather than simply promoting the tool. Ultimately, use of videoconferencing increased by several hundred percent. The cultural approach was necessary, because at the time the company lacked a collaborative culture.

Mayo's culture receives "democratizing" tools more readily, because its founders weaved collaboration into the organizational fabric.

In contrast, Mayo's culture receives "democratizing" tools more readily, because its founders weaved collaboration into the organizational fabric. As Mayo makes available a web conferencing tool with interactive video capability, the challenge for the implementation team differs from that in other organizations. Rather than focusing on internal marketing, the team must figure out how to fend off mounting requests for the new capability. The team is gradually integrating the new tool throughout the organization, meantime monitoring technological developments so that the capability remains state of the art. Because of its collaborative culture and track record using other collaborative tools, Mayo braces for soaring demand.

THE PRINCIPLE-DRIVEN CULTURE

Toyota is another organization that has exported a collaborative culture. The Toyota Way consists of ingrained principles, which are the foundation of its culture. Among the principles is *nemawashi*, which means to prepare a tree's roots for the soil.

Before Toyota changes the wheel base on a car model, it gets broad input from those who design and assemble the vehicle.

The metaphorical meaning is to make decisions slowly by consensus. For example, before the company changes the wheel base on a car model, it gets broad input from those who design and assemble the vehicle.

Toyota's culture grew out of the 1950s when the company faced limited access to capital and small domestic markets in post-World War II Japan. Because there were severe resource constraints, Toyota's concept of lean thinking emerged. The company had to rewrite the rules of the industry by engaging its workforce, creating customer value, and continually improving processes. The company became flexible in manufacturing, producing several cars on the same production line.

In Toyota's view, lean thinking frees people to solve problems, inspires people to innovate, and encourages people to collaborate without the burden of unnecessary rules and management models. Management has never used lean thinking to justify layoffs. In the

Lean thinking frees people to solve problems, inspires people to innovate, and encourages people to collaborate.

challenging environment of 1950s Japan, Toyota nevertheless wanted to create a stable workforce. *Nemawashi* emerged as a way to get all of the stakeholders involved and give them a chance to speak. While *nemawashi* means that Toyota goes slowly up front, the company moves relatively quickly on the back end. Because it has carefully considered a decision, achieved the necessary buy-in, and aligned the organization behind the change, the company can implement decisions faster.

SHORTCOMINGS OF STAR CULTURES

Toyota's culture provides a stark contrast to many organizational cultures that value internal competition. In such cultures, colleagues may view being collaborative as a weakness. In *The Origin of the Species*, Charles Darwin writes about natural selection in which the fittest survive. Many competitive organizational cultures apply a similar concept to workforce development. So that the best rise to the top, a company may eliminate the bottom performing 15 percent of its workforce. Out the door along with the underperformers is trust. Such cultures often pit one colleague against another in that a manager may ask two or more people to prepare proposals. The manager then picks the best one.

COLLABORATIVE

~~Toyota's~~ culture provides a stark contrast to many organizational cultures that value internal competition.

In such cultures, fear dominates as people worry whether their names appear on the elimination lists or whether they can beat out colleagues for recognition and promotion. Such star cultures reward

Without understanding the need for business partners to succeed, competitive companies may negotiate too aggressively and therefore sacrifice partner trust.

individualism rather than collaboration. Why would you trust Joe and share your ideas with him? He will steal your concepts so that he can get promoted over you. Such cut-throat cultures often extend beyond the enterprise to relations with business partners. Without understanding the need for partners to succeed, companies with competitive cultures may nego-tiate too aggressively and therefore sacrifice partner trust.

Many companies that foster competitive, star-oriented cultures chalk up impressive results for stockholders. General Electric is the classic example. In their book, *The War for Talent* (Harvard Business School Press, 2001), Ed Michaels and his McKinsey & Company co-authors quote Chuck Okosky, former GE vice president of executive development as saying, "Bet on the natural athletes...don't be afraid to promote stars without specifically relevant experience, seemingly over their heads. Generally you will be surprised at how well they do."

Malcolm Gladwell, writing in *The New Yorker,* notes that McKinsey, America's largest management consulting firm, advocates a process officially called "differentiation and affirmation" that is commonly referred to as "rank and yank." The idea is to identify a, b, and c players, and treat them according to their ranking. One McKinsey client that adopted the approach with relish and created a star culture was Enron. "The management of Enron, in other words, did exactly what the consultants at McKinsey said that companies ought to do in order to succeed in the modern economy. It hired and rewarded the very best and the very brightest—and it is now in bankruptcy," Gladwell writes, noting that the reasons for Enron's collapse are obviously complex.

In contrast, a key tenet of The Toyota Way is basing decisions on a long-term philosophy, even at the expense of short-term financial goals. Mike Morrison, dean of Toyota's internal university, believes that internal competition delivers results short term but that collaboration builds long term value. "If your suppliers don't trust you and you kind of beat them up on price and your employees don't trust you and you're in a situation of having to throw some of them overboard continuously, it's hard to have that collaborative environment," Morrison insists. "We have such a stable workforce, which is probably one of the reasons the environment is so collaborative. We don't vote anyone off the island. We're all here. It's kind of like a small town. By

Internal competition delivers results short term but collaboration builds long term value.

Figure 2.3   Using Toyota's V-comm system (see profile, page 150), engineers collaborate in a culture that makes decisions slowly by consensus.

nature, the work environment is collaborative." Whenever Toyota integrates new tools into processes, the introduction occurs within the context of consensus-building and the other tenets of The Toyota Way. Therefore, adopting collaborative tools into work styles happens more naturally (see figure 2.3).

CULTIVATING A SHARING CULTURE

The Dow Chemical Company, which creates value through collaboration, was perhaps the first company of its size to conduct all of its videoconferencing over a converged IP network. To leverage the network, called DowNet, Dow has introduced what it calls iRooms (see profile, page 176). The rooms let users in forty-three countries connect via Polycom videoconferencing to any Dow site while collaborating on applications, data, and digital whiteboards (see figure 2.4). Dow managers describe a historic "culture of sharing." Engineering, manufacturing, distribution and sales have always interacted regularly, and the dreaded "silos" or insulation of functions has never developed at Dow as it has at many other large companies.

The collaborative culture has evolved in part because of cross-pollination. Dow regularly reassigns people to different functions, different businesses and different regions so that they understand

Courtesy of The Dow Chemical Company

**Figure 2.4   Collaborating in an iRoom at The Dow Chemical Company.
iRooms extend Dow's historic "culture of sharing."**

many facets of the overall business and can appreciate multiple points of view. Because a collaborative culture existed before the iRooms, most Dow people began using the new tools immediately. Those tools, in turn,

Dow's collaborative culture has evolved in part because of cross-pollination.

enabled Dow to build on its cultural legacy by collaborating more effectively and more broadly.

However, new tools often impact culture; and after Dow provided each of its forty-three thousand employees with notebook computers as replacements for desktop computers, the culture shifted. The implementation team calls it "the changing dynamics of how Dow meets." Notebook-based collaboration plus voice skyrocketed, because mobility fit many work styles.

Dow debated whether to equip its next generation of laptops with cameras for video interactions. The question of whether to make cameras an "orderable service" or a bundled capability was cultural. Dow realized that creating demand for tools was more likely to enhance collaboration than pushing capabilities to people. Ultimately, it made more sense culturally to let users decide whether they want cameras. Even though Dow people regularly use notebook-based collaborative tools and frequently connect via video from iRooms, accepting a camera on one's laptop requires a greater leap of culture. It's one thing to walk down the hall to attend a video-enabled meeting or to use non-video web conferencing from your laptop or desktop computer while talking with colleagues. However, a PC is a personal zone—and using video from that zone requires more trust and a greater propensity to share.

We have to feel enough of an emotional bond with colleagues that we would feel comfortable letting them look at us in our work spaces or, in many cases, our homes. Even though we can control the level of access, uneasiness may linger. Nevertheless, we are becoming increasingly comfortable with web cams and we will increasingly embrace cameras on laptop and notebook computers.

SPONTANEOUS VS. SCHEDULED INTERACTIONS

In companies with Cultures of Collaboration, people are quicker to embrace capabilities that allow spontaneous interaction.

Presence and converged networking, discussed in chapter 1, allow collaborators to connect spontaneously. While technically no appointment may be necessary, culturally it's another ball game. In companies with Cultures of Collaboration, people are quicker to embrace capabilities that allow spontaneous interaction. At Mayo, doctors frequently practice "curbside counsel" during which they grab a colleague, describe a patient's symptoms and get immediate input. So, it's a relatively easy leap from scheduled room-based video meetings to spontaneous, real-time data, voice, and video interactions from desktops and mobile devices.

Procter & Gamble has embraced spontaneous interaction since the company first made instant messaging available to employees in 2000. P&G now leverages presence to enable greater spontaneity in web conferencing and videoconferencing. "With the advancement, evolution of these tools to where they're more broadband and more full duplex, they make more sense in an ad hoc context, whereas before they had to be planned out, laid out, and uploaded," notes Laurie Heltsley, P&G's director of computer and communications services. "A web conference tended to be more of an event and was, of course, scheduled and prearranged."

P&G has focused on deserializing interactions. The company is nudging employees away from the pattern of sending email or leaving voice mail and awaiting a response. This pattern turns interactions that could be completed in minutes into dialogues that may last more than a week, impeding decision-making and slowing problem resolution. Instead, P&G people increasingly connect with each other in real time so that ideas can fly and team members can concurrently make better, quicker decisions. "Urgency is driving us to be faster and more productive than ever. And so we're finding that minutes and days matter," says Laurie Heltsley of P&G. "So when you can shave those off of conversations and get the business outcome sooner, you're driving business forward."

It takes more than tools to spark spontaneous interaction among collaborators.

IM has had unintended consequences for P&G in that it has increased phone use, because sometimes IM interactions escalate into phone calls. Using IM also avoids the need to leave a voice mail. "I know you're not going to call me back until tomorrow. And I really needed to talk to you right now. So the whole idea that I can see right away... are you in the office? Are you working? Can I ask you a quick question?" according to Heltsley. "It's that immediacy and urgency. Immediacy is a big, big thing. Chat mechanisms give you that. Presence mechanisms give you that."

W.R. Grace & Co., the chemical and materials manufacturer, recognizes that fear of failing derails collaboration, particularly in interactions involving real-time tools. So, the internal communications team has worked with business units to ensure that the consequences of making mistakes are small. Mistakes could include everything from choosing the wrong tool to etiquette. This approach has increased the comfort levels of collaborators. As collaborators at Grace increase the frequency of their interactions, they grow less concerned about making impressions and more focused on achieving results.

Collaborators must get accustomed to less structured interactions as ad hoc sessions become more commonplace.

More ad hoc interaction requires a shift in thinking. We traditionally associate many tools with scheduled presentations and meetings. During these higher-profile scenarios, we want to look our best and sound organized. If we have time to plan, the expectation is that we will plan. Spontaneous or serendipitous interactions emphasize chaos and brainstorming over organization. The idea is to let the sparks fly rather than deliver one's ideas from a script or outline. So collaborators must get accustomed to less structured interactions as ad hoc sessions become more commonplace.

HOARDERS VS. SHARERS

While some cultures encourage sharing information, others promote hoarding. Within a hoarding culture, organizations often reward subject matter experts for keeping their expertise to themselves. In their evaluations, these experts will get kudos for attending conferences, reading trade journals, and participating in professional networks that enhance their knowledge of a particular subject area.

However, the reward system is based on gathering knowledge rather than on sharing knowledge. Such cultures cultivate "information hoarders" who consider their professional knowledge a personal asset that increases their power and influence within the organization. Such hoarders avoid contributing to team workspaces, team portals, and interactive brainstorming through web conferencing.

The greater the dependence on knowledge, the more likely a company will have a sharing culture. Management consulting companies rely on knowledge sharing for revenue. Therefore, they often reward and promote employees who share. Companies with a sharing culture may still encourage subject matter experts, but these companies reward those experts based on their dissemination of knowledge rather than for keeping what they know to themselves. Information sharers know instinctively that they will increase their influence if collaborative synergy creates value. While information hoarders and

The greater the dependence on knowledge, the more likely a company will have a sharing culture.

sharers coexist in companies, cultures determine the dominant approach. In short, sharing cultures breed information sharers. And sharers make better collaborators.

MENTORING AND IMENTORING

Cultures that encourage mentoring are prime breeding ground for collaboration. While mentoring is perhaps an uneven relationship in which the protégé defers to the mentor, it is nevertheless a sharing relationship—and sharing must be present for collaboration to occur. At The Dow Chemical Company, where cross-pollination is key to its culture, a tradition of mentoring moves employees gracefully from role to role. When someone wants to change jobs within Dow, the first step is to find a mentor. The mentor informally shows the protégé the ropes before the job shift occurs. Once the protégé is in the new position, the mentor more formally takes responsibility to ensure the protégé's success.

Cultures that encourage mentoring often make prime breeding ground for collaboration.

Because of globalization and the availability of Dow's iRooms, which offer a range of collaborative tools over a converged network, traditional mentoring has morphed into iMentoring. Protégés find mentors who, regardless of their location, have the knowledge and experience they wish to tap. These mentors may work in different business units or in the same unit but in a different region. Protégés learn how their skills may translate into a new role and how the needs of a new business or region may require the protégé's capabilities. However, mentors and protégés rarely share the same physical space. This is in keeping with team composition at Dow where collaborators, using collaborative tools, typically work from multiple countries linked by DowNet.

COLLABORATIVE CHAOS AND CULTURE

Cultures that tolerate collaborative chaos promote collaboration. Of course, chaos conjures up plenty of negative images like food fights in school cafeterias and, worse yet, demonstrations that turn into riots. In chapter 1, we defined *collaborative chaos* as the unstructured exchange of ideas to create value. Collaborative chaos creates value by inviting unintended consequences.

In *Only the Paranoid Survive* (Currency Doubleday 1996), former Intel CEO Andy Grove writes about navigating through strategic inflection points, which are times when a business's fundamentals are about to change. Grove writes that at such times, organizations must loosen up control and allow experimentation. "The operating phrase should be: 'Let chaos reign,'" according to Grove. During Grove's strategic inflection points, it would seem that chaos is really collaborative chaos. Such chaos leads to a shift in strategic direction that ultimately creates value. It makes sense to extend collaborative chaos beyond times of crisis so that organizations can create value 24/7.

IDEO, the product design firm based in Silicon Valley, has institutionalized brainstorming and has created guidelines to advance the art. One such guideline, described by Tom Kelley in *The Art of Innovation*, is "get physical." IDEO encourages its designers to use sketches, diagrams and a range of materials that can be used for crude models. This process precedes actual prototyping.

Despite the guidelines, brainstorming IDEO-style is a form of collaborative chaos in that it encourages people to stretch their creativity, exchange ideas, and create value. Similarly, geographically-dispersed collaborators in many companies can "get physical" virtually by sharing 3D modeling applications at a distance

Collaborative chaos is part and parcel of cultures that inspire collaborators to create value. The Mayo Clinic has created a prototype environment so that collaborators can explore new approaches to patient care. Traditionally, research and development has been geared towards products. However, Mayo conducts R&D for its services, a unique concept in healthcare. Mayo calls the program SPARC, which stands for See Plan Act Refine Communicate. Patient care processes, team design, team communication, and collaboration are the SPARC unit's focus (see figure 2.5).

Typically, SPARC assembles cross-functional teams that come together for a project and then disband. One project example is

Courtesy of Mayo Clinic

Figure 2.5   A cross-functional team conducts R&D for health care delivery at Mayo Clinic's SPARC unit.

refining a process like patient admitting. Mayo has used SPARC to prototype self check-in terminals like those airlines use. The SPARC staff briefs the team on the rapid prototyping process and then facilitates the free flow of ideas. The team monitors the action via video from a space that is steps away from the prototype. Almost everything about this program support space is designed to encourage brainstorming. We will discuss SPARC's physical environment in chapter 3. The point is that SPARC, though based on a specific process, provides a climate that encourages collaborative chaos and creates value for Mayo.

BRIDGING COMMAND AND COLLABORATIVE CULTURES

If you're married or living with somebody, you know the challenges of bridging the habits of two people. You leave the toothpaste tube on the sink, but your partner always puts it in the medicine cabinet. Your partner loves eating a big dinner, but you prefer your largest meal at lunch and a light meal in the evening. You like to exercise at night, but your partner prefers yoga in the morning and watching television or listening to music after dinner. Linking habits and lives requires patience, time, and compromise.

Mergers and acquisitions often create similar challenges for companies. When a cultural divide persists, often the problem is that management has failed to anticipate and acknowledge cultural differences. A classic example is AOL and Time Warner in which a fast-moving Internet-oriented media company merged with an old-line media firm with disastrous results. Numerous analysts have blamed the clash of cultures for at least part of the merger's problems.

Ford Motor Company has acquired several brands in recent years, and the company has wrestled with cultural integration. Any visitor to Ford's world headquarters in Dearborn quickly learns that the culture embraces hierarchy. The tenth and eleventh floors are reserved for executives. Employees talk about vice presidents in hushed tones, and their language suggests command and control. In describing the use of presentation software, one graphic artist who works in the basement tells me that she creates slides "for management to cascade information down through the ranks." Down the road at the information technology organization's home base, the low-slung buildings suggest Silicon Valley. Nevertheless, senior managers park their cars in reserved spots.

Ford Motor Company's Premier Automotive Group does a cultural balancing act in housing its four brands—Jaguar, Land Rover, Aston Martin, and Volvo—under one organization. A command-and-control culture similar to that at headquarters pervades the group's operations in the United Kingdom. However, Volvo is a different story. Consensus defines Volvo's culture which has historically promoted job rotation, small work groups, and management/employee councils. Volvo, based in Sweden, derives its culture from Swedish business culture, which emphasizes cooperation and results over power and position.

If Volvo's CEO were to propose a new strategy or direction during a meeting, a junior person would feel very comfortable telling him that his ideas require further discussion. Volvo people spend considerable time reviewing, negotiating, and discussing. Once they come to agreement, "everybody's all aligned, and they proceed with paced discipline, and it's great to see," according to Kevin Timms, IT Director for Ford Europe and the Premier Automotive Group. In contrast, Timms notes that in his group's UK operations, "If our boss says jump, we usually say how high?"

Ford's Premier Automotive Group has so far succeeded in bridging the two cultures by taking time to understand the differences and by resisting the temptation to shove Ford's dominant culture down Volvo's

Forcing a cultural change could sacrifice the brand.

throat. Ford PAG leaders recognize that Volvo's brand reflects its culture and that therefore forcing a cultural change could sacrifice the brand and hurt the bottom line. UK-based Ford people anticipate how their Volvo colleagues in Sweden feel about issues and vice versa, and the entire group receives cross-cultural training.

As Ford "commonizes" certain commodity parts across its brands, Sweden-based Volvo teams must collaborate with counterparts in the UK. Ford's Premier Automotive Group uses a broad range of tools in bridging the cultures (see figure 2.6). The IT team has discovered that videoconferencing works effectively in closing the gap only if collaborators already know each other from face-to-face meetings. Often the key is the data. Since the language gap only compounds the organizational culture barrier, Ford PAG collaborators have found that they need more than spoken words, more than body language to achieve results. Working simultaneously on diagrams

Courtesy of Ford Motor Company

Figure 2.6   Bridging regional cultures while collaborating across brands within Ford's Premier Automotive Group

and documents shared electronically, cross-cultural colleagues can achieve some meeting of the minds and collaborate effectively despite the barriers of geography and culture.

COLLABORATING IN A LESS-COLLABORATIVE CULTURE

While culture paves the way for collaboration, people nevertheless collaborate in more traditional organizational environments that favor control. Culture often takes years to change and must be inched along in new directions that benefit the organization. Many HR departments have fallen on their faces trying to drag a corporate culture where it doesn't want to go. Indeed, senior leadership often deludes itself that it can order a cultural shift. Ultimately, cultural changes blow across—rather than down—an organization.

> Cultural changes blow across—rather than down—an organization. — Leadership

Companies with traditional cultures that successfully introduce collaboration sometimes leverage a "skunk works." A skunk works is a loosely-structured group of people who, to foster innovation, work on projects in ways that are outside the usual rules. The original was Kelly Johnson's skunk works, the nickname for Lockheed's Advanced Development Projects that began during World War Two. Johnson, considered the best aerodynamicist of his time, hand picked most of his skunk workers. They set up shop in windowless Building 82 next to the Burbank, California airport's main runway.

The intensely-cohesive group of fifty engineers and designers and about a hundred machinists and shop workers built a handful of technologically advanced airplanes for secret U.S. Central Intelligence Agency and Air Force missions. Lockheed's dominant culture favored bureaucracy and command-and-control leadership. In *Skunk Works: A Personal Memoir of My Years at Lockheed* (Back Bay Books, 1996), Ben R. Rich writes that he felt "stymied and creatively frustrated" at Lockheed before Johnson asked him to join the skunk works. The skunk works' relationship with the Air Force was love-hate, according to Rich, because Kelly knocked heads to keep his unit relatively free from "bureaucratic interlopers or the imperious wills of overbearing generals."

To enhance collaboration, companies can implement two types of "skunk works."

To enhance collaboration, companies can implement two types of skunk works. The first, which more closely resembles Kelly Johnson's model, focuses on R&D for products. A small, fast-moving team with a flattened hierarchy can more easily embrace sharing, innovation, and collaborative tools. The second type of skunk works focuses on spreading collaboration—through strategy, tools, and work styles—throughout the organization. This is the kind of skunkworks that W.R. Grace & Co. leverages. William Corcoran's office at Grace is right next to that of CEO Fred Festa. When Corcoran joined Grace several years ago as vice president of public and regulatory affairs, he realized that increased regulation required more effective communication and collaboration within Grace.

Corcoran discovered that a tiny team reporting to human resources had chalked up early successes in training through video and had introduced videoconferencing. The team was bubbling with good ideas but needed freedom to thrive. Corcoran realized the value the team could create, and leveraged his close relationship with Grace Chairman and former CEO Paul Norris to bring the team under his umbrella. Under the leadership of Barry Kuhn, the electronic media group enhances collaboration and communication within the traditional confines of Grace's culture.

The team uses a mix of psychology, journalism, technology know-how, and subtle salesmanship.

With the "protective umbrella" that Corcoran has created, Kuhn and his colleagues push the envelope by integrating new tools and approaches into business processes. The team uses a mix of psychology, journalism, technology know-how, and subtle salesmanship to nudge Grace towards a more collaborative culture. Consequently, business units and functions that rarely interacted before the skunk works kicked into action now collaborate and communicate (see figure 2.7).

Courtesy of W.R. Grace & Company

Figure 2.7 At W.R. Grace & Company, the electronic media group operates as a "skunkworks" with the freedom to jump start collaboration. Now people collaborate across business units and functions.

CRISIS AND CULTURAL SHIFTS

> When industries and companies face crises—and face up to crises—cultures can shift.

The most entrenched corporate cultures can shift because of crisis. After the terrorist attack on the World Trade Center September 11, 2001, many companies that had shunned collaborative tools suddenly embraced them. With airline schedules disrupted, companies sought alternatives to travel. Meantime, with mounting pressure from their families to stay home, employees became open to using tools that they previously might have avoided. These tools included non-video web conferencing and videoconferencing.

A child, fearing a repeat of September 11, tells a parent, "I don't want you to ever get on an airplane again." That type of exchange multiplied by hundreds, perhaps thousands in a company has far more impact on how the organization collaborates and communicates than does any management edict. Such sentiment blows across—rather than down—a company and therefore the cultural shift is natural rather than contrived.

While September 11 created changes to our collective culture, many smaller crises in industries and companies can spark a cultural shift—even in companies with entrenched, non-collaborative cultures. In the textile industry, an artificially-low Chinese currency has allowed companies in China to underprice textile exports. This has caused considerable consolidation, particularly in the United States. Markets have evaporated, mills have closed, and the industry faces an unprecedented crisis. In the pharmaceutical industry, researchers must currently replace a pipeline of products that face patent expiration in the next few years. This combined with increased FDA regulation of the drug manufacturing process has created a challenging environment.

When industries and companies face crises—and face up to crises—cultures can shift. Executives who once stayed in their mahogany-lined offices begin walking through plants. Hierarchies diminish as cross-functional teams tackle problems, sometimes from war room-type settings. While in some cases, the shift happens too late for a company to survive a crisis, in other situations the cultural shift creates new opportunities.

ROLE OF REGIONAL CULTURE

Regional culture impacts collaboration as much as organizational culture does. Often, both regional and organizational forces are at work. Teams may include members from several companies—in the case of business partners—and multiple regions or countries. The habits, expectations, and preferences differ substantially from one region to the next. Because of these differences, regional approaches to collaboration vary.

> Regional culture impacts collaboration as much as organizational culture does.

Italian business culture promotes free-flowing discussion with less structured interaction. In contrast, German business culture favors tightly organized meetings with concrete agendas. Managers often take courses in dealing with other cultures—and sometimes these courses overlook the nuances of communication. A client of mine in Germany, who likely has taken such courses, frequently begins conversations with a rather forced "How is the weather in San Francisco?" Clearly, he has learned that Americans often begin phone calls by discussing the weather. His inclination otherwise would be to dive right into the business at hand as many Germans do. In Chinese business culture, hierarchy plays a major role. Therefore, meetings often revolve around the highest-ranking executive in the room.

Often, there are a variety of regional cultures within a country. These might be termed sub-regional cultures. In India, each region has its own dialect, cuisine, customs and dress. Within the United States, regional cultures vary—though much less now than they did before television and the Eisenhower Interstate System of highways paved the way for a more dominant national culture. When I do business with people in the southern United States, they frequently want to make more small talk, speak more slowly, and stay on the phone longer than people do in other regions. In New York City, where I grew up, the culture is state your business, talk fast, and end the call as quickly as possible. The Midwest perhaps offers a compromise between these two extremes.

The World Bank, comprised of ten thousand employees from 184 countries, provides loans and shares knowledge globally. To help developing nations deal with globalization, the World Bank encourages collaboration among its globally-dispersed staff. The bank has been an early adopter of many collaborative tools, and the organization understands more than most the role that regional culture plays in collaboration.

The Bank is realizing that the appointment model for virtual meetings often falls short. Since Friday is a holy day in Moslem countries, problems arising the previous Wednesday or Thursday in the United States traditionally must wait until the following week before global collaborators can connect and resolve them. This is because team members frequently send an email to arrange a video-conference or web conference, and they typically receive an answer at least one business day later.

To shorten the "time to the goal," The Bank is laying the groundwork for increased ad hoc interaction. Rather than sending email, collaborators are gaining the capability of launching interactive, full-motion video interactions over IP from their PC's through a customized, multi-mode tool. Hajrudin Beca, who taught tele-communications for more than two decades at The University of Belgrade, directs the bank's communications technology strategy.

Cognizant of a range of factors impacting collaboration, Beca takes into account *virtual distance*, a term used by Karen Sobel Lojeski. Virtual distance describes the sense of separation among people regardless of whether they work in the same building or across the ocean. Lojeski's model measures factors that determine how connected team members feel to one another. When there are higher levels of virtual distance, according to Lojeski's research, team members are less likely to share ideas. Beca of the World Bank considers components of virtual distance including geographical, temporal, cultural, gender, educational, and management style as he integrates tools into the World Bank culture. His goal is to reduce virtual distance so that World Bank collaborators feel interpersonally connected regardless of geography.

At Dow Chemical Company, the entire organization has become increasingly aware of regional culture and its impact on collaboration. When senior leaders conduct interactive "broadcasts" to North America, they always encourage questions but may not receive any. During broadcasts to Asia, however, they get flooded with questions. This is because many Asian cultures, particularly Japanese, encourage politeness. If you are given the chance to ask a question, the feeling is, you should accept that opportunity. This notion impacts not only high-profile executive encounters, but also day-to-day interactions among virtual teams.

Despite the role of regional culture, organizational culture increasingly dominates. Companies export their cultures formally through policies and training and informally through jargon, habits and emulating colleagues. People may begin their day from a common company intranet portal and work in a virtual and physical environment that looks similar at all company locations. Interacting constantly with colleagues, they may feel more "Intel" or "Dow" than German or Japanese.

Despite the role of regional culture, organizational culture increasingly dominates.

While China has historically had animosity towards Japan, those tensions recede when people from both countries work for the same company. The same is true of the friction between India and Pakistan. The friction evaporates when Indians and Pakistanis join the same corporate team. "When people come into town and we go out to dinner, regardless of what country you're from, everything is the same," insists a manager at Dow. "Kids are the same…arguing about the same things at home. I mean it's no different. You just live in a different country."

IS WHAT THEY SAID WHAT THEY MEANT?

Dow used to employ 110 freelancers in Montreal to translate seven million words per year in thirty-four different languages. The translations were technically correct. However, translation is an inexact science. In French *une grosse légume* translates literally into *a big vegetable*. However, the meaning is *a bigwig* or *a VIP*. There are countless expressions that mean little if translated literally. Also, language frequently takes on regional dialect and slang. The problem at Dow was that the translation lacked the local flavor and therefore missed the meaning. The company fixed the situation by farming out the translation work around the world.

In collaboration that involves multiple languages or multiple people with different native languages speaking English, meaning can easily escape collaborators. Often, the ability to see one another helps bridge that gap more effectively than using audio, text, or audio plus data and shared applications. When the data becomes more important, the video can be minimized. The key is to read people.

"We know what they said. Is it what they meant? And the only way to get to that is to see people's faces," according to Christopher Duncan, Dow's global leader of communications resources. Americans prefer—and are accustomed to—yes or no answers. Other cultures, including Chinese, are less direct. In such cultures, a flat out *no* would be an insult and a business *faux pas*. But Americans may read the lack of a *no* as a *probably* when in fact the

Americans may read the lack of a "no" as a "probably" when in fact the meaning may be "probably not."

meaning may be *probably not*. Such a gap in communication can certainly impact collaboration!

BUILDING TRUST AMONG MULTI-CULTURAL COLLABORATORS

[handwritten margin note: Are Boolean Virtual teams]

BMW achieved its goal of slashing product development time from sixty to thirty-five months when it introduced the X5, because it considered culture when it introduced telecooperation and focused on building trust among collaborators. To recap from this book's preface, BMW defined telecooperation as technology-supported collaboration and communication allowing globally-distributed teams to design and produce a product.

BMW developed *mirror organizations* in its Spartanburg, South Carolina plant and Munich design facility. Each team member had a counterpart across the ocean with whom he or she collaborated in real time during the shift overlap and asynchronously the rest of the time. This extended the collective work day and accelerated the development schedule. The X5 design team used video when necessary but emphasized sharing designs and data. Standardizing on practices, systems, platforms, and tools ensured that BMW's extended enterprise could collaborate. Ultimately, the ability to telecooperate became a key criterion as BMW selected suppliers.

Leveraging time zone differences requires tackling cultural differences. BMW quickly realized that revolutionizing the way people work is by no means automatic. While some engineering-driven organizations overlook

> *Leveraging time zone differences requires tackling cultural differences.*

culture and instead emphasize tools, the X5 team focused on integrating new work methods into the corporate culture. To that end, the company enlisted thirty employees to become telecooperation promoters, putting one in every department. The promoters coached collaborators and relayed feedback to a centralized telecooperation department. The department's responsibility was to remove obstacles so that people could collaborate more effectively.

The promoters participated in a group called the Roundtable Telecooperation. The roundtable met monthly in Munich with video links to BMW locations and supplier sites globally. The group shared experiences, resolved cultural issues, and made decisions for the strategic implementation of telecooperation tools. Since the telecommunications and information services departments also participated in the roundtable, they understood user concerns and fixed problems faster. Also, the roundtable gave promoters insight into what other departments had learned about telecooperation.

Building trust is a critical success factor in effective collaboration, particularly when bridging regional cultures. Many companies have found that effective collaboration at a distance usually requires collaborators who have shared the same physical space at least once—and preferably multiple times. This helps establish trust, bridge cultural differences, and create a team. With this foundation, distance becomes less of a barrier to effective collaboration. Another approach in building trust is exposing one culture to unique aspects of the other culture. To this end, the German members of the X5 team experienced Thanksgiving—a uniquely American holiday—through a video link.

THE DYNAMIC DIMENSION OF CROSS-CULTURAL COLLABORATION

Build trust and bridge cultures so that collaborators can benefit from their differences rather than fail because of them.

Bridging cultural gaps creates a dynamic dimension perhaps unattainable with homogenous groups of collaborators. Diversity of cultures produces broader perspectives that give collaborators an edge, particularly in solving complex engineering problems. Team members trained in one country's aerospace engineering tradition may view a creative challenge completely differently than their colleagues who were trained in a different country's system. Drawing from their collective global knowledge, cross-cultural collaborators can spark synergies and create greater value. The trick is to build trust and bridge the cultures so that collaborators can benefit from their differences rather than fail because of them.

Boeing achieves the dynamic dimension of cross-cultural collaboration by leveraging the rich tradition of Russian aerospace

Common attributes of collaborative cultures

- Frequent, cross-functional interaction
- Leadership and power spread around organization
- People are accessible regardless of their level
- Reduce fear of failure
- Broad input into decisions
- Cross-pollination of people
- Spontaneous or unscheduled interaction
- Less structured interaction
- Formal or informal mentoring
- Tools fit work styles

engineering. After all, the former Soviet Union chalked up many successes during the dawn of the space age. Sputnik 1, launched in 1957, became the first satellite to successfully orbit the Earth. Boeing learned in the mid-1990s how input from different cultures could create greater value when it asked contract engineers in Russia to help redesign the first class overhead bins on the 777. Instead of having the bins drop down like they do on a 737, Boeing wanted to have them fly out and then dip in an H pattern. The idea was to make it easier to place luggage in the bins.

Boeing provided the initial design for the brackets that the bins slide onto and the initial design for the hangers, the part of the overhead bin that is riveted to the inside of the airplane. The company informed the Russian engineers about the specific changes it wanted and explained the design constraints. Rather than tackling the assignment exactly the way Boeing expected, the Russian engineers redesigned not only the overhead bins but also the brackets. Using a bracket cut out of a single piece of metal, the Russian engineers produced a prototype overhead bin that included few moving parts and no fasteners. The Russian design required less labor. Also, the assembly was lighter and stronger and was easier to put in the airplane. The cultural difference and the difference in aerospace tradition allowed the Russians to think about the problem differently. Input from another culture had created a broader perspective for tackling a complex engineering problem and ultimately delivered greater value.

Now Boeing has multiple design partners located in different time zones throughout the world. To link those partners, Boeing has designed electronic conference rooms, the larger of which resemble small theaters. One example of this synergy with partners is the Moscow Design Center where contract engineers collaborate with colleagues in Everett, Washington. Engineers in Everett, just in to work at 7:00 a.m., may view 3D renderings of parts and assemblies on one monitor, while viewing their colleagues in Moscow, who are working at the end of their work day at 6:00 p.m., on another monitor. They collaborate on the so-called *packages* of design work, meaning colleagues on both sides of the ocean annotate the design together.

Sergey Kravchenko, the President of Boeing Russia and an outspoken and colorful scientist, has spent the last decade building the Moscow Design Center from seven to one thousand engineers. In one of Boeing's more successful executive-level collaborations, Kravchenko has worked closely with CIO Scott Griffin, whose organization implemented the tools and processes to make the collaborative design environment happen. Kravchenko studied mobile work sharing models before persuading Boeing leadership that the design center in his home country would increase efficiency and reduce costs. Kravchenko and Griffin have helped bridge two regional cultures plus two engineering traditions.

A key success factor has involved focusing on what Kravchenko calls the four T's—terminology, tools, trust, and team. While engineers use the rules of physics everywhere, they often use different terms. This breeds confusion and can potentially compromise collaboration. Once both cultures agree on terminology, the next step is to address tools. Engineers in different cultures and different environments often use different tools. Once both groups agree on tools and receive training on those tools, the next step is trust. This step often takes weeks as people get used to each other, understand and negotiate differences, and determine how to work together. "When you build trust, then you move to the final T and this T is team.

And when you have a team that agrees on the terminology, is equipped with the same tools and has trust, you can do miracles," notes Kravchenko.

While the Moscow Design Center reduces design costs for Boeing, Kravchenko points out that the benefits are as much about knowledge as about hard dollars. "The main driver is the access to the critical skills and access to the critical mass of really well trained, experienced aerospace engineers," Kravchenko explains. "It's also about the speed, time to market, having the opportunity to work using time differences twenty-four hours per day, and having an engineering team that never sleeps. I would put access to experienced, global people as number one." Today Boeing uses mobile work sharing models throughout its operations, linking engineers in Italy, Japan and elsewhere.

From aerospace to healthcare to the chemical industry, culture determines how people collaborate. Regional culture, organizational culture, and even personal experience all play a role. As societies, organizations, and individuals, we are creatures of our influences. On a personal level, these may include mentors, teachers, family, friends, and environment. These influences help determine our prejudices and points of view and become part of our composition. As we meet constant challenges, this legacy or baggage comes along for the ride. It is inescapable! Likewise, culture, which reflects our collective experience, governs collaboration.

CHAPTER 3

THE COLLABORATIVE ENVIRONMENT

At a San Antonio bar called St. Anthony's Club in 1966, businessman Rollin King drew a triangle on the back of a cocktail napkin as he and lawyer Herb Kelleher discussed air routes in Texas. King's doodles would become Southwest Airlines.

In December of 1981, Rod Canion and Bill Murto met with industrial designer Ted Papajohn at a House of Pies restaurant in Texas. Using a napkin, Papajohn conceived the company that was to become Compaq Computer and would later merge with Hewlett-Packard. These are two of the seemingly endless examples of entrepreneurs hatching their companies on napkins in bars and cafes.

INFORMALITY DRIVES BIG IDEAS

We often think more creatively and collaboratively when we get away from cubicles, offices and conference rooms.

Why do so many successful business plans begin on napkins? Why are so many companies born in bars and restaurants? Informality! We often think more creatively and collaboratively when we get away from cubicles, offices and conference rooms. We can brainstorm more freely when surrounded by the trappings of relaxation such as beer taps and sports memorabilia. In traditional office environments, however, we are more likely to feel constrained.

In my work coaching leaders to communicate effectively, I have found that executives often connect with audiences better when they perceive a lack of formality. This perception turns off the pressure and creates a feeling that the presentation or interaction is lower stakes. Intellectually, they understand that presentations matter; nevertheless, these executives sense that when formality decreases, they relax more. They also feel more accepted and less judged. The same phenomenon applies to job searches. If the interview environment is a restaurant or café, often we come across more relaxed and animated than in an office setting. Consequently, there is more of a connection with the interviewer.

Environment contributes to our perception of whether the pressure is on and whether the presentation or interview is make or break. During communication coaching sessions, many leaders initially appear stiff, "corporate" and overly formal when I ask them to stand and talk in a conference room or auditorium. When they sit, they become more animated and engaging. And when they sit in a less formal venue such as the cafeteria, they connect with people even more effectively.

In short, we are often more believable as communicators when we sense informality in the situation and setting. Andrew Liveris, CEO of Dow Chemical Company, knows this instinctively. That's why he often prefers the informality of the cafeteria to the high-tech auditorium at headquarters for quarterly satellite broadcasts (see figures 3.1 and 3.2). The more formal the situation and the environment, the less people connect.

Standing at a lectern in an auditorium is perhaps the least natural and most formal of situations and environments. Subconsciously, we may recall reading to the class as the teacher graded the presentation or, worse yet, speaking at a school assembly with all the teachers and administrators present. That's why I encourage many CEO's and other executives to wear a

The more formal the situation and the environment, the less people connect.

Courtesy of The Dow Chemical Company

Figures 3.1 and 3.2   Two "town meeting" broadcasts from The Dow Chemical Company's headquarters in Midland, Michigan. On the left, CEO Andrew Liveris holds forth from the more formal auditorium environment. On the right, Liveris and other Dow leaders interact with employees from the more relaxed environment of the cafeteria. Besides taking audience questions, Liveris verbally responds to email appearing on the monitor next to him.

wireless microphone, abandon the lectern and walk around the stage and into the audience. The informality of walking relaxes us and helps us connect with people we hope to reach. We can infer that environmental factors impact demeanor and interaction.

When I reported news for television stations, I often walked during live remotes so that the viewer could experience the story with me. Because I could interact with people and the environment, walking seemed more natural than standing in front of a building. In fact, I frequently got jitters doing those overly formal live shots in which the reporter stands in front of the courthouse or city hall and is supposed to be the authority on what's happening inside the building.

Therefore, whenever possible, I asked the photographer to pull the camera off the tripod and walk with me through crowds, around buildings, and into City Hall as I reported live on the six and eleven o'clock news. I felt more relaxed, because it was a more natural approach.

Reviewing tapes of those live shots confirmed what I suspected—that I engaged viewers far more by taking them on a tour of the story. Because walking created a more natural and less formal environment, I felt more comfortable, thought better on my feet and connected more effectively with the audience. Similarly, leaders motivate audiences more effectively when they move away from the formality of a lectern and, if appropriate, abandon the stage. An informal environment makes a difference.

How Environment Determines Behavior

Just as informal environments can improve presentation delivery, job interviews and television news reporting, informality enhances collaboration. Part of the reason a cocktail napkin is seductive for brainstorm-

A cocktail napkin is seductive for brainstorming, because it seems so temporary.

ing is that it seems so temporary. You could easily crumple it up, stuff it in a dirty glass, and it would be gone forever. The impermanence of the napkin eliminates the pressure involved in writing on a white board or even on a sheet of paper.

Since what we write on a napkin could be gone in a flash, we feel perhaps that we will escape accountability for mistakes. The environment of a bar or restaurant with glasses clinking, people laughing, and music playing reinforces the perceived absence of risk. We might as well write the wildest notions on that napkin, because nobody will see or hear about them anyway. The paradox is that these crazy concepts are often our best ideas.

The opposite environment of the corner cafe is probably the traditional boardroom. When we enter, we see mahogany walls and twenty leather chairs around a seemingly endless table and perhaps framed images showcasing the company's legacy. Everything we write may appear on a sixty-inch screen for all to see.

If we use a boardroom or conference room to collaborate, how relaxed and comfortable do we feel? Probably not very. This is because the formality of the environment makes us feel that we're being judged, and that the stakes of the interaction are too high for our wildest—and perhaps best—ideas. And how much value do we create? In most cases, little. If, on the other hand, we move the group to the neighborhood watering hole and start sketching ideas on cocktail napkins, we are more likely to brainstorm wildly, collaborate effectively, and create substantial value.

In short, environment impacts collaboration.

Of course, it's impossible—and often undesirable—to escape the workplace whenever we need to collaborate. And even if we wanted to sit in a cafe with colleagues, our collaborators may be spread around the globe. Therefore, let's consider how our physical and virtual environments contribute or detract from collaboration and discuss optimum collaboration environments.

OPEN VS. CLOSED WORKPLACES

When people work in close quarters, a collaborative culture is more likely to develop. Part of the reason that Toyota's culture—and more broadly, Japanese culture—involves consensus is that the company was born in an island environment. Islands provide limited space, and therefore people work and live together in close quarters. Consequently, greater interdependency develops. In Toyota's facilities in Japan, three people have traditionally shared the space normally allotted one person in the United States. In essence, when working shoulder-to-shoulder in a tight environment, it's necessary to figure out ways of collaborating.

The best physical environment for collaboration depends on the industry, the culture, the type of work, and the nature of collaboration. In the most general terms, workplace environments are either open or closed. Closed environments typically include private offices for non-clerical employees. In a true open environment, every employee including senior leadership works from desks without dividers.

In some open environments, everybody except senior leaders sits in a room without dividers. This approach is often used for newsrooms and financial trading environments. However, most environments considered "open" are actually semi-open, meaning that people work from cubicles. Low-walled cubicles allow seated people to see seated colleagues. High-walled cubicles obstruct that view and create an environment closer to that of private offices.

Some workplace designers are looking for new ways to blend open and closed environments. The late Michael Brill of BOSTI Associates conducted a twenty-year study of the impact of environment on work satisfaction and performance. The study, which focused on forty organizations, indicated that the top two predictors of job performance are the ability for individuals and teams to do distraction-free work and have easy, frequent, informal interactions. BOSTI has experimented with fifty to sixty square foot, acoustically-private offices with sliding glass doors. These smaller, "cocktail offices" surround an open team space. The concept, while enabling face-to-face collaboration in the common area, also allows work without distraction.

To understand the powerful message that office environment sends, let's consider body language. When executives deliver presentations, there is often a disconnection between the message they seek to convey and their non-verbal communication. If a CEO stands in front of a thousand employees and tells them he or she welcomes their input, the message gets derailed if the CEO puts his hands behind his back or in his pockets. Such gestures are closed, while the message is about openness. There is therefore a disconnection. The audience senses a problem, and the CEO's credibility can suffer. Closed gestures become noise that interferes with the message.

When a CEO tells an audience that he or she is enthusiastic about the company's prospects and confident in the market for its products but the CEO's facial expression is one of worry rather than joy, there is a disconnection between the message and body language. Tom Kelley, General Manager of the design firm IDEO, has equated office design and environment with body language. Kelley has said that organizations should align workplace design with verbal and written communication. Companies often embrace words like *innovation* and *collaboration*, but their workplaces may say something else.

> Companies often embrace words like innovation and collaboration, but their workplaces may say something else.

The purpose of an open environment is to stimulate the free flow of information, increase idea generation, and bring egalitarianism to the workplace by eliminating the trappings of position. The other benefit, not always acknowledged, is economic. It usually costs less to construct open environments than to build offices.

THE EVOLUTION OF OPEN WORKPLACE ENVIRONMENTS

The history of the cubicle dates back to 1954 when Modern Products, now called Haworth, Inc., developed modular office partitions. However, many of today's open and semi-open office environments have their roots in the work of Robert Propst and his colleagues at Herman Miller in the 1960s. Propst, Herman Miller's research director, was interested in maximizing what he called the "human performer." He believed that the right environment could significantly enhance thinking, sharing ideas, and performance.

Propst sought to balance the benefits of interaction with the drawbacks of interruption. His work culminated in the Action Office, which Herman Miller introduced in 1968 (see figure 3.3). "We can start with the premise that we all are vastly more comfortable and productive with a territorial enclave," Propst wrote in *The*

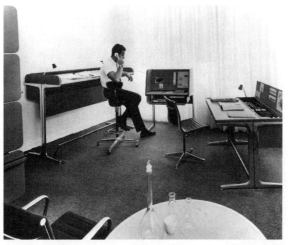

Photo by Louis Reens. Courtesy Herman Miller, Inc.

Figure 3.3   Herman Miller's original Action Office concept designed by Robert Propst, 1964. Propst believed that environment could enhance thinking, sharing ideas, and performance. He sought to balance interaction and privacy.

Office: a Facility Based on Change (Herman Miller, 1968). "However, we must immediately couple this with the need for vista, opening, or expression of access."

The concept version of the Action Office included mobile panels that could be configured based on the user's activities. Since Propst was concerned with the health hazards of sitting all day, he studied options for increased mobility including the stand-up desk that Winston Churchill used. Likewise, Action Office provided options for standing within the workspace. Propst also designed a stool called the Propst Perch and a wall-mounted roll top desk with foot rail that could be used in the Action Office (see figure 3.4).

Propst also conceived the "Arena Effect," which placed multiple work stations around an individual's workspace, forming a "U" which opened onto the entrance to the space. Action Office work stations occupied a 240-degree arena, while the remaining 120 degrees provided the opening and visitor area. This environment would allow greater variety in tasks, increased mobility and more options for how the user interacted with his or her colleagues and visitors.

Courtesy of Herman Miller, Inc.

Figure 3.4   An executive works on a Propst Perch within the Action Office in 1971. The Action Office could be reconfigured on the fly. Today collaboration-oriented environments including the Mayo Clinic's SPARC unit and the Stanford Center for Innovations in Learning (SCIL) enable users to change the seating configuration based on the project.

Propst understood that the more contact colleagues had either on demand or by accident, the more people would generate ideas and solve problems. Therefore, Propst's approach to space allowed increased visibility among colleagues. Action Office included options for glass inserts in panels for enhanced transparency. Propst also advocated putting lounge spaces in high-traffic areas.

Herman Miller developed early computer models to analyze interaction within and among functions and departments and to determine where people should sit in relationship to others. A researcher would interview each member of a department and then enter the data into a mainframe computer. "This would give us an idea of where Eric should sit in relationship to Joe, in relationship to Jack, in relationship to Sarah, so that it recognized the communication process between these groups and the teams within the groups so that the layout that the interior designer produced reflected this," according to Joe Schwartz, who headed sales and marketing and later product development for Herman Miller.

The first company to adopt Action Office was the Citizens and Southern National Bank, which needed an unorthodox interior design for a circular building in Atlanta (see figure 3.5). MasterCard quickly followed suit, followed by Northwestern Mutual Life Insurance Company, and Texas Instruments. IBM rejected the concept, because the company was dedicated to private offices.

While Propst's concept for the Action Office centered on a productivity model for the human performer, the product veered away from the concept. This was because of architectural requirements, computer and telecommunication wire management concerns, and market demand for cost effective warehousing of workers. "So instead of using Propst's open plan concept or Arena Effect concept, workplace environments started to look like boxes," Schwartz explains. What began as a research-driven concept to enhance communication, health and performance ultimately became an environment more like a cubicle.

Newer cultures—organizational and regional—embraced open workplace environments faster than did older, more established cultures. In New England and the East Coast of the United States, people were accustomed to private offices and saw little reason to

Figure 3.5 In 1969, The Citizens and Southern National Bank became the first company to adopt Action Office. Production versions of Action Office veered away from Robert Propst's prototype.

Courtesy of Herman Miller, Inc.

change. The recognition and reward systems in organizations centered around moving to the highest floor in a corner office, preferably the northeast corner away from the heat and glare of the setting sun.

Silicon Valley and the northwest United States, where cultures embraced results over hierarchy, rapidly adopted open environments. Hewlett-Packard was one of the first companies to adopt an open approach, mostly because William Hewlett and David Packard were modest guys who believed executives and managers should roll up their sleeves and work with their teams rather than remaining sequestered in offices. Though Hewlett and Packard worked from adjoining offices, they left the doors open and frequently employees stopped in with questions or concerns. During that time, other senior HP executives worked either from high-walled cubicles or from "high-visibility" glassed-in offices with open doors.

While HP set the standard for open environments in Silicon Valley, Intel went a step further. At Intel, every employee including the CEO works from a cubicle. While the vast majority of Silicon Valley companies favor open workplaces, not all organizations using open environments carve up space equally among the workforce. Some companies seek open communication and collaboration, but maintain space perks for executives. In such environments, using words from George Orwell's *Animal Farm*, "All animals are equal, but some animals are more equal than others." In other words, executives may work from plush cubicles with better furniture that are, in some cases, triple the size of the standard cubicle.

In Europe, where governments often pay for healthcare, many countries have mandated that office workers use ergonomic furniture and have access to natural light. The light requirement impacts environment in that furniture and panels must let light into workplaces. Therefore, a concept called desking has taken hold in Europe. Desking features adjoing L-shaped workspaces without partitions.

There is a correlation between movement around the workplace and collaboration. In *The HP Way: How Bill Hewlett and I Built Our Company* (Harper Business, 1995), David Packard notes the importance of management by walking around (MBWA). MBWA lets leaders learn first hand about team members' thoughts and opinions. "MBWA needs to be frequent, friendly, unfocused and unscheduled," Packard writes. At Toyota, leaders frequently leave their personal work spaces. Many managers spend time working on the production line, and leaders know their way around factories. Leadership training programs include selling cars door-to-door, which is common in Japan.

At The Dow Chemical Company, the environment encourages walking. Alden Dow, son of company founder Herbert Dow, was a protégé of Frank Lloyd Wright. He designed Dow's headquarters with long walkways linking sections of the building. Consequently, working at Dow involves plenty of walking. This increases opportunities for serendipitous interaction. Also, walking enhances circulation and may encourage clear thinking. Cultures and environments that encourage leaders and team members to walk around enhance the Culture of Collaboration.

PRIVATE OFFICES AND HIERARCHY

In contrast to the openness of desking, the other extreme is an environment in which every person, except possibly administrative assistants, works in a private office. My father, Gerald Rosen, has spent almost all of his career in business journalism. His one foray outside of writing and editing was a job, which lasted several weeks in 1969, analyzing economic trends and advising the board of directors of Mobil Oil Corporation, now ExxonMobil. This was in the days of bloated corporate payrolls. There was little work to do and my father was expected to arrange golf dates, join clubs, and eat in the executive dining room. However, my dad is a native New Yorker who doesn't play golf and preferred to duck out of the office at noon for an hour and meet his buddies for a burger.

Formality prevailed. My father suddenly had a big office and a secretary. To interact with superiors, he was expected to write memos and send them through channels. He often received no response. After a couple of months, he resigned and returned to his journalism job.

The Mobil experience helped my father develop a sensitive hierarchy meter. And twenty years later when he took a job editing newsletters at the International Monetary Fund, his hierarchy meter went off big time. HR used a system of letters and numbers, suspiciously reminiscent of Army pay grades, to rank executives. Those ranks corresponded to the square footage of offices.

In fact, some managers reportedly even measured their offices to ensure that they received every inch that their position accorded them. The environment was particularly formal, and many colleagues called my father "Mr. Rosen." In part, this is because the IMF appoints people from many countries where business cultures are less relaxed than in the United States. The point is that private offices reinforce hierarchy.

How Industries Influence Workplaces

Some industries tend to favor particular workplace environments. In newspaper and television newsrooms, most people work without walls. Magazines, in contrast, are more likely to give writers and editors offices. In television news, the staff must react to constant developments, create content for several broadcasts daily and provide material for online portals. Since teams must constantly collaborate to produce stories and newscasts, it would seem counter-collaborative and certainly counter-productive to put team members in offices.

I can recall many instances while working as a reporter when a six o'clock producer would call across the newsroom and ask me for a line the anchor could read during a programming break to "tease" my story and draw viewers to the newscast. There were times when producers had only a minute to write such teases. If they had to find me in an office or call me, the product would suffer.

While real-time group writing is a relatively recent phenomenon in education and business, reporters and producers frequently write story introductions and newscast headlines together. Typically, it's five minutes to air and the story is late breaking. With the producer at the keyboard, the reporter verbally helps craft some lines that will hopefully hoist viewers out of their easy chairs. The reporter may begin a sentence, and the producer may finish it. The lack of walls makes this possible.

But the value of the open environment in newsrooms goes beyond efficiency; informality develops when everybody sits in the same room. I worked at one small-market television station in Joplin, Missouri where there were no cubicles. Reporters, assignment editors and anchor/producers sat at adjacent desks in an environment reminiscent of police stations in TV cop shows. Everybody was engaged in a constant dialogue with everybody else. If we had worked from offices or even high-walled cubicles, we would have interacted differently.

A reporter might have asked the assignment editor, "Excuse me, Marilyn…do you have a moment? I need to clarify something with you regarding tonight's live shot at City Hall. What time is the Mayor's news conference?" Instead, a reporter would just look in the assignment editor's direction and ask "When is the Mayor's newser?" The difference is that professional intimacy developed, because we were engaged in a continuous conversation throughout the day without tiptoeing by offices or playing phone tag. Also, we could anticipate each other's moods and evaluate the best time to bring up issues just by glancing at one another.

Other industries favor open workplaces as well. In the financial industry, traders often work shoulder-to-shoulder in big rooms. In fact, some rooms are so large that traders use video to interact with colleagues on the other side. Just like the speed of news, markets move quickly and traders must anticipate developments and respond. Surrounding each trader with walls could detract from the camaraderie and intimacy that enhance collaboration.

Firefighters not only work without many walls; they also live together a few nights a week. Constant interaction helps firefighters anticipate the actions of colleagues during emergencies. In firefighting and financial trading, putting people in offices certainly runs counter to the culture and would likely interfere with results.

COMPARING WORKSPACE APPROACHES

The advantage of open workplaces is that they encourage faster, more free-flowing communication. Working without walls flattens hierarchy and encourages bonding with colleagues, greater professional intimacy, and the informality that often leads to better brainstorming. The drawbacks of such environments are that people lack privacy, and it's harder to focus on work.

Some professionals, including writers and software developers, need to "get in the zone" before they can create their best work. The zone is a mental gear that requires focus, and it's usually easier to get in that gear when there's a private space. Ironically, some professionals who benefit from getting in the zone have limited access to private spaces. That's part of the reason why TV reporters sometimes prefer writing their stories in news trucks than in the newsroom. At least, they're less likely to encounter interruptions.

When I covered the automobile industry in Michigan and Ohio, I was accustomed to hierarchical environments in which plant managers wore suits and worked in offices comfortably separated from the people who were assembling parts and cars. The first time I encountered a manufacturing environment that departed from the American norm was when Mazda invited me and a photographer in the late 1980s to tour its new plant in Flat Rock, Michigan. The plant was producing the Probe, the product of a joint venture with Ford.

In what seemed novel at the time, the plant manager wore the same uniform as every other worker and sat at a desk that adjoined those of others. Similarly, Toyota uses open environments in its plants. Rather than issuing orders through direct reports or writing officious memos, leaders work shoulder-to-shoulder with team members and help people implement their ideas. The environment, born out of a consensus-driven culture, enhances collaboration.

Clearly, both open and closed workplace environments have benefits and disadvantages. Private offices reinforce hierarchy, because those with bigger titles usually get larger offices. Traditionally, offices can create barriers to communication because colleagues feel less free to interact. Companies with private office environments also run the risk of establishing formality that can impede brainstorming and effective collaboration. However, offices do provide the physical and mental space that often helps people focus.

If we trade intimacy and informality for the privacy of four walls, it becomes even more critical to provide the right kind of spaces throughout buildings where team members can congregate and collaborate. The traditional conference room falls short. Such rooms are sterile, formal environments that conjure up thoughts of restructurings, downsizings, and shape-up-or-ship-out encounters. The elongated table which encourages a single person to chair the interaction does little to stimulate creativity or problem-solving. Often, there is a white board on which one person at a time—and often one person for the whole encounter—writes. The alternative is an environment designed for collaboration.

ENVIRONMENTS THAT ENCOURAGE BRAINSTORMING

The Mayo Clinic's SPARC unit offers a shared physical environment optimized for brainstorming and innovation (see profile, page 72). The program involves bringing R&D to Mayo's patient services. The SPARC team creates prototypes for new service delivery systems and environments and brings Mayo professionals from many functional areas into its unit where they can brainstorm about how to improve services and examine prototypes in action.

The SPARC unit has received much attention inside Mayo, and many employees know how the unit has helped improve the organization's services. During a visit to Mayo, I noticed that whenever I mentioned SPARC to people, their faces changed. Facial muscles relaxed, and frowns melted into the almost ecstatic smiles of students on the brink of discovery. Voices shifted from monotones to the varied pacing and pitch more common during cocktail party chat.

It was as if the mere mention of that environment took them back to the time spent at SPARC. Clearly, their experiences brainstorming and innovating had brought new energy and commitment to their work. While SPARC is about much more than physical environment, the unit's atmosphere undoubtedly enhances collaboration. We will discuss SPARC's methodology in chapter 5.

FORMALITY AS AN ENVIRONMENTAL TOXIN

Environments like SPARC that are designed with informality in mind produce emotional responses, because people feel different when they're there (see figure 3.6). The atmosphere lets them step outside of their traditional roles with the security that their organization endorses their behavior. They can break away from typical thought patterns which often reflect the responsibilities of their role.

Without sounding overly psychedelic, informal environments open people's minds. And having open minds is essential to

Courtesy of Mayo Clinic

Figure 3.6   The hub of the Mayo Clinic's SPARC unit features an informal environment with a variety of furniture that can be reconfigured based on project needs

collaboration! "You have to be willing to explore and understand other areas outside of your specific realm. The casualness of the environment helps do that, and the flexibility of space helps that too," explains Ryan Armbruster, director of operations and design for Mayo's SPARC.

Formality poisons creativity and collabora-

Formality poisons creativity and collaboration, and it does little for effective communication.

tion, and it does little for effective communication. Unfortunately, many people feel that their role, position or their organizational affiliation requires that they become stiff, humorless and devoid of emotion. I see this constantly when I coach senior executives. There is a relationship between informality and passion. One of the biggest hurdles executives face in communicating is the lack of passion. But without passion, how can a leader expect to motivate others? People respond to passionate people. Look at how Richard Branson of Virgin or Steve Jobs of Apple inspires colleagues and customers. They have succeeded in creating epidemics for brands and products in part because of their charisma and informality.

Often, people have plenty of passion for hiking, soccer, leading scouts, scuba diving, wine tasting, and many other activities outside of work. So, exhibiting passion is part of their personalities. The problem is that they feel constrained by their roles at work, believing they must keep on their "corporate face" at all costs and remain formal in the work environment. This is shortsighted. *Informality creates value!*

There is a tendency to confuse informality with what can get you fired, and nobody wants to pop up on HR's radar screen as a problem employee. There is, however, a clear distinction between informality and inappropriate behavior. Informality is about the perceived freedom to brainstorm and create new approaches, rather than a license to crack off-color jokes or make others feel uncomfortable.

Informal environments create a more relaxed mindset allowing The Ten Cultural Elements of Collaboration to flourish. While a formal atmosphere curbs collaborative chaos, informal surroundings let collaborative

There is a tendency to confuse informality with what can get you fired.

chaos flourish. When it comes to constructive confrontation and communication,
we are more likely to refrain from engaging when we're sitting in a traditional con-

Informal surroundings let collaborative chaos flourish.

ference room. If we are sitting with colleagues over coffee in a cafe,
we are more likely to confront them constructively and reveal what's
really on our minds.

It is far easier to trust our colleagues and share ideas and insights
when we are comfortable, and clearly we feel more comfortable
interacting in relaxed settings. Consider the emotional reaction
Mayo people have to their SPARC unit, and how they visibly relax
when they think of the space. Innovation happens when people feel
freedom of thought and the desire to discover, and these are more
likely when we leave traditional corporate trappings behind. And
together we create far more value when we are brainstorming,
exchanging concepts, and creating new approaches.

THE COLLOCATION MOVEMENT

Ideas fly and innovation happens when people who typically have
little to do with one another gain opportunities to interact. Mayo's
SPARC unit brings people from a variety of functions together in a
relaxed environment to create innovative healthcare services. These
are typically scheduled encounters. However, organizations can also
encourage cross-functional, serendipitous interaction that may lead
to collaboration. To this end, some organizations design workplaces
to maximize chance encounters.

When companies put coffee bars, snacks, and comfortable seating
in high-traffic areas, they increase the possibility that people from
different functions will meet, interact, and form networks. These
networks, in turn, create new ideas and innovative approaches.
Therefore, chance meetings produce intellectual capital which
becomes an organizational asset.

Cafeterias are less useful for chance meetings, because they tend
to be clique-oriented; we are more likely to sit down with people we
know. When I was in high school, a studious and reserved classmate
frequently approached the table at which I was eating and asked,

SPARCing Innovation and Collaboration at Mayo Clinic

Doctors Will and Charles Mayo built the Mayo Clinic on a foundation of collaboration by assembling a cross-functional team of doctors, laboratory experts, business people, and communications specialists in the 1880's. The Mayos with their father, Dr. William Worrall Mayo, introduced private group practice, shunned individualism, and promoted medicine as a cooperative science.

The Culture of Collaboration continues to define Mayo as leaders, doctors, nurses and staff practice principles including teamwork and putting patients first. "We take research out of the laboratory and translate it in a very quick and meaningful way right to the patient's bedside, says Dr. Glenn Forbes, CEO of Mayo's Rochester, Minnesota campus. "That takes a lot of collaboration, because you're crossing cultures and you're often times crossing a lot of internal organizational structures and silos."

Mayo's SPARC unit extends the Culture of Collaboration. SPARC stands for see, plan, act, refine, communicate; the acronym refers to the research and development process for services. SPARC focuses on live prototyping in which patients experience new service approaches while a cross-functional team of industrial designers, patient education experts, doctors, administrators, facilities people, financial analysts and others gather data and observe.

SPARC breaks down barriers among functions at Mayo by forming multidisciplinary teams to improve patient care delivery. SPARC uses well-honed processes and an informal environment to develop new patient care approaches. "SPARC enables people to step outside of their traditional roles," explains Ryan Armbruster, SPARC's director of operations and design. "You know. This is my environment. These are my job responsibilities. It opens their minds, which is essential to collaborating."

Cross-functional teams brainstorm in an open area called the "program support space," essentially SPARC's hub. The idea is to promote patient-centered service design by including rapid feedback in the service R&D process. Surrounding the hub are prototypes that include patient check-in counters and examination rooms. From the hub, the team that developed the approach can observe prototypes in action through glass and via video.

In designing the space, SPARC leadership sought to inspire innovation and collaboration. Therefore, informality pervades the hub, and collaborators can easily change the seating configuration based on the project. At times, the multicolored space resembles an Internet café with bar-type stools and high tables. As they brainstorm, collaborators use two dozen Steelcase Huddleboards (see figure 3.7). These are mini, two-sided, dry-erase white boards.

Courtesy of Mayo Clinic

Figure 3.7   In the hub of the Mayo Clinic's SPARC unit, collaborators use two-sided, dry-erase Huddleboards for brainstorming. SPARC provides two dozen Huddleboards, wall-mounted in a double layer. Collaborators can move Huddleboards around, take them down, and pass them around.

"When we go to small groups, two or three people take a Huddleboard with them. They write all of their notes on that Huddleboard," explains Armbruster. "Then when they come back to share or communicate their notes with the larger team, they can put all of the Huddleboards back on the wall." A ceiling-mounted camera captures a digital image of the Huddleboards and preserves the fruits of collaboration. Thanks to SPARC, people in many functions who previously had minimal contact now collaborate.

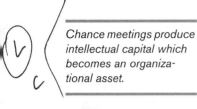

Chance meetings produce intellectual capital which becomes an organizational asset.

tray in hand, if he could join me. I recently attended a high school reunion that included a series of events including—guess what?—lunch in the school's new cafeteria. As I was about to bite into a sandwich, I heard the distinctive voice of my classmate, now an architect, asking whether he could join me. Old habits die hard.

Flexible team workspaces allowing people to move walls and furniture based on project needs have their roots in the research that Thomas Allen conducted at MIT in the 1970s. Allen investigated the relationship between distance and communication. The results of that research, known as the Allen curve, indicate that the more physical distance that exists among people, the less they communicate. Allen also discovered that the number of informal contacts people have outside their departments and disciplines increases performance in R&D settings. Without broad interaction across functions and business units, people become insular and their thinking turns stale. As exposure to varied influences and cultures increases, so does the opportunity to develop great ideas.

In *Workplace by Design* (Josey-Bass, 1995), Franklin Becker and Fritz Steele introduce the concept of the "rugby" vs. the "relay-race" approaches to organizational ecology. In the relay-race model as applied to product development, each function completes its work and then tosses it to the next function. Marketing, for example, may conduct research and then toss the results to a design group, which then throws its work product to engineering, which then tosses its results back to marketing. "Unfortunately, what goes over the fence has a tendency to be thrown back," according to Becker and Steele. "Like a neighbor whose yard serves as the outfield for the kids next door, it can tend to create hard feelings and harsh words."

The rugby model brings all the players together at the start of the project. As the team moves towards the goal, different players may take a stronger lead at one point or another. The key is that the entire team stays in the game all the time, so that each member participates in decisions and knows the status of work constantly. The rugby approach involves constant communication, much of which is spontaneous, whether at the water cooler or in the hallway.

Designing the space is part of the equation in encouraging the rugby approach. Another significant factor is how the organization assigns desks or work areas within the environment. Traditionally, space is allocated by department or function. Marketing people work near and around other marketing people. Information technology professionals are physically located with their IT colleagues. This builds department-oriented cohesiveness and identity. However, an "us and them" mindset also tends to develop.

In some industries and companies, there is a movement towards collocation. This involves putting people from different departments and disciplines together. In many cases, collocation is based on projects.

Collocation puts people from different departments and functions together.

In a product launch, a corporate communications person might sit across from an engineer or designer. The idea is to create synergy.

Industrial Light & Magic, founded by director/producer George Lucas in 1975, creates visual effects for films including the Star Wars series. ILM has experimented with collocation in a variety of workplace environments. ILM artists are usually project—rather than process—oriented, because their work is tied to the production schedule of films. Because the climate is particularly creative and clients often determine the tools and approaches to collaboration, the culture varies from one project to the next. Animators, compositors, modelers, view painters, and technical directors must collaborate to create the latest films.

In the past, ILM has put animators shoulder-to-shoulder with other animators and compositors with other compositors, and so on with each job classification. The problem with this arrangement is the inevitable disconnection that develops among departments. This communication and collaboration breakdown often becomes apparent after the daily review sessions—called "dailies'—during which the supervisors, and sometimes the client, view the day's work.

During dailies, the technical director might comment that the dragon looks too green, but it remains unclear who will solve the problem. So the viewpainter goes back to the viewpaint area and changes the paint, making the image less green. The technical director goes back to another area and reduces the green in the lighting.

A compositor goes to the composition area and takes green out of the element.

And the next day, the color of the image is an ugly magenta, because everybody reduced the green. This time and resource-wasting scenario suggests ILM should assign workspace based on the project rather than on the discipline. If the viewpainter, the compositor, and technical director sit near each other, they are more likely to communicate who is doing what and also more likely to avoid redundant effort.

Depending on the project, ILM also uses a variety of workplace environments. These range from offices to open space. Tim Alexander, a visual effects supervisor at ILM, has worked on projects ranging from *Star Trek* movies to *Harry Potter*. Alexander believes that collocation combined with open environments enhances collaboration, and he therefore advocates this approach.

Typically, supervisors work from separate offices, and artists and technical people come to these offices for work reviews. For the *Harry Potter and the Goblet of Fire* project, Alexander flattened the hierarchy and increased collaboration and communication by collocating the supervisors in an open space, which became a sort of production hub. The team also used the hub for what we might call *distance dailies* in which the film director, ILM's client, reviews the day's work via videoconferencing.

Without walls, the hub environment allowed information to flow and encouraged team cohesiveness. Therefore, Alexander could review a shot with an artist while the sequence supervisor sitting next to him was listening, albeit casually, as he was doing something else. "I think many times in the process we lose that communication, because the visual effects supervisor is sitting in an office and everybody that might be interested in hearing what they're saying is not around or is not available," explains Alexander. "So by sort of pulling down the walls and having everybody sit in one big room together, that information gets disseminated freely and makes the task of tracking all of this easier because everybody's heard it and everybody has heard it first hand."

THE FLIP SIDE OF COLLOCATION

Despite the benefits of collocation, there can be a downside. ILM has found that arranging physical space based on productions sometimes helps projects at the expense of the company. That may sound like a contradiction, because what's good for the project and the client should also benefit the company. However, when a tightly-knit group gets swept away in the needs of a project, the group may lose site of the big picture. For instance, technologists may develop software that works for one show but is of little value to the company once ILM finishes the project.

There are other arguments against collocation. When people in the same department occupy the same physical space, they gain greater insight into their function. Instead of focusing only on painting a moose for *Rocky & Bullwinkle*, for instance, an ILM viewpainter may listen to peer discussions that give him or her insight into issues arising on other projects. Similarly, a communications specialist who sits near other communicators gains a more complete picture of how the organization is interacting and disseminating information. However, he or she sacrifices the collaborative benefits of constant interaction with project colleagues in other functions that collocation allows.

Another down side to collocation is the cultural shock of breaking up a departmental team. At many companies, people spend more time with their colleagues than with their spouses and families. When a department gets along well, those relationships can make people look forward to their work day. Therefore, suddenly relocating people near those from other departments with whom they have less of a rapport can be a morale buster.

On balance, the collaborative benefits of collocation at ILM outweigh the big picture advantages of assigning space based on function. "I think it's better to have the information flow about the show going on," notes Tim Alexander of ILM. "It's just up to us to work harder at making sure we still are looking at the bigger picture, that we're not just doing something on our show that's going to be wasted later if other shows can't use it."

*People in the same disci-
pline tend to interact even
if their workspaces are further away.*

People in the same discipline tend to interact even if their workspaces are further away. However, people with different specialties on the same team are less likely to interact unless they occupy the same space. To prevent myopia, departments can encourage interaction and sharing information that may apply to multiple projects. This exchange can happen during formal gatherings, informal or chance meetings, and through tools including departmental team spaces, instant messaging and even videoconferencing.

HOW VIRTUAL ENVIRONMENTS IMPACT COLLABORATION

The design of physical environments is just part of the equation in determining how space affects collaboration. Since geography gets between us and our colleagues, we use a variety of tools, which we will describe in chapter 7, to bridge the gap. Tools help us

*While we are unable to
share physical space with
colleagues across the
ocean, we can share
virtual space.*

recover some of the intimacy that we sacrifice to distance, but they also create another dimension to environment. While we are unable to share physical space with colleagues across the ocean, we nevertheless can share virtual space.

The composition of virtual environments and our relationship to them impacts collaboration. Virtual environments include everything from digital whiteboards and team sites to the "look and feel" of a videoconference. Whether digital whiteboards feel informal and approximate the experience of jotting down great ideas on cocktail napkins is a virtual environment design issue. The move towards high-definition video significantly impacts the virtual environment of a videoconference, because we can see greater detail in facial features and the remote location.

3D immersive systems and some media spaces create perhaps the biggest challenge in virtual environment design, because the goal is to make us feel as if we occupy the same physical space with our distant colleagues. Media spaces provide always-on, real-time audio and video links between two or more locations. Like physical environments, virtual environments should enable collaboration rather than getting in the way.

When DreamWorks Animation CEO Jeffrey Katzenberg wanted to enhance collaboration in the globally-dispersed company, he realized the need for a virtual environment that felt natural, maximized human interaction and would bridge the distance gap. In short, Katzenberg wanted to approximate face-to-face encounters while creating an environment that would allow artists to engage in shared creation of computer graphics. There was particular urgency, because DreamWorks had recently acquired Pacific Data Images (PDI) of Redwood City, California near San Francisco. Katzenberg wanted seamless integration of PDI with other DreamWorks operations globally, particularly the headquarters in Glendale, California, which is about three hundred and fifty miles south of PDI.

Also, DreamWorks Animation was planning an initial public offering, and eliminating geography as a barrier was part of the company's strategy to create shareholder value. "Part of what we needed to solve was being able to repeatedly and reliably produce two of these films a year with a talent pool that was scarce and scattered. And so we had to develop this technology to solve this problem," explains Ed Leonard, chief technology officer of DreamWorks Animation. Ultimately, DreamWorks met Katzenberg's challenge by creating its own environment which it calls Virtual Studio Collaboration (VSC). The company partnered with Hewlett Packard to enhance the technology, and HP now markets a similar system as Halo Collaboration Studio.

The DreamWorks Animation virtual environment involves more than a dozen physical room environments across three continents. The rooms are optimized for two locations with six people at each location, though more locations and people are possible. Each beige-toned VSC room includes a table which curves outward at the ends in a near semi-circle. This helps create an optical illusion that remote participants are sitting across the table. In front of the table is a row of three screens each showing two of the six participants who may be seated at the remote table. Above those screens is a fourth screen that displays work product including 3D animation.

Animation artists require natural virtual environments for collaboration. Because their work involves making imaginary things real, anything that seems forced or awkward falls flat. Using VSC, collaborators can talk over each other without any perceived delay or latency, allowing more natural voice communication. "You need to be able to look at somebody's eyes and you need to be able to have the texture and the human connection where you feel part of the same space," says Leonard. When geographically-distributed collaborators look at each other on DreamWorks VSC screens, it appears as if they are looking almost directly into one another's eyes. There is no need to look at the cameras.

Bringing animated characters to life on screen requires keen attention to such details as body language. To show that a character has an idea or is thinking about something, artists may lift the character's eyebrow. Therefore, there is increased sensitivity to body language in the DreamWorks Animation culture. To capture this nonverbal communication, DreamWorks focused on realism in developing VSC.

"If you miss the non-verbal, you're missing half or more of the communication, particularly when you're doing creative collaboration in which you want to be able to have the finesse and the timing, the jokes. Do you cut three frames? And when do you loop back? Do you need a reaction shot? All of that really senses detailed finesse in the craft of making films," according to Leonard. "We needed to replicate that in a way in which the experience was as good as being there in person."

A DreamWorks Animation film often involves more than two hundred people scattered around the globe devoting some fifteen million hours rendering computer graphics. The company has about a dozen projects in production simultaneously. Because the best artists are in short supply in any one region, DreamWorks recruits globally. Some artists work for DreamWorks affiliates or business partners.

Using VSC, DreamWorks can operate as a single virtual studio by linking many physical studios. The environment brings together highly-skilled specialists including story developers, storyboard artists, physical artists, visual developers and even niche software experts. "I don't know how many people there are on the planet that have PhD's in doing long hair simulation, but I know we have one, maybe two or three at the most. And you see that in other areas," Leonard explains. "And what we wanted to do was be able to leverage that skill set and talent regardless of geography."

The VSC rooms throughout DreamWorks remain on, so when people enter the rooms at each location, they can interact immediately. Also, there is no "self-view" mode so that collaborators avoid becoming self conscious seeing themselves on screen. This approach helps remove technology from collaboration.

One element missing in DreamWorks' use of VSC is spontaneous interaction. We have discussed how chance meetings in physical environments encourage collaboration. The same is true of serendipitous encounters in virtual environments. Media spaces, which encourage on-the-fly interaction, work best in high-traffic areas such as lounges and break rooms.

Parker Hannifin's Virtual Hallway, which we will describe in chapter 7, is an example of a media space. While the DreamWorks VSC rooms are always on, they're also almost always scheduled. Often, interactions must finish promptly because people are waiting their turn. Putting VSC environments in heavily-trafficked common areas would open windows between DreamWorks facilities.

While I was eating lunch in the DreamWorks cafeteria in Redwood City, it occurred to me that artists in northern California could interact informally with colleagues in southern California if there were some manifestation of VSC in the cafeteria. While the noise level might preclude detailed discussions, colleagues could exchange small talk and feel more connected. As we have discussed, the cafeteria is less than ideal for physical chance encounters because the same people often eat together regularly. However, the cafeteria could enable virtual serendipitous interaction.

CUSTOMIZING VIRTUAL ENVIRONMENTS

Virtual environment also involves presence. In a significant shift, we can now launch collaborative capabilities from business productivity applications such as word processing and spreadsheet programs. We can also launch spontaneous interactions from "line of business" systems such as enterprise resource planning (ERP) applications.

Since many people spend much of their day using these systems, they are less likely to collaborate if they must leave their work and launch separate tools to interact with their colleagues. Therefore, tools vendors have figured out how to bring collaboration to people rather than forcing people to go somewhere to collaborate. Instead of viewing collaboration tools as distinct applications, it is increasingly accurate to think of these tools as an array of always-available capabilities. This means that shared virtual space is blending with our desktop environment.

Industrial Light & Magic has created its own desktop virtual environment in which animators, modelers, technical directors and others share information and collaborate. The space, called Dome, is an umbrella for collaborative capabilities and a "central hub" for interaction and creating the visual effects that are the company's stock-in-trade (see figure 5.2, page 131). Several collaborators, for instance, may be creating a dragon and animating the dragon in many scenes of a film. Everybody involved uses Dome to access their work. If supervisors determine that the creature requires fundamental changes, they will use Dome to quarantine the dragon. This prevents people from wasting time and energy on a figure that will be overhauled.

Also within Dome, an animator can instigate a review request from a supervisor to ensure that his or her work fits in with the overall project. He or she typically does this by sending an instant message to a technical director. The IM may include the link to a movie file or a request to meet in an area of Dome that includes a shared white board. As they review frames of animation, the animator and technical director may use electronic writing tools to mark up film frames in real time. This gives the animator visual cues so that he or she can remember the necessary changes after the review session ends.

The Stanford Center for Innovations in Learning (SCIL) is trying to make virtual encounters more similar to in-person interactions. The approach is creating a contiguous working space that is partly virtual. To test the approach, SCIL arranged a concert with two musicians in Stockholm and two others on Stanford's campus in Palo Alto, California. There was an audience in both locations. Using strategic placement of multiple cameras and a video synchronization program, the musicians appeared to both audiences as if they were in the same room. When the audience in Stockholm looked to the right, they saw the Stanford audience. When the Stanford audience looked to the left, they saw the Stockholm audience.

In lounge areas at both locations, SCIL placed seven-feet-tall video screens so that both audiences could socialize after the performance. A six-foot-tall person would appear that height to the remote audience. Also, SCIL placed the cameras so that people could easily maintain eye contact with one another regardless of location. Besides more obvious cues, the virtual space allowed nonverbal, non-visual cues normally present during interactions in physical space. For example, inhaling often signals that a person is about to speak and therefore all eyes may move in his or her direction.

Organizers of the event never informed the audience that they would be able to interact with their cohorts in another continent. Nevertheless, people walked into the lounge areas, immediately saw the remote participants and began interacting. "They felt that this was a genuine person on the other side. So it's not that hard, right?" insists Robert Smith, SCIL's technical director. "It's not like we have to go out and create some whole new scratch-and-sniff, high-definition, surround-sound thing. We just have to present people at the scale of people."

PHYSICAL MEETS VIRTUAL ENVIRONMENT

The shift in workplace culture and environment supporting collaboration parallels trends in education. Hidden behind the turn-of-the-last-century facade of building 160, Stanford University has created a state-of-the-art collaborative learning facility called Wallenberg Hall. The hall is named for the foundation that contributed $15 million to create eighteen classrooms, five of which are highly-collaborative, plus break-out areas and a theater. While the Stanford Center for Innovations in Learning (SCIL) runs the building, the facilities are available to any Stanford professor who reserves them. The Mayo Clinic used Wallenberg Hall as inspiration for the design of its SPARC unit.

Classrooms provide a flexible environment allowing faculty and students to reconfigure the tables and chairs in about a minute. White boards surround the rooms, and digital cameras let students capture on-the-board brainstorming and publish it to a class web site. At the front of each room are two, rear-projection, forty-inch, flat panel displays. Students and faculty can push web sites and other content to the displays from notebook computers with wireless modems housed in each classroom.

Suspended from the ceiling are four microphones designed to capture all of the classroom discussion. These microphones feed into a digital signal processor programmed to create a continuous mix and favor whichever microphone is closest to the person talking the most. There are two digital whiteboard systems that can be displayed on the flat panels. Four video cameras allow students to capture images and push them to the class web site. Videoconferencing capability provides a learning environment that often extends to classrooms in other parts of the world.

The concept behind the environment is to shift the role of the teacher from "sage on the stage to guide on the side." It is essentially a leveling of hierarchy in the classroom to encourage collaboration. Rather than the class focusing on the front of the room, the action can be anywhere around the room. When I was in school, it was the rare teacher who encouraged his or her students to work together. In fact, collaboration was typically considered cheating in many American schools, mine included; the work one submitted was supposed to be his or hers alone. That approach no longer makes sense as collaboration takes hold in the workplace.

Schools and universities are realizing that establishing collaborative work styles in the classroom not only prepares students for an evolving work environment, but also helps them learn more effectively. In a parallel paradigm shift, the focus is moving from teacher to student, from delivering knowledge to facilitating the acceptance and integration of knowledge. And using collaborative tools can reinforce and extend the Culture of Collaboration.

When I visited SCIL, an undergraduate writing class was group writing an assignment from notebook computers linked to five "writing stations" or digital whiteboards around the classroom. The collaborative result appeared on a rear-projection display. The principle on which the writing class is based is that writing is inherently a collaborative activity.

Of course, the image many people have of prominent writers is that they sit in solitude and create great works. In reality, many eyes and fingers are involved. Content editors review and change magazine articles and book manuscripts; copy editors insert punctuation. However, writing traditionally involves asynchronous collaboration, which is essentially the relay race approach. The writer hands off a draft to an editor who works on it. The editor then hands the draft back to the writer for changes and additions.

Instead, the Stanford class pushes writing into the realm of real-time collaboration. The idea is to change students' concept of writing by removing it from the personal realm of notepads and laptops and transfer it to the group arena of a forty-inch screen. Also, the large display places some psychological distance between the students' efforts and the words. Therefore, it's easier to view the work objectively and remain open to edits and changes, rather than getting defensive about one's creative product.

During SCIL classes, students often IM each other. In this case, IM is the contemporary equivalent of passing notes, which schools once frowned upon. No trip to the principal's office is required if you're caught. However, not all Stanford professors embrace the cultural shift that tools often create. After seven students began laughing one-by-one while exchanging IM during a communications class, the professor asked a technologist to disconnect the wireless network.

Preventing people from using a tool simply invites them to find another, often more revolutionary, method of interacting.

However, it is impossible to get the genie back in the bottle. Countless repressive regimes have ultimately failed in banning communication methods and channels. Preventing people from using a tool simply invites them to find another, often more revolutionary, method of interacting. The better approach is to create a shared space on a display in which the entire class can IM. If a Stanford communications professor freaks out over side conversations through IM, there are perhaps greater etiquette issues regarding IM chat among corporate meeting participants.

BRIDGING VIRTUAL DISTANCE

Karen Sobel Lojeski has researched *virtual distance*, the sense of distance among people. Virtual distance plays a role regardless of whether collaborators work in the same building or in different countries. Lojeski's model measures factors that determine how close team members feel to each other. When there are higher levels of virtual distance, according to Lojeski's research, team members are less likely to share ideas. Productive, spontaneous interactions would seem more difficult within teams with high virtual distance.

Certainly, larger, more life-like displays and more strategic videoconferencing camera placement that enhances eye contact can bridge virtual distance. Bonding in person before establishing a virtual relationship can do wonders in bridging virtual distance, particularly when there are multiple regional cultures among the collaborators. Stanford engineering students learned this when they collaborated with students at Kungliga Tekniska högskolan (KTH) in Stockholm, also known as the Royal Institute of Technology

Using a dedicated high-bandwidth connection for video and audio, SCIL created a media space. Because of cultural differences, both groups defined the projects differently. By the end of the quarter, the Stanford students disliked the Swedes, insisting that they were standoffish, stuffy, and just about any negative adjective and accompanying emotion that one might imagine developing in the worst work situation. Therefore, the Stanford students dreaded their trip to Sweden during which they would meet their Swedish counterparts in the flesh.

However, after three days of staying with the Swedes and eating and drinking with them, they returned to Stanford. The small-screen videoconferencing system that had been inadequate for the students to develop a useful relationship with the Swedes suddenly became a porthole to friends. There was lots of walking by the monitors, tapping on the glass, and laughing. This illustrates how establishing an in-person, informal connection reduces virtual distance when using collaborative tools.

We have discussed how the industry and the organizational culture may determine the ideal physical environments for collaboration. In an interesting twist, the increased flexibility of virtual environments may impact physical environments. Companies that have abandoned or avoided private offices to increase communication and stimulate creativity may reconsider walled environments. Indeed, office-oriented workplaces may become more viable for some teams, companies, and industries that have previously favored open floor plans.

A key factor is presence. With presence-enabled tools, we can find our colleagues and spontaneously collaborate through IM, audio, or video without leaving our offices. The advent of IP-based videoconferencing means that people can more easily interact via video from their desks, and having four walls may decrease distractions. Also, videoconferencing environments are evolving so that there is increased realism. This gives us some—though certainly not all—of the intimacy of working in the same room without the need to give up offices and forfeit privacy.

While the technology industry typically favors open workspaces, Microsoft has traditionally put most of its professionals in offices. Since the company develops virtual environments, perhaps it is in a better position than most to leverage the benefits of privacy and focus that offices provide while maintaining collaborative chaos and informality through presence-enabled tools. Nevertheless, Microsoft is considering a workplace redesign that would include more open spaces.

The same factors that are making private offices more viable for collaboration are also making telecommuting more attractive. The primary drawback of telecommuting is isolation; people are often cut off not only from formal meetings and interactions but, perhaps more importantly, from the informal face-to-face communication that occurs in workplaces. As virtual environments evolve, however, people will overcome much of the isolation associated with telecommuting. In chapter 4, we will explore the relationship between telecommuting and collaboration.

CHAPTER 4

LIFESTYLES AND
WORK STYLES

The Culture of Collaboration pays off by creating value, which typically refers to hard-dollar returns. But there are other, less tangible and more personal benefits to collaborators that translate into organizational gains. Effective collaboration enhances lifestyles and work styles by giving us more freedom and flexibility. Companies benefit, because employees who balance work and personal concerns are less likely to burn out and are easier to retain. The most effective tools let people integrate collaboration into their lives, rather than forcing people to put aside their work and abandon activities so that they can collaborate. However, we can also become slaves to tools and to the perceived expectation that we must remain available day and night.

CONVERGENCE OF BUSINESS
AND PERSONAL TIME

The lines between business and personal time are becoming blurred. Whether we work from home, from the road, or from a cubicle or office, many of us mix tasks from multiple worlds throughout the day. Besides our roles at work, we wear multiple hats. These may include spouse, parent, caregiver, home renovator, soccer coach, condo or home association board member, volunteer firefighter, scout leader, among many others.

As we receive and initiate instant messaging (IM), email, voice calls and other interactions, our multiple roles overlap. During a meeting at work, we may respond to an IM from a contractor. While watching the kids play softball in the evening, a business-oriented message may pop up on a mobile device. When we get home, a colleague in another time zone may track us down with a question. Once upon a time, the quittin' whistle blew at 5:00 p.m. And, short of an emergency, there was no reason to deal with work until 9:00 the next morning. Those days are long gone.

The flexibility that collaborative tools allow can become either a blessing or a curse—or, perhaps, a little of both. Presence, which allows people to remain available and reachable throughout the day, raises new concerns about balance. Progressive organizational cultures encourage employees to set boundaries, so that they avoid becoming overwhelmed by the prospect of twenty-four-hour availability.

People must feel that it's acceptable to become unavailable. Realizing that he was overly reachable, one Ford manager turned in his handheld device. The technology disrupted his private time, and he believed that it "crossed the line." "I think we're going to have to be able to set those boundaries and parameters somehow in these tools and say either by logging off or signing off or shutting off, that is an indicator that we are no longer working," says Laurie Heltsley, P&G's director of computers and communications services. "And that's OK."

Some people do their best work at midnight. And in global organizations, this may sync well with colleagues in another time zone. But if somebody is working at midnight, the organization must accept that they may be unavailable at 10:00 a.m. Therefore, an "on/off" designation replaces the traditional time or shift-oriented designation. The old thinking was, "Joe works until 5:00 p.m. Where is he?"

An "on/off" designation replaces the traditional time or shift-oriented designation.

The new thinking is, "Is Joe on or off? If he's on, what's the best way to reach him?"

TELECOMMUTING: A COLLABORATION DILEMMA?

Telecommuting presents a dilemma. Does the isolation of working from home interfere with collaboration? Or does telecommuting encourage the use of collaborative tools and therefore enhance collaboration?

In chapter 3, we discussed how the island culture, out of which Toyota's organizational culture emerged, has created interdependency and encouraged collaboration. The environment forced people to figure out ways of working together, thus instilling elements of collaborative culture. Telecommuting is a different sort of island environment—a figurative island of one. On one hand, telecommuting eliminates close proximity to other collaborators, and therefore telecommuters miss out on chance encounters in hallways, break rooms, and cafeterias.

On the other hand, working from home may encourage us to collaborate. When we are physically cut off from our colleagues, we are more likely to maximize tools. In

When we are physically cut off from our colleagues, we are more likely to maximize tools.

much the same way that the lack of personal space forced Toyota people to work together, the lack of face-to-face interaction encourages telecommuters to integrate tools into their work styles—and tools can provide a more robust collaborative experience than face-to-face meetings. When teams were mostly comprised of people in a single location, tools were less important in creating value. Because being at the office determined the degree to which a team member could participate in shared creation, telecommuting often disrupted collaboration. This is old news. Now teams increasingly include people from multiple countries.

At Dow Chemical Company, it is the rare team in which all members are based in the same continent. Therefore, it is impossible for these teams to occupy the same physical space regularly, and collaborators must rely on tools to help them create value. With broadband connections and the right tools, globally-dispersed team members may collaborate more from home than from the office.

As collaboration becomes more tool-focused, collaborators gain the flexibility to use tools from cubicles, from offices, from home, from hotels, and even from planes, trains and automobiles. Though organizational culture sometimes lags behind that flexibility, it eventually catches up because of the potential value. Team members may have to work early in the morning or late at night to connect in real time with colleagues in other time zones. Driving to the workplace during these times makes little sense. Also, commuting on clogged highways in major metropolitan areas can waste valuable time, frustrate employees, and dampen the spirit of innovation.

If the goal of telecommuting is mostly about saving money on real estate, the initiative is less likely to succeed. Telecommuting works if the organization commits to creating value through collaboration and balancing personal and professional lives. Though tools are a key enabler, whether organizations embrace telecommuting has more to do with culture than tools. Cultures that favor control and internal competition are less likely to encourage telecommuting. Though these organizations may offer telecommuting programs, management often prefers promoting people who show up at the office. Managers who grow up in these cultures fear that employees goof off when they're away from the workplace. If they can't see them working, the thinking goes, they must be doing something other than work.

With potential distractions like preparing dinner and helping the kids with homework in the late afternoon, it would seemingly be easy to back burner work. However, these managers often fail to consider the distractions that occur in the workplace! These include unproductive meetings, the kinds that are more about producing hot air than about creating value. If, on the other hand, home-based employees are better able to balance family and work concerns, they may be less likely to burn out and more likely to deliver results.

BRIDGING REGIONAL WORK STYLES

Work styles vary from one region to the next. In the southern United States, the informal chit chat or warm up period before talking business lasts longer than in the Northeast. And globally there are many such regional work style differences. A software developer in the United States may do his or her best work with maximum flexibility and without close supervision. Telecommuting two days a week and working a later shift may help balance work and family demands. Such flexibility in many other countries runs against the grain.

"We certainly aren't sitting here saying you have to be here eight to five," says Mark Conway, chief technical officer of Monster Worldwide, which operates online job search and career development web sites in twenty-three countries. "We're very much oriented around project goals and meeting your objectives. When you do it and how you do it is more on you." Monster perpetuates a collaborative, creative culture and provides an informal environment. In the red and purple "monster den," team members can play ping-pong, Foosball, or shoot pool.

In encouraging collaboration between its Prague, Czech Republic and Boston, Massachusetts area development centers, Monster has found that regional culture impacts integrating tools and approaches into work styles. Prague developers and managers are accustomed to greater formality and hierarchy and less flexibility in how, where, and when they work. Nevertheless, developers on both sides of the ocean embrace most tools. They use wikis and blogs to disseminate technical information internally; and they post all project requirements, definitions, design specifications, and meeting notes on team sites. For design reviews and brainstorming, the collaborators often choose IP videoconferencing.

Although developers in both time zones use IM extensively, Monster has had mixed results in adding video to IM. The company put cameras on desktops at the request of some of its Boston area developers, who began using video instant messaging (VIM). However, the Prague group prefers scheduled video-conferences and feels less comfortable with spontaneous video interaction. VIM runs

VIM runs contrary to more formal, hierarchical cultures.

contrary to the more formal, hierarchical culture among the Prague developers. Language is also an issue. "They typically have different degree levels of English language skills," according to Conway, the CTO. "But a lot of them have a much better time with written English verses spoken English." In contrast to VIM, videoconferences are occasional and involve greater numbers of people. Therefore, each person participates less and language is less of a problem.

Beyond these issues, another key factor impacting the adoption of VIM is the nature of the work. Software developers are typically more concerned with sharing data than with seeing each other spontaneously. If the cross-continental team were developing market strategy or advertising concepts, the collaborators would likely focus more on facial expressions. They might want to study their colleagues to evaluate whether everybody agrees that a new campaign will work. In such a case, video would enhance IM regardless of the language and cultural gap.

As the cross-cultural teams develop closer relationships through in-person gatherings and joint coding at a distance, Monster is infusing the Czech development team with a more collaborative culture. Recognizing cultural differences has helped Monster bridge global work styles, and the company is applying that knowledge as it opens additional global development centers.

CREATING VALUE THROUGH INSPIRATION

The challenge for any organization is to inspire people.

The challenge for any organization is to inspire people. If people feel inspired, they are more likely to collaborate and innovate. This is true whether they work from home, from a hotel, or from a train or plane. Software developers, entrepreneurs, writers, graphic designers and others often work remotely and create value through collaboration, because they are inspired. Start-up technology companies often inspire home-based, geographically-dispersed collaborators to think and innovate. Besides the often vague possibility of financial rewards from start-up work, employees embrace the lack of control and the informality of the start-up culture. Collaborators appreciate that the organization values their input, and they often contribute their best.

Taiichi Ohno, the father of Toyota's production system, inspired manufacturing workers by encouraging them to think. Ohno conceived a "pull" system in which demand at each step of the manufacturing process determines production levels. Traditionally, companies have pushed production based on schedules that anticipate demand. In such environments, workers are paid to do, rather than to think. Therefore, there is little opportunity for workers to gain wisdom or to innovate.

Toyota's pull system, in contrast, not only pulls—rather than pushes—inventory, but it also pulls more from each worker. Toyota's approach asks workers to collaborate in the development and improvement of manufacturing processes. "An environment where people have to think brings with it wisdom, and this wisdom brings with it *kaizen* [continuous improvement]," Teruyuki Minoura, Toyota's chief business development and purchasing officer, told an audience at the Automotive Parts Solution Fair in Tokyo in June of 2003. He added that developing people who can come up with unique ideas and revolutionary techniques is key to Toyota's success.

Toyota's approach asks workers to collaborate in the development and improvement of manufacturing processes.

The same control paradigm that governs push systems on assembly lines also prevents organizational cultures from embracing telecommuting and "work from anywhere" approaches. Borrowing the concept from Toyota's production system, organizations can apply a cultural pull approach in encouraging employees to think, innovate, contribute, and collaborate. If the organizational culture reinforces this mindset, employees will perform at their best—regardless of whether they work from home or from elsewhere. In a push system, employees will find ways to avoid thinking, contributing, and collaborating even if they are sitting fifteen feet from their supervisors.

Organizations can apply a cultural pull approach in encouraging employees to think, innovate, contribute, and collaborate.

PROCTER & GAMBLE: COLLABORATION BUILT ON TRUST AND INTERDEPENDENCY

Procter & Gamble has embraced collaboration since brothers-in-law William Procter, a candle maker, and James Gamble, a soap maker, partnered to create the company in 1837. Operating in eighty-six countries, P&G assembles teams that typically include people from multiple regions and functions. The culture embraces cross-fertilization, so employees gain broad experience across P&G's operations. This exposure reduces barriers, inspires innovation and can give people a sense of the bigger picture. The culture also encourages promoting from within, which builds trust.

As P&G integrates collaboration practices and tools throughout its enterprise, both cultural legacy and senior leadership play a role. "If you don't collaborate and yet you have interdependencies, you can never succeed," according to CIO Filippo Passerini who also has responsibility for human resources, facilities and many other services shared by P&G's business units. When A.G. Lafley became CEO in 2002, he extended collaborative culture to the executive suite. P&G created more open space on the executive floor and added a livingroom area for spontaneous chat and chance meetings. The environment throughout P&G includes low-walled cubicles and "huddle rooms," informal meeting areas which offer phones and laptop connections. The huddle rooms are strategically placed to encourage casual, cross-functional encounters.

With 300 brands sold in 160 countries, P&G must design region-specific packaging for each product. Package design across business units and regions involves considerable coordination in that business units manage thirty thousand pieces of artwork each year. P&G has developed a system allowing collaborative design and approval. The system lets globally-dispersed team members design packaging in real time. Many business units and functions participate in the art work process including legal, regulatory, marketing, translation, and design. Business partners including printers also participate in the process.

Historically, P&G has adopted tools quickly. In the early 1990s, the company developed its own internal email system to unite its geographically-dispersed workforce. Using presence-enabled IM and web conferencing, colleagues can find one another and determine availability without leaving the application in which they are working. During and after P&G's acquisition of Gillette, the two companies used these tools to integrate processes and organizational structures more rapidly and more effectively. Also, P&G uses videoconferencing to link geographically-dispersed teams.

To enhance collaboration, P&G is integrating such tools as web conferencing and IM with 3D computer-aided design/manufacturing (CAD/CAM). This creates a virtual design environment for product development, manufacturing systems development, and product testing. The ability to visualize a prototype and the production process lets P&G people and business partners conduct virtual design reviews.

In one case, collaborative visualization saved a product package from cancellation. P&G was planning to replace a metal can with a plastic AromaSeal canister for its Folgers coffee brand. However, the new packaging was falling short in quality control testing and needed to withstand stacking and shipping tests. Additional physical tests would have been too costly and time consuming. At a fraction of the time and cost, the team virtually tested the canister and brought the packaging up to quality standards by the launch date. P&G's coffee volume and sales subsequently rose 4 percent. This creation of value is a manifestation of the company's Culture of Collaboration.

ENGAGING MOBILE AND DESKLESS WORKERS

In chapter 1, we outlined the trends that are enabling collaboration. These trends have particular impact in integrating collaboration into lifestyles and work styles. While convergence and the availability of broadband are making home offices more viable, Third Generation (3G) and Fourth Generation (4G) wireless allow us to collaborate from almost anywhere. Clearly, using collaborative tools over broadband wireless gives managers flexibility. But besides road warriors and telecommuters, there are many other peripatetic professionals who would benefit from richer collaboration. These are people who spend most of their day in motion rather than sitting at desks or in meeting rooms. These include doctors, nurses, insurance adjusters, photographers, police officers, factory workers, emergency personnel and many others.

The work style of Richard Parry-Jones, Ford's group vice president of global product development and chief technology officer, illustrates the significance of mobility in collaboration. Parry-Jones spends much of his time in the back seat of a car en route to company locations in Europe. His only tools are a notebook computer and a mobile phone (see figure 4.1). Using those two devices, he collaborates with colleagues globally. In the mid-1990s, the CTO would have been part of an elite group of executives and other road warriors using laptops. Now organizations provide notebooks to a broader population. With broadband wireless and a camera, notebook users can see each other when necessary.

Some mobile workers spend most of their day in motion and part of their day at a desk. Others could be classified as deskless workers. These people often work on the front lines providing care, tabulating damages at disaster scenes, photographing news, responding to crimes, or assembling the products on which a company stakes its reputation.

Deskless and mobile workers can effectively collaborate only if the approach and tools fit into their work styles.

Deskless and mobile workers can effectively collaborate only if the approach and tools fit into their work styles. Expecting people to abandon their work to collaborate makes

Figure 4.1   Richard Parry-Jones, Ford Motor Company's group vice president of global product development and chief technology officer, collaborates with global colleagues from the back seat of a car.

little sense. But it's in the best interests of organizations to include the input of mobile workers in collaborative endeavors. After all, they're often the people who have insight from the front lines. Rather than make process decisions in a vacuum, smart organizations encourage deskless and

Smart organizations encourage deskless and mobile workers to collaborate with people across functions, departments, levels, and regions.

mobile workers to collaborate with people across functions, departments, levels, and regions. This means making it easy to participate in synchronous and asynchronous collaboration.

Collaboration success requires bringing connectivity to people rather than forcing people to leave their work.

Collaboration success requires bringing connectivity to people rather than forcing people to leave their work and walk to desks, conference rooms or other locations. Many companies have installed monitors displaying company news and information throughout their facilities. This often works well for one-way communication, because video monitors incorporate information into people's work styles rather than forcing people to attend informational meetings. This is particularly true for deskless workers who may lack a device on which to view streamed video. However, collaboration requires two-way interaction. The next step for companies who value collaboration is to extend collaborative capabilities to front-line workers who are often mobile or deskless. The most effective approach is recognizing how and where people work and fitting the tools and collaborative approaches into their work styles.

Dow's global sales force works—in most cases—virtually. This means rather than showing up at a Dow facility, salespeople move from one customer site to the next. Dow supports salespeople with a telecommuting program, but discourages them from spending more than eight hours a week in home offices. So that salespeople can share in Dow's culture and interact with colleagues in multiple business units, Dow is opening sales "hubs" or regional centers providing drop-in office facilities. At these hubs, Dow schedules such group interactions as health screens, safety meetings, and investment seminars. These activities spark interaction among otherwise isolated colleagues and help establish informal relationships that lead to the exchange of ideas and approaches.

Because face-to-face interaction is occasional, Dow is considering how to integrate collaborative tools into the work styles of salespeople without cutting into their sales time. "It needs to be wireless for it to be effective in my book. Otherwise, you're sitting somewhere," insists Robert Long, who manages sales administration and coordinates Dow's telecommuting program for salespeople globally. "If you're sitting somewhere, you're probably not spending time with customers."

COLLABORATING FROM THE SKY

While broadband wireless fits many work styles, wireless is typically useless at thirty-thousand feet. Boeing is bridging the connectivity gap by equipping many commercial airplanes with what we might call broadband to the seat. Besides exchanging IM and reading email, passengers can participate in web conferences and videoconferences (see figure 4.2).

In May of 2002, Boeing announced what it called the first public demonstration of "true broadband" videoconferencing between an airplane and the ground. Specifically the videoconference linked Boeing 737 passengers flying thirty-seven thousand feet above Arizona with participants at Boeing's annual investors' conference in St. Louis. The demonstration via satellite ran at a speed of 256 kilobits per second (kbps). The event came seventy-two years after AT&T's first public demonstration of two-way video telephony.

The down side of airplane connectivity, of course, is the expectation that we're available in one of the few places where we, until recently, were out of contact. I know several road warriors who relish their quiet time in the sky. For many frequent business travelers, however, sitting on an airplane has meant being out of the loop. If those travelers can interact with colleagues around the world from an airplane, collaboration can more closely fit their work styles.

Of course, full participation in a videoconference may be challenging outside of the relatively-private seat environment of first class. Nevertheless, airplane connectivity allows people to interact

©*Boeing*™. *Used under license.*

Figure 4.2   Collaboration from the sky: using videoconferencing from an executive jet.

when necessary through multiple modes. Presence awareness means that people can determine how, when, with whom, and for what reasons they wish to communicate and collaborate. This applies whether they're at their desks, at home, driving, or flying.

MEETINGS REVISITED

Meetings, while an integral part of most organizational cultures, provoke strong opinions. "Meetings are a waste of time" is the comment I hear most frequently. On one hand, meetings can reduce productivity and even interfere with collaboration. People who face project deadlines and other workflow concerns must leave their work and go someplace else. This may involve walking down the hall, running to another building, driving across town, or traveling. Then they must spend perhaps two hours listening to colleagues and others who may enjoy the sound of their own voices. Participants exchange many words, but often say little.

People complain that meetings distract them from real business and interfere with accomplishment. The temptation is to zone out and think about other work or sneak peaks at mobile devices. Sales people have particular disdain for meetings, because attending reduces valuable sales time and therefore costs them money.

Meetings are most effective for establishing and rekindling relationships rather than for disseminating information.

On the other hand, meetings pull some people from the cocoon of solo work and encourage interaction and the exchange of ideas. Meetings are most effective for establishing and rekindling relationships rather than for disseminating information. Anybody who attends trade shows knows that the real deal happens in parties, bars, and hospitality lounges rather than on the show floor or during endless conference sessions. Trade shows provide far more value by building social networks than by passing out marketing kits and news releases. People fly into a city and check into a hotel on the company dime primarily to establish contacts, enjoy informality with colleagues and partners, develop opportunities and make deals.

Similarly, the best meetings allow people to press the flesh and establish closer ties. After an effective meeting, people leave the room feeling more professionally intimate. Meetings work better if they're for a specific purpose. Calling a brainstorming session with a particular goal lets people know that the purpose is to tap their creativity in developing new approaches rather than to hold forth on any topic.

The least effective meetings are often regularly scheduled ones, such as the Monday 8:00 a.m. sales meeting. Often, there is no agenda and no purpose. Many sales people view such meetings as nothing more than a command-and-control mechanism. A friend of mine who is a news manager for a major market television station detests the scheduled daily meetings ostensibly for producers, assignment editors and other managers to discuss which stories to cover. Often there are delays in getting reporters and photographers to news scenes, because managers are too busy blowing hot air.

The Culture of Collaboration changes meetings. We no longer must gather in an overly-formal environment for a data dump. There is no need to watch somebody show slides and pass out materials as we struggle to remain engaged—or to stay awake! For disseminating data and information, our options include email and team sites. For reviewing slides in real time, web conferencing makes more sense. We can review the material more effectively on our own PC's or notebook computers in our preferred work environments. For face-to-face brainstorming, we might choose a more relaxed setting than the typical conference room..

THE INTERRUPT-DRIVEN CULTURE

The increasing availability of collaborative capabilities on desktops, notebooks, and mobile devices encourages shorter, more plentiful interactions. Keeping interactions brief increases both our absorption of information and our motivation to collaborate. Also, it makes more sense to collaborate when we have our work at hand. Web conferencing lets us discuss data while reviewing it in real-time, while personal videoconferencing permits a more intimate exchange while sharing applications and a digital whiteboard.

The culture of work is evolving to accept interruption. The interrupt-driven culture means that we are getting increasingly agile in moving from one world to the next— from our roles at work to our roles in our personal lives. While we are engaged in one activity, another role interrupts us via IM, voice, or perhaps video. We engage briefly

> *In the interrupt-driven culture, we are getting increasingly agile in moving from one world to the next—from our roles at work to our roles in our personal lives.*

and switch gears. Our days become a series of interruptions via multiple modes of collaboration and communication. These relatively brief interactions let us deal with small issues before they become big problems and also free our schedules from unnecessary meetings.

Though meetings have their place in establishing and advancing relationships, increasingly we are using spontaneous rather than scheduled interactions to collaborate. In this regard, the collective culture is perhaps ahead of many organizational cultures. On a whim, we play games online with people we've never met. And many of us have mastered our buddy lists for IM and think nothing of initiating spontaneous chat with our friends. With this conditioning, it is a smaller jump to collaborate with more spontaneity at work.

The chief information officer of the software company, SAS, manages her to-do list through presence. Suzanne Gordon begins her day by checking the status of people she needs to reach. "That kind of dictates who I work with that first hour of the morning," she says. Between meetings, she again checks the availability of colleagues, connects via IM with those who are "on" and then crosses more items off her list. "If I stay late, sometimes I can pick up the people in the international offices for a quick little chat," says the CIO.

As presence-enabled tools gain traction in our work styles and spontaneous interactions increase, meetings become less formal. When we're accustomed to collaborating with someone through IM or VIM, formality falls flat. A more effective face-to-face meeting may occur in the kind of spaces, described in chapter 3, that the Mayo Clinic's SPARC unit or the Stanford Center for Innovations in Learning (SCIL) utilize to encourage collaboration. Or, it may make more sense to bond with colleagues over drinks or meals. The conference-room approach for many meetings makes less sense.

THREE MODES OF WORK: PROCESS, PROJECT AND INCIDENT

Let's consider three modes of work:

1. Process
2. Project
3. Incident

Process-oriented work involves continuity. Project-oriented work requires clear start points, check points and end points. Incident-oriented work involves responding to developments or crises of a limited duration.

Clearly, some people are better suited to one of the three, and many jobs are more geared towards one mode. Technical support, emergency medicine and uniform police work are more incident-oriented. The distinctions, however, are vague in that there is plenty of crossover. A given job may be mostly process-oriented but occasionally project-oriented. For instance, working in staffing, a subset of human resources, for a large company revolves around a process. The process may involve recruitment, interviewing, meeting equal opportunity guidelines, interfacing with business units, and maintaining employee records. However, the mode may shift to project-oriented when there is a major hiring initiative or an acquisition.

Public relations and sales are more process-oriented but have project elements. PR people must develop and maintain relationships with reporters and fulfill the function of disseminating the organization's point of view. When there's a major product introduction, however, PR becomes project-oriented. Sales, with the exception of telemarketing and other quick-score endeavors, also involves developing and maintaining relationships. Trying to land a major account, however, is a project.

Project-oriented work includes building and designing products, producing films and videos, and writing books. However, there are elements of process in each of these disciplines.

Creating animation for movies is project-oriented. When the film is finished, animators move on to the next one. Nevertheless, improving one's skills as an animation professional is a process. Journalism is also project-oriented. When the story runs, the project ends. But developing sources is a process. Psychology is process-oriented. A psychologist sees patients regularly, sometimes for years. However, if a patient threatens suicide, the work temporarily becomes incident-oriented.

Let's consider how to integrate capabilities into work styles in dynamic environments. Organizations must recognize that as the work mode shifts, the modes of collaboration may also shift. This means not only providing the right mix of capabilities, but also making those capabilities manifest themselves in multiple ways and appear in multiple devices.

As the work mode shifts, the modes of collaboration may also shift.

An HR manager might normally use email, phone and room videoconferencing to collaborate on the staffing process. In the faster-paced environment of a merger project, however, the HR manager may spend more time away from his or her desk, perhaps at factories or other facilities. The relatively slow turnaround time of email exchanges may fall flat. IM allows the merger team to interact in near real-time, fitting the bill better than email.

Despite the HR manager's involvement in the merger team, he or she may still need to participate in a weekly videoconference with a geographically-dispersed HR group. Under normal circumstances, walking down the hall to the videoconference room fits the manager's work style. But now the work style has morphed into a project-oriented classification. Therefore, gaining the ability to join the videoconference from a video-enabled notebook computer makes sense.

If, on the other hand, a merger colleague is working in an application and needs to collaborate with the HR manager on the fly, presence awareness lets him or her know whether the manager is available for IM, video or some other mode of interaction. A team site, the use of which has particular relevance for the HR manager engaged in a merger, also indicates how to track down team members. Understanding the dynamic nature of process, project, and incident-oriented work helps organizations become more flexible in providing capabilities, tools and collaborative approaches that fit work styles.

LIVING WITH LONE WOLFS IN COLLABORATIVE CULTURES

We've discussed how different types of workers spend their day and how this relates to collaboration. But what about various types of people and their personal work styles? Some people prefer to get direction and then go off in a corner and make their mistakes in private. When they get their work just right, then they're willing to show it to colleagues. To others, this approach feels wrong. They hate toiling away on work without knowing whether they're going down the right path. They crave interaction with their colleagues in part to validate their ideas and approaches. "The kind who likes to go off in the corner is not going to like working collaboratively that much," notes Steve Sullivan, director of R&D for Industrial Light & Magic.

Those who prefer going off in a corner may believe their work is superior and want full credit for their contributions. But can work be truly superior if it's performed in the vacuum of individualism? Probably not, because the work becomes infused with the viewpoint and prejudices of a single person. Even if that worker tosses his or her work "over the fence" to a colleague or supervisor who makes changes and additions, the work retains the often limited point of view of a single creator.

In contrast, letting multiple minds share creation of a product or service often produces greater value because of the broader perspective and talent involved. For the lone wolf to collaborate, he or she must overcome fear. The lone wolf guards territory, because of concern that sharing data will disrupt the franchise and diminish his or her value to the organization.

Letting multiple minds share creation of a product or service often produces greater value because of the broader perspective and talent involved.

ILM's new integrated systems approach blends capabilities and data once available only to particular disciplines in isolated systems. As ILM encourages greater knowledge among artists of multiple disciplines, the company faces a trade-off in system design. Each component must be less tailored to specific specialties so that artists from other disciplines can "duck in" and do a little paint work or a little lighting. This means that the tools more closely match the work styles and knowledge of specialists who morph into generalists in a cross-functional collaborative environment.

"Some people take to it immediately and they can do a little bit of everything and they'll do a single shot from end to end and they'll thrive in that environment," explains Sullivan. "Some people have no interest in doing other stuff, like they just paint and that's all they'll ever do. And that's fine. We have room for them too."

Nevertheless, kudos-craving lone wolfs may ultimately warm up to collaboration once they comprehend the order-of-magnitude increase in credit that they will receive as key players on collaborative teams. Instead of getting kudos from the boss as an individual, a specialist may appreciate receiving broader internal, and perhaps external, recognition as a collaborator.

BRIDGING TIME ZONES

While collaborative tools enable people in home and satellite offices to collaborate with headquarters from almost anywhere at any time, how does an organization ensure that people retain work and life balance? If people at a New York headquarters usually schedule web conferences, audio conferences or videoconferences during their work day, team members in Japan may be expected to interact with colleagues in the wee hours of the morning. We can all understand occasional crises, but such expectations get old quickly.

Arranging interactions on a headquarters-driven schedule runs against the grain of true collaboration.

Arranging interactions on a headquarters-driven schedule runs against the grain of true collaboration. Also, expecting people around the globe to join spontaneous collaborative sessions throughout the nine-to-five work day in the Eastern time zone makes people in other regions feel like they are participating in a command-and-control, headquarters-driven, U.S.-oriented culture. Being global and collaborative means considering the lifestyles and work styles of all team members, regardless of location. This applies to scheduled sessions and the use of presence to determine how and whether people are available for spontaneous interaction.

Being global and collaborative means considering the lifestyles and work styles of all team members, regardless of location.

At Dow Chemical Company, team members and managers at headquarters have become sensitive to the work clocks of geographically-dispersed collaborators. Cindy Newman, Dow's director of corporate communications, leads a global team that includes a Singapore-based member. Based at Dow headquarters in Midland, Michigan, Newman constantly considers the work styles and lifestyles of global team members when arranging interactions. To avoid a headquarters-driven collaboration schedule, Newman sometimes holds virtual meetings at 10:00 p.m. Midland time with her Singapore team member.

"Managing balance of life with technology is a double-edged sword. Technology is great, but it comes with expectations that bring headaches," says Newman. "I don't really want to work 24/7. And I don't really think my people should have to either. As responsive as we want to be and as responsible as technology allows us to be, at the end of the day you have to make judgments about how you're going to spend your time and what's important to you."

Many global companies with collaborative cultures solve time zone problems by scheduling interactions that rotate convenience among regions. So a virtual meeting may fit a Paris collaborator's schedule better one week, but the next week a session is more convenient for a colleague in Boston. Other solutions include choosing asynchronous modes of collaboration, if appropriate to the situation.

When an interaction requires the higher touch of video, video mail may enable a collaborator in one region to show and explain a maintenance problem. In another region, a collaborator can respond via video mail and perhaps demonstrate a proposed solution. When someone is unable to participate in a web conference or videoconference, the virtual meeting can be archived and made available so that the collaborator remains in the loop and can offer input through video mail or email.

Clearly, the impact of collaboration on lifestyles and work styles involves a dichotomy. Effective collaboration enhances our lifestyles and work styles by giving us freedom and flexibility to live and work where

> *Effective collaboration enhances lifestyles and work styles by giving us freedom and flexibility.*

and how we choose. We can engage in shared creation with globally-dispersed colleagues from planes, trains, automobiles, and from home. However, collaboration tools can blur the boundaries between personal time and work hours. Therefore, we must ensure that tools reflect our preferences which might preclude receiving work-related IM or calls at 3:00 a.m. Also, organizational cultures must evolve to embrace flexibility in regional and personal approaches to work.

CHAPTER 5

BREAKING DOWN BARRIERS

First, a disclaimer: I have never been a smoker. Now, the shocking truth: smoking forms communities and breaks down barriers.

This notion dates back to the schoolyard when those who smoked formed a special bond. Social relationships among smokers carry over into the workplace. And, in fact, anti-smoking laws have enhanced those ties, because now smokers must congregate outside buildings to light up. Within organizations, barriers develop among departments and functions. Marketing develops its own culture and has difficulty interacting with sales. Finance and engineering may avoid interaction. However, smokers from all of these departments interact. They often get a heads up regarding new policies and directions, because they have formed bonds and broken down barriers.

Barriers develop among departments and functions within organizations.

I know a retired manager at a large Silicon Valley company who developed a close relationship with the former CEO, in part because they both stepped outside the headquarters building several times a day to smoke. The CEO, though several levels above this manager, frequently bounced ideas off of him and vice versa. So, smoking can break down both departmental silos and hierarchical barriers.

I know what you're thinking. Rosen thinks we should take up smoking, jeopardize our lives and livelihoods, and put our families at risk all in the name of collaboration. Absolutely not! What I am suggesting is that we can learn something from how smoking impacts interaction in the workplace and apply it. We can then learn more about breaking down barriers to interaction and gain insight into cross-functional collaboration.

So, how does smoking break down barriers? For one thing, smoking forces people who are otherwise distributed around a building to share the same physical space—namely, the area a few feet beyond the building doorway. Smoking also involves sharing in that smokers often light each other's cigarettes and mutually engage in a common pastime. Since smokers are often a minority, they feel connected to each other as if they belong to a club. Those ties often eclipse departmental and hierarchical structures.

CURING SILO SYNDROME

While smoking involves sharing only among those who smoke, collaboration breaks down barriers across the organization. Unlike smoking, collaboration works its magic independent of geography. Rather than sharing a flick of the lighter in physical space, collaborators may share ideas in virtual space. The result is that we form bonds and relationships with people across functions, business units and levels. Let's explore how collaboration reduces what we might call *silo syndrome*.

Almost no organization is immune to this syndrome in which each department or function interacts primarily within that department rather than with other functions and departments. Marketing interacts with marketing, but avoids interacting with sales or IT. Product design avoids interacting with manufacturing. In a sense, this is natural. People within particular disciplines may have similar training and use certain jargon. They are more comfortable with one another than with people in other departments. In

Almost no organization is immune to "silo syndrome."

hierarchical organizations, it is sometimes necessary to use the chain of command just to talk with another department. A manager might need to run an idea "up the flagpole" and let a more senior person involve another function or silo.

When silo syndrome infects an organization, one symptom is finger pointing. If a business unit leader fails to meet gross margin targets, he or she may insist the problem is that the purchasing group failed to buy materials at the right price. Or, he or she might blame the problem on incompetence within the accounting function. Often the real problem is a lack of collaboration among people in multiple functions and business units whose complimentary skills are necessary to create value.

HOW CULTURE IMPACTS SILOS

I have coached numerous sales executives, most of whom believe marketing screws up strategy, produces poor "collateral" or brochures, and generally does more to complicate sales than anything else. If only marketing understood the needs of salespeople, the thinking goes, sales could exceed targets. I have also coached many marketing people who think if only sales knew how to sell that the company would succeed in the marketplace. Often salespeople prefer communicating one-on-one, while marketing people prefer presenting to groups. Clearly, there is a cultural divide between these functions and this difference contributes to silo syndrome in many organizations. Effective collaboration requires breaking down the barriers and bridging the cultures.

A large telecommunications company once invited me aboard a cocktail cruise around San Francisco Bay to promote a mobility initiative. It was a great idea that was poorly executed. The company figured it could lure industry analysts and consultants to an information dump if the event were on a boat rather than in a meeting room. Both marketing and salespeople participated in the event, which began with meeting, greeting and cocktails. During this period, the salespeople introduced themselves and relished the one-on-one interaction.

The marketing people, seeming uncomfortable amid unstructured interaction, retreated to the corners of the floating room. Half an hour into the cruise, the marketing people interrupted the party—and many good conversations—and announced that participants should take their seats. Then, one-by-one, marketing people took the floor and delivered presentations. The salespeople began drifting to the edges of the room, and then disappeared one by one.

Growing bored with the presentations, I left my seat for a walk around the boat. On an upper deck, I found most of the sales team laughing, sharing drinks, and anxious for me to sit down so that they could connect one-on-one. They even commented about the ridiculously formal nature of the event that was clearly driven by marketing. The salespeople believed that a more effective approach would have been to continue the meet-and-greet cocktail party for the entire cruise. Clearly, silo syndrome was so engrained between sales and marketing that it manifested itself in the limited physical environment of a cocktail cruise boat.

When I worked as a television reporter at a CBS affiliate in a mid-sized, midwestern market, the news department rarely interacted with people in other station functions. Reporters, producers and photographers typically had journalism and communications backgrounds. Reporters, working closely with photographers, interviewed presidential candidates and cabinet members. We hit crime scenes at a moment's notice, trudged through chemical spills, and flew with police in choppers as they swooped down on marijuana fields.

In short, we lived lives of adventure as compared with the more routine existence of people in other station departments. Also, most of us were from other parts of the country—sort of TV nomads—whereas the non-news people were mostly local. Therefore, we had difficulty finding common ground with those who worked in accounting or the folks who decided when to schedule commercials or the engineers who kept the station on the air. We interacted with accounting only when we wanted something such as reimbursement for a business meal. I remember one accountant telling me that the pizza I had while out of town on business was too expensive and was cheaper in his neighborhood. "But we weren't in your neighborhood," I explained.

There was tension between departments perhaps because of the relative freedom many news people had to chase down stories, have lunch with sources, and spend most of the day outside the office. Reporters and anchors appeared on the news each evening and received recognition for their work. Others worked in relative obscurity. In short, silo syndrome existed.

The department that news people interfaced with best was sales. Sometimes salespeople would hang around the newsroom or chat with reporters in the parking lot. That's because, like news people, salespeople spent most of their day outside the office and focused on communicating with many external people. So, the two departmental cultures shared some elements.

Despite the negatives, silos have some advantages. They allow departmental and functional cultures to develop and increase professional intimacy within those areas. One disadvantage of collocating people from multiple functions is that this approach can disrupt the chemistry within departments. However, people who share the same training and discipline will establish relationships regardless of where they sit, and therefore the cross-functional collaboration benefits of collocation outweigh the disadvantages.

> The more companies collaborate, the more barriers disintegrate among departments.

Whether, how, and why departments interact is certainly within the province of culture. Companies with collaborative cultures have less defined barriers among departments and functions, and therefore it's easier to avoid silo syndrome and enable collaboration. Also, the more companies collaborate, the more barriers disintegrate among departments and the less of a negative role silos play. Using tools that enable collaboration can increase cross-functional interaction and decrease silo syndrome. The companies that use tools most effectively, typically those with collaborative cultures, experience more mild cases of silo syndrome.

At Dow Chemical Company, people from different departments and functions form informal teams to investigate new business process approaches. Implementing iRooms providing a range of capabilities has enhanced cross-functional collaboration and allowed informal teams to flourish. It makes little difference if team members transfer to other locations, because it's relatively easy to continue relationships via iRoom tools such as videoconferencing. This, in turn, has prevented silo syndrome from impeding innovation.

In another example of breaking down barriers to stimulate innovation, Monster collocates product managers and engineers. The company wants to cross-pollinate its people so that each function learns more about the other and develops sensitivity and understanding regarding what makes each function tick. Sometimes engineers feel, "This person is just giving me things to do. They don't make any sense," says Monster CTO Mark Conway. "Then on the other side, you have the product person saying 'Why can't these guys get anything done? What are they doing down there?'" Rather than the traditional "waterfall approach" in which work pours from one function to the next, Monster is using collocation to stimulate cross-functional collaboration and create new approaches to old problems.

DISCUSS FISHING ON COMPANY TIME!

There was a time when many organizations refused to give employees Internet access, because of fears that people would surf instead of work. This was a manifestation of command-and-control cultures. Most organizations now realize that blocking access interferes with information flow and idea generation. In collaborative cultures, providing tools and collaborative spaces for people with common interests further breaks down barriers among functions, departments and regions.

Shortsighted organizations worry that IM, wikis and virtual chat rooms will decrease productivity. Innovative companies recognize the value of increasing interactions among employees, regardless of the nature of those interactions. IM, wikis and related tools enhance socialization, allowing innovation and light bulb moments along with cross-functional collaboration.

Organizations benefit by providing ways for people to find others with common interests. This builds community, one of the Ten Cultural Elements of Collaboration. One approach involves virtual

Encouraging interactions among people with common interests reinforces cross-functional collaboration.

spaces on company intranets where people who share interests like chess or fishing can meet. This may also spark informal business-related teams dealing with everything from recycling programs to the use of new tools. Presence awareness indicates whether members of these interest groups are available and how to reach them. Undoubtedly, people from many departments, functions, and regions will interact in these ad hoc teams. Encouraging interactions among people with common interests reinforces cross-functional collaboration.

If people from different departments are accustomed to interacting about fishing or recycling, they are more likely to embrace collaborating in designing a new manufacturing process or marketing a new product. Putting cameras on notebook computers, as Dow is doing, provides even greater opportunity for cross-cultural interaction. Now people in different regions with similar interests can find each other in virtual spaces, determine each other's availability, and—if appropriate—launch video interactions without having to schedule conference room time. These interactions may be real-time or near real-time in the case of VIM.

USING TOOLS TO BREAK DOWN BARRIERS

Like most companies, W.R. Grace & Co. has struggled with silo syndrome. "People create their own little fiefdoms or kingdoms or empires or whatever you want to call them, and it's kind of a not-invented-here type mentality," says Barry Kuhn, manager of electronic media for W.R. Grace. "And groups that could benefit from a lot of wonderful ideas don't, because of these silos."

Part of the reason that silos develop among functions and regions at Grace and at other companies is the direct travel cost and indirect cost of lost productivity involved in getting people together. This is true even if all of the people who should be collaborating work on the same corporate campus. In some cases, it may take twenty minutes to get from one building to the next. For an IT professional to leave his or her work, walk or drive to a meeting, participate in the meeting and then walk or drive back to his or her workspace takes a bite out of productivity.

Integrating tools including videoconferencing and web conferencing into workflow and culture has increased cross-functional collaboration at Grace. This has helped tear down walls among departments. If a team charged with improving a business process schedules a videoconference, members will often inquire whether anybody else in the company is working on a similar problem. If the answer is yes, says Kuhn, then they can include them. "It's wonderful, because these narrow little silos are starting to get broader and broader."

This means that people from more departments and more regions provide input, and this improves the quality of decisions because they include a broader perspective. If people, because of time zones or conflicts, are unable to participate in real-time interactions, they can review archived audio, video, slides, and meeting notes.

HOW PRINCIPLES AND PROCESSES ENCOURAGE COLLABORATION

Tools are more likely to break down barriers among departments, functions and regions if the policies, principles and culture encourage collaboration. Such is the case at Toyota. Nevertheless, the company acknowledges the need to keep silo syndrome in check. The approach involves developing work processes and routines based on the Toyota Way.

"We have silos within Toyota for certain. The only way you can break down the silos is when you collaborate, form a team where you're interdependent. You need to work together and have clear processes that allow you to move fast," according to Mike Morrison, dean of the University of Toyota. Toyota recognizes that loyalty to one's department or function is natural, but institutes processes that require people from many functional areas to interact while designing and manufacturing vehicles. While tools including videoconferencing combined with advanced computer-aided

Tools have limited impact on silo syndrome without processes, practices, and principles.

design/manufacturing (CAD/CAM) enhance efforts to break down barriers, tools use would have limited impact on silo syndrome without processes, practices, and principles.

Toyota's view is that if you think of organizational culture as a person who over time becomes orderly and values organization as a principle and practice, he or she will use an electronic calendar program effectively. The same concept applies to breaking down barriers through collaborative tools. If the organization institutes practices that encourage interaction among functions, departments and regions, people will effectively use tools and collaborate more effectively.

Perhaps the most important role that the SPARC unit plays at the Mayo Clinic is breaking down barriers among functions. This in turn enhances collaboration and stimulates innovation in care delivery processes. Because of its methodology for innovation and a physical environment that encourages brainstorming, SPARC consistently succeeds in cross-functional collaboration (see profile, page 72).

Besides bringing tremendous improvement to patient care processes, the SPARC unit brings together people who historically have rarely interacted. For instance, SPARC engages audio visual technicians and doctors simultaneously. In the past, doctors and administrators made decisions that impacted the AV technicians. Rather than involve them in the process, the decision makers simply informed the AV people what needed to be done. "What you're basically encouraging everyone to do is engage in the exploration up front and not just engage in the back-end exploitation, if you will," says Ryan Armbruster of Mayo's SPARC unit. "How about we all think about what needs to be done?"

The Stanford Center for Innovations in Learning (SCIL), from which SPARC drew inspiration for the design of its physical space, is breaking down barriers in education. While silo syndrome is less of an issue in the classroom than in organizational structures, barriers nevertheless form between professors and students and among students. Before integrating tools and collaborative environments into teaching, SCIL began with principles and processes. As we have discussed, a central principle was shifting the role of the professor from "sage on the stage" to "guide on the side."

In traditional education, a barrier exists between the professor who stands and lectures from the front of the room and students who sit and take notes. Clearly, the environment and approach reinforce hierarchy. The professor delivers the lesson and the students, hopefully, absorb it. Formality rules.

In SCIL's world, students and professors explore learning together. And that learning occurs all around the classroom, using whiteboards on side walls, pushing content

> *Students will enter the business world conditioned to collaborate.*

from notebook computers to the front of the room, linking another classroom via videoconference, and exchanging IM. Informality and, yes, collaborative chaos come into play. As this approach takes hold more broadly in education, students will enter the business world conditioned to collaborate and ready to interact with multiple functions, departments, regions and levels.

> *Collaboration shifts roles and relationships and smashes barriers.*

So, collaboration shifts roles and relationships and smashes barriers. When I coach executives to deliver keynote speeches, I frequently encourage them to abandon lecterns, get off the stage, and instead walk out into the audience. This helps eliminate the barrier that often exists between speaker and audience and gets people more engaged. Theater in the round was a movement that gave rise to such venues as New York City's Circle in the Square. The idea was to break down the barriers that exist between actors and audience. Some directors extend this concept by having actors perform some scenes from the audience, an approach that late-night television hosts have also adopted.

SIX SIGMA: THE SILO KILLER?

Six Sigma is playing a significant role in increasing collaboration and in breaking down barriers within companies. There are countless books and other sources on Six Sigma, so there's little need to complicate this book with details of this quality control approach. Suffice to say that the Greek letter sigma can denote variation from a standard; and Six Sigma statistically measures how far a process deviates from zero defects. Developed by Motorola, Six Sigma comprises disciplined practices to reduce defects and increase quality in manufacturing. Six Sigma has also been applied to processes in service industries. An overall Six Sigma process called DMAIC stands for define, measure, analyze, improve and control particular processes that affect customer satisfaction.

Six Sigma encourages people throughout the organization to get involved in quality improvement projects early.

Advocates insist that the approach reduces product cycle time, produces more reliable products and services, reduces costs, and increases customer satisfaction. Six Sigma, adopted widely by leading companies, spells out key processes and sub-processes and identifies process owners. For our discussion, what's compelling about Six Sigma is that it encourages people throughout the organization to get involved in quality improvement projects early rather than waiting until a production line fails or a customer complains about service. Part of this approach involves *information democracy*, the notion that data should be available to every employee at any level whose work touches on quality. This access to data and information breaks down barriers. The idea is to analyze the data and discover root causes of quality problems

Six Sigma initiatives also promote cross-functional teams. If a hotel chain is increasing quality by improving the customer experience, this activity crosses multiple functional areas. Housekeeping, food and beverage, front desk, business center employees and others must abandon silo

Information democracy is the notion that data should be available to every employee at any level whose work touches on quality.

mentality and collaborate. The same principle applies in manufacturing. If an office equipment company wants a higher-quality manufacturing process using Six Sigma, people from multiple departments and functions must get in the game. This reduces functional, business unit, and regional silos.

Since team members are selected regardless of level, Six Sigma reduces the impact of hierarchy in organizations. Cross-functional teams led by process experts and "black belt" facilitators brainstorm improvements. In a departure from shoot-from-the-hip management, teams focus on sharing pertinent data. The entire organization relies on the same data to improve processes, and teams make decisions collaboratively. Since these teams are often geographically dispersed, participants can use a range of collaborative tools to accomplish their objectives.

At Dow Chemical Company, Six Sigma has enhanced the collaborative culture and increased the use of collaborative tools. Teams implementing Six Sigma are typically located in multiple countries, so they rely on Dow's iRooms to bridge the distance gap and enhance collaboration. Because of Six Sigma, people who previously had no contact with one another now collaborate regularly. So, the approach extends Dow's collaborative culture. "It's including people that haven't been included in the collaborative decision-making process," explains Chris Duncan, Dow's global leader for communications resources. "You can come up with the greatest process in the world, but if the people who are required to implement it don't buy in, you're never going to achieve your goals."

To remove defects from manufacturing processes, Dow assembles a cross-functional team that includes plant operators, the people with their hands on the controls. Traditionally, plant operators received marching orders and would simply carry them out. But Dow's philosophy in implementing Six Sigma is that quality depends on plant operators collaborating with people in other functions and contributing input.

The concept is similar to how Mayo's SPARC unit involves audio/video technicians in designing processes that impact them. By including the entire chain of people involved in manufacturing processes, Dow injects realism into the result of its Six Sigma collaboration.

Six Sigma breaks down barriers and keeps silo syndrome in check.

The changes in processes are more likely to improve quality, because the people who work with the processes daily have collaborated on the changes. As people from multiple levels, multiple regions, and multiple functions and departments collaborate on Six Sigma, the process breaks down barriers and keeps silo syndrome in check.

INFORMATION DEMOCRACY AND THE CULTURE OF COLLABORATION

Policies that overly restrict access to data can foster a culture that rewards secrecy and internal competition.

The concept of information democracy and access to data occurs repeatedly in organizations with collaborative cultures. Access is about sharing, one of the Ten Cultural Elements of Collaboration. While companies clearly must safeguard their data from competitors and interlopers, they nevertheless must share data with all of the people who participate in data-driven processes. By sharing information and data, companies promote innovation and collaboration. Policies that overly restrict access to data can foster a culture that rewards secrecy and internal competition. In such cultures, information hoarders thrive.

I once worked for a news director at a television station who encouraged information hoarding. Only producers and one investigative reporter, ostensibly for cost reasons, could gain access to certain research databases. If they needed access, most reporters had to ask a producer or manager to search the databases for them. Considering the compressed deadlines of broadcast journalism, producers rarely had the time or the inclination to conduct searches for reporters.

The news director considered himself a computer guru, often hoarded his knowledge, and assumed most newsroom staff knew little about computing. This made him the go-to person for computer questions. One day, a reporter began exploring the nooks and crannies of the newsroom computer system which everybody used and came upon a folder called "print/send." The reporter realized that the folder contained copies of everything that had been printed.

One such item was a gossip-ridden letter from a co-anchor to a friend. The letter pulled no punches in making fun of the sports anchor's "bad toupee" and the news director's looks and personality. Before long, word got out about the letter. The news director was red- faced and furious—not at the person who wrote the letter but at the reporter for discovering it! Rather than inform the staff that anything printed on the newsroom system is far from private, his solution was to bar reporters from accessing the "print/send" file. This reinforced a culture of secrecy and information hoarding.

BACKLASH FROM ARTIFICIAL DEADLINES

Perhaps the most widespread violation of information democracy is the artificial deadline. Most companies and many individuals create fake finish lines. Engineering managers at chip companies tell their teams

Perhaps the most widespread violation of information democracy is the artificial deadline.

that the customer must have the product in hand by Friday, even though the real deadline is the following Tuesday. Creative team leaders at advertising agencies pretend the work must be complete on Monday, even though the client expects it the following Friday.

Management erroneously believes that artificial deadlines encourage people to do their best work and get it done before the real deadline.

Management erroneously believes that artificial deadlines encourage people to do their best work and get it done before the real deadline. The theory is that managers will look like heroes to their team if, at the last minute, they extend the fake finish line by another day or so. Then they can still meet the real deadline. In fact, this approach breeds a culture of secrecy, compromises trust, and makes people feel out of the loop.

My wife and I communicate openly and trust one another implicitly. However, I will go to great lengths to avoid being late. I used to think I was being smart by telling her that whatever flight we were making was scheduled to leave fifteen minutes earlier than the actual time. I justified this tactic by assuming that my wife was less concerned about deadlines than I and that the artificial deadline would ensure that we would make the real deadline.

On the way to the airport, I was frequently relaxed because I knew we had plenty of time. Meantime, my wife was looking at her watch, concerned that we might miss the plane. When we arrived at the airport with time on our hands, my wife would realize items she could have packed or things she could have done had she had a few more minutes at home. Ultimately, I realized that this seemingly small violation of information democracy was compromising the trust that otherwise defines our relationship.

Tim Alexander, visual effects supervisor at Industrial Light & Magic, has learned that sharing information builds trust, breaks down barriers, and encourages collaboration. In the past, Alexander and his fellow supervisors would tell their teams that clients expected their work two days earlier than the actual deadline. Their justification was that demanding clients expected prompt delivery and that large sums were at stake. Therefore, it seemed better to filter information—including actual deadlines—so that team members would keep their noses to the grindstone and get their work done well before it was due.

"But in the end, all that does is cause people to really feel like you're hiding things from them, they're not collaborating or that you don't trust them," says Alexander. "I've been finding more and more that as much information as you can give everybody that is true and the more you try not to have corporate secrets and try not to hide the reality of the situation, the better." Besides which, two days can be an eternity to creative people, who can use the time to make their shared creation—and the company's product—better.

How Big Changes Create Silo Syndrome Cures

Sometimes the cure for silo syndrome can come from a technological trend, a change in the industry or business landscape, or regulatory requirements. The convergence of voice, video, and data over IP has forced people, who previously had little or no contact, to collaborate. In many organizations, IT traditionally had nothing to do with voice communications and video. A separate telecommunications group ordered phone lines and negotiated with local exchange carriers and long distance providers.

In some cases, the telecom group managed videoconferencing integration and use, because telecom people were familiar with integrated services digital network (ISDN), the standard transport for videoconferencing during the 1990s. In other organizations, the group that managed video production—often a subset of corporate communications—managed videoconferencing. And because video-conferencing began as a training tool for many companies, the tool was sometimes the province of human resources.

In those years, people in many departments regarded IT folks as misguided Star Trek fans at best and, at worst, people who had no understanding of the organization's business. IT people often considered business unit workers Luddites. However, convergence means that IT gets involved in integrating video and almost any other tool into work flow. Therefore departments that previously had occasional contact with IT now regularly interact with that function. The convergence has encouraged geographically-dispersed, cross-functional teams to collaborate in integrating IP-oriented tools into work processes. Barriers among functions have collapsed, in some cases literally as well as figuratively, as people from multiple departments tackle convergence implementation, tools use, and cultural issues.

Exigent business circumstances can break down barriers. Ford's Premier Automotive Group, which the parent company runs from its European headquarters, includes Jaguar, Land Rover, Aston Mar-

> *Executives running each brand who previously retreated into silos must now collaborate.*

tin, and Volvo. In years past, each brand independently made decisions about parts including batteries. In today's competitive environment, this approach lacks efficiency. Therefore, executives running each brand who previously retreated into silos must now collaborate. They hold frequent videoconferences to discuss how one brand's battery, for instance, might work in another brand's model. This collaboration has helped reduce silo syndrome throughout Ford's Premier Automotive Group.

COMMON PROCESSES AND SYSTEMS AS BARRIER BUSTERS

Another trend that is enabling collaboration and breaking down barriers is the implementation of common processes and systems throughout organizations. The Mayo Clinic is uniting its three previously autonomous group practices. The move is part of a broader program to reduce expenses by up to 14 percent in four years. Those savings could translate into as much as $200 million. Part of this process is an initiative called MAGIC, which stands for Mayo Administrative Goal for Integrated Coordinated Systems (see figure 5.1).

Courtesy of Mayo Clinic

Figure 5.1   The Mayo Clinic's MAGIC team combats silo syndrome by merging systems and processes.

MAGIC involves merging all key administrative functions—including accounting, human resources, and materials management—of its three geographically-dispersed group practices. Centralized purchasing means that Mayo can negotiate better deals when it buys pacemakers and other medical devices. In the past, patients entering one Mayo facility would have to provide billing information. Then, they would cross the street for another procedure and have to provide the same information again. Mayo is eliminating this inefficiency by merging billing systems for various accounting units.

As Mayo replaces a twenty-year-old general ledger system and an eighteen-year-old HR system, for the first time these islands of technology can "talk" to each other. And, guess what? The people who work in these functions are increasingly communicating and collaborating. In a broader sense, Mayo is establishing common business practices among all of its locations. Besides the better balance sheet derived from greater efficiency, the change creates more synergy among the three locations.

The impetus for MAGIC was competition in healthcare and a more challenging economic environment. Mayo leadership wanted the organization to work together more closely without duplicating services. The shared services concept, which many companies are implementing, means that some Mayo locations must get by without an on-site staff to perform each function. Besides coping with the usual departmental and functional silos, Mayo has faced regional silos. Each of the three group practices—Rochester, Minnesota; Jacksonville, Florida and Scottsdale, Arizona—have operated independently of each other and have developed separate cultures. MAGIC breaks down those barriers by encouraging leadership of each practice, and subsequently the entire organization, to share information and collaborate.

To build trust, MAGIC's Rochester-based project leader goes out of her way to include input from other Mayo locations. That means some travel, the use of team sites, and frequent videoconferences. "You can't be just driving this from one place. If you try and you don't have their buy-in and their support, at some point down the road they're going to rebel, according to Teresa Knudson, operations manager for MAGIC. "People are not going to feel part of it and there's going to be resistance when you try to get to an implementation mode."

Since exchanging data while looking each other in the eye can help break down barriers, MAGIC is adopting personal videoconferencing with integrated application sharing, IM, shared whiteboard, and the ability to archive entire sessions for those unable to attend. This will integrate tools into work styles rather than force people to leave their work and walk to conference rooms for videoconferencing.

On a much larger scale, Boeing is also driving towards common processes and information systems, two interrelated elements. Because Boeing recognizes that interrelationship, CIO Scott Griffin is leading the move towards not only common systems, but also towards common processes. As part of this effort, Griffin is dramatically reducing the number of systems that Boeing uses to conduct business. All business units will use these core systems.

Boeing, like many other companies, has inherited a mixture of systems and processes in part because of mergers.

Common processes and systems will allow Boeing to move people to work and work to people. If business processes and information systems are identical across all Boeing aircraft programs and projects, people can move from one aircraft program to another and they can share work. This means greater collaboration among functions and the disintegration of barriers.

Besides the ability to share work, common processes and systems allow business units to share best practices and more effectively participate in common initiatives. The move to common systems and processes reinforces Boeing's mandate to design anywhere, build anywhere, move work around the world, and move work around the clock. We will explore this further in chapter 10.

Boeing has implemented a program that tracks all portable and perishable tools used in factories. The program, called Cribmaster, is a compelling example of the value created by moving to common processes and systems. Because both the commercial and defense aerospace business units use Cribmaster, each group gains the opportunity to find available tools elsewhere in the organization before buying them new.

Besides obvious cost savings, using Cribmaster reduces silo syndrome. There is less of an us-and-them attitude in functions, departments, business units, and regions. Instead, common processes and systems create more of a Boeing consciousness, reducing the myopia that often develops within business units. Breaking down the barriers among silos enhances collaborative culture, encourages the use of collaborative tools, and sparks the formation of cross-functional teams.

We have discussed the benefits that Industrial Light & Magic derives from collocating multiple functions in one physical environment. In another push to break down barriers, ILM is reducing specialization and adopting common processes, tools and systems (see profile, page 130). Now that ILM has created the integrated environment, everybody has access to the same data and information. Rather than pass work over a fence, artists can perform many cross-functional tasks. This is the first step in ILM's campaign to open the flow of information among silos and encourage greater collaboration. The next stage, which we will discuss in chapter 10, involves turning ILM into a global collaborative enterprise.

COMMON THEMES IN ELIMINATING BARRIERS

There are distinct parallels between ILM and Toyota in approaches to collaboration and in fostering a collaborative culture. ILM's move giving all artists, regardless of specialty, exposure to multiple functions is a page out of Taiichi Ohno's playbook. Ohno, the father of Toyota's production system, conceived a pull system that involves production based on demand rather than on schedule and inspires team members to think and contribute to the process. Ohno also advocated job rotation to give workers an understanding of many phases of production. Similarly, ILM is improving its production process by engaging artists across multiple functions to share data, systems and work.

As organizational cultures shift from supporting scheduled interactions to encouraging on-the-fly collaboration, people feel more comfortable reaching outside the comfort zone of their functions, departments, business units, and regions to interact with others. Consequently, a marketing team member may welcome VIM from IT or an HR manager may embrace the opportunity to receive an unexpected video call from a business unit process manager seeking input.

Increased spontaneity in collaboration helps break down barriers. This, in turn, encourages information democracy, sharing, and flattened hierarchy. Overly hierarchical structures usually embrace scheduled interaction as a control mechanism, but this approach can stifle innovation. Converged networking over IP plus presence awareness, allowing easy access to available colleagues, is fueling the shift from scheduled to spontaneous interaction and collaboration. In the past, calling a colleague at the wrong time could reinforce barriers. But presence allows us to connect and collaborate with others according to their preferences. This essentially brings greater efficiency to collaboration and communication.

INDUSTRIAL LIGHT & MAGIC COLLABORATES ACROSS SILOS

In creating visual effects for Hollywood movies, Industrial Light & Magic places a premium on collaboration. Founded in 1975 by director and producer George Lucas, ILM has created visual effects for some two hundred feature films including all of the Star Wars movies.

To link film directors in southern California or those on location with effects artists and supervisors at ILM in San Francisco, the company uses a range of collaborative tools including an internally-developed virtual environment for application sharing and whiteboarding called Dome (see figure 5.2). For dailies, the director's review of the day's work, ILM often uses videoconferencing. On one screen at each location is the work product and on the other screen is the videoconference.

To enhance collaboration, ILM is reducing specialization among functions and adopting common processes, tools and systems. Traditionally, experts—including painters, lighters, compositors, shade sculptors, and animators—each mastered their own specialty but knew little about other complementary disciplines. This slowed down the production process, because a lighter, for example, had to wait for a painter to make a relatively simple change. Even if one specialist did know how to perform another discipline, processes and technology prevented cross-functional activity because each specialty used a different system. If a lighter needed to perform a task involving composition, a compositor would get involved. This caused back-and-forth delays, segmenting ILM's pipeline and forcing specialists into an assembly-line approach.

The transition to common processes, tools, and systems allows ILM to move from specialty-oriented teams to what it calls a "digital artist" concept in which multiple functions can collaborate without constant concern for turf and specialty. The digital artist will ultimately know enough about each discipline to do basic work. Since only the most complex tasks require a specialist, ILM can keep its production pipeline moving. This approach speeds production, enhances quality, and reduces costs.

"The most obvious benefit, and often it translates into time savings and sometimes into quality, is the number of iterations that you can accomplish when you have everybody looking at and conversing about

Courtesy of Industrial Light & Magic

Figure 5.2   Industrial Light & Magic's Dome virtual environment lets visual effects artists annotate frames of films in production. To eliminate barriers and enhance collaboration, ILM is reducing specialization among disciplines.

the situation all at once, says Steve Sullivan, ILM's Director of Research and Development. "The director is more likely to get what he or she wants and is able to see things in context to see if they'll all work together instead of having to piece it together in their minds and hope it fits."

The integrated approach helps ILM operate like a smaller, more nimble company. In many small post-production houses, three or four people do all the work. They're typically in the same room and share roles and disciplines. As small shops get bigger, they often use specialization to get more work done. Since ILM has already built a specialization infrastructure, it has experienced the downside. Therefore, the company is now recapturing the benefits of a small, collaborative environment through integrated systems and reduced specialization.

Understanding how collaboration breaks down barriers gives us insight into organizational efficiency. Trends towards information democracy and flattened hierarchical structures, quality systems including Six Sigma, and such processes as Mayo's SPARC increase interaction across departments, functions, business units and regions while reducing silo syndrome. In short, removing the barriers that impede interaction and eliminating impediments to information flow enhances shared creation and creates value.

CHAPTER 6

INTEGRATING COLLABORATIVE TOOLS INTO CULTURE

Tools that we use outside of work take hold in organizations more readily than those we never use in our personal lives. If we have already incorporated a tool into our lifestyles, it's a shorter leap to integrate the tool into our work styles.

Almost everybody in business uses mobile phones, but that happened as the home or personal market for these devices became saturated. Today if you hop into a New York taxi, you may think the driver is talking to you. "What did you say, driver?" But he may actually be chatting with a relative in a distant land using a hands-free device.

As we increasingly use IM to interact with our friends, children and parents, we are becoming more receptive to IM use at work. What once felt like an interruption now feels more efficient in certain situations. If we read or write blogs for parent-teacher associations or wine tasting groups, it's easier to accept the role of blogs in the workplace.

The same is true of VIM, wikis, vlogs and podcasts. Personal use of tools lets us make mistakes and discover a tool's shortcomings and

Personal use of tools lets us make mistakes and discover a tool's shortcomings and potential in a lower-impact context.

potential in a lower-impact context. When we use the tool in a higher-stakes work situation, we can approach the tool with greater confidence and perhaps use the capability more appropriately.

BUILD IT AND THEY SHALL COME?

In the mid-1990s, many organizations believed that if they introduced videoconferencing, teams would rapidly adopt its use. The thinking was *build it and they shall come*. However, organizations found that video systems were often gathering dust in the corners of conference rooms. The problem was that few organizations had anticipated cultural factors in integrating tools into work flow.

One of the many cultural reasons videoconferencing has experienced so many false starts in organizations is that people rarely use the tool in low-impact situations. Part of the reason is that homes have traditionally lacked the bandwidth necessary for effective video interaction. The bandwidth issue persists, because consumer-oriented broadband typically provides minimal upload speed. While time will resolve bandwidth issues, the lack of use in low-impact situations requires more thought.

Many organizations seeking rapid adoption of videoconferencing have found the need to create their own low-impact uses among collaborators. Examples include holding parties at two or more locations and linking the events through video or inviting the children of traveling employees to video with mom or dad from one company location to another. This has increased familiarity with interactive video and has given people a low-risk opportunity to use the tool. Subsequently, it becomes easier to incorporate videoconferencing into collaboration with colleagues.

With the increasing availability of broadband both at home and through wireless connections and the advent of IP as a transport, videoconferencing is rapidly becoming more viable for personal use. Meantime, comfort level for business-oriented use is increasing. This is a boon for collaborators in home offices who would like to see and hear each other. Nevertheless, some corporate cultures are slow to embrace videoconferencing and other, newer tools.

What we can learn from the history of videoconferencing use is that the technical hassles of implementing new tools in organizations often pale in comparison to cultural issues. Collaborative tools take hold more effectively in organizations with a Culture of Collaboration. However, culture is dynamic and tools play a role in cultural evolution.

> *Culture is dynamic and tools play a role in cultural evolution.*

TO PLAN OR NOT TO PLAN?

There are two basic strategies for introducing an organization to a new tool: carefully plan the integration of the tool into work styles and business processes or make the tool available and see what happens. Either strategy may be viable depending on the nature of the tool, the organizational culture, and the priorities and pressures of collaborators. Some companies, including Dow Chemical, conduct internal market research that mirrors external research techniques used to verify product concepts. Approaches may include focus groups and interviews with prospective users with the goal of identifying employee needs and concerns.

Dow calls its internal research *Voice of the Customer*, a term adopted from Six Sigma. In this context, Voice of the Customer helps determine how tools may enable people to do their jobs more effectively. Research also includes analyzing how much business units are willing to pay for tools and related services. Ultimately, the integration team determines value cases, develops timelines, and approaches executives with the hard dollar benefits, the soft costs, and soft benefits. The soft costs are those that are hidden and difficult to quantify, while the soft benefits could include everything from increased employee morale to a better corporate image.

Dow has learned that Voice of the Customer works best when it filters the research. When Dow introduced global collaboration suites called iRooms, the integration team wanted to ensure employees in all functional areas could use the facilities for almost every kind of collaboration. Research and development people wanted to attach microscopes to videoconferencing systems and use multiple cameras. The team placed significant emphasis on this input, because Dow is an engineering-driven company.

However, including all of the functionality that each "customer" requested made the first generation of iRooms unnecessarily complex. While R&D users love test driving tools and appreciate maximum functionality, most users care less about bells and whistles than about collaborating with colleagues. Therefore, the integration team has insured that the second generation of iRooms reflects the needs of most, rather than all, users. This approach is streamlining collaboration at Dow.

The other extreme in introducing tools is to "throw them out there" and see what happens. This is the approach Ford Motor Company took when it introduced application sharing capability with shared digital white board. The tools came bundled with the Windows 2000 operating system, so there was no additional hard cost to consider and, therefore, less of a need to make a business case. Overnight every PC in the company gained the new capabilities.

At the time, sharing applications and white boards screen-to-screen was an abstract concept that few people understood. "We put it up almost as a trial and sent a note out saying give this a try and let me know what you think...and we were killed in the rush," remembers Kevin Timms, information technology director for Ford's Premier Automotive Group. Timms, now based in the UK, used to lead the team at headquarters responsible for collaborative tools. "What we found is that within a matter of weeks, because of word of mouth, it was just staggering. People were really using it. So it really, really took off."

Then Timms and his colleagues scrambled to consider the inevitable questions that are ideally considered in advance. These include bandwidth allocation, impact of conferencing tools on the data network and infrastructure, and the cultural implications. "We kind of ended up with a tiger by the tail," according to Timms.

Now application sharing, digital white boards and team sites are part of the fabric of how Ford works. How could this happen considering the lack of surveys, market research, and usability studies?

Perhaps the shock of a barely planned universal rollout of a collaborative tool allowed Timms and his team to circumvent a formal, hierarchical culture and integrate new collaborative tools into work flow. Clearly, there are increasing pressures on teams to bridge the distance barrier and work more efficiently as Ford pushes its business units to cut costs and develop common processes.

DEPLOYMENT *AS A BAD WORD*

Procter & Gamble has chalked up greater collaboration successes in making tools available and generating buzz about them than in "deploying" them. When P&G introduced IM in 2000, the IT organization had difficulty convincing people that text chat was a viable business tool. Most employees perceived IM as merely a way for teenagers to gossip. Because there were so many doubters, the IT organization avoided "deploying" the tool and instead told several key champions about the availability of IM. A few years later, sixty thousand P&G people were using IM, and surveys indicated it was the tool employees would miss most were it eliminated.

The IM example was the first time P&G offered a tool without "deploying" it. "Now that we know we can do it, we're fully expecting many of these tools will *The word* deployment *works against collaboration.* get legs and they will build their fan base on their own, and we don't need the word *deployment*," according to Laurie Heltsley, P&G's director of computers and communications services. The word, with its combat connotation, works against collaboration; *deployment* suggests that IT is trying to force people to use tools. Therefore, Heltsley has banned use of the word *deployment* in her organization.

TOP-DOWN VS. BOTTOM-UP

A key question for any organization seeking value from collaboration is whether a top-down or bottom-up tools and practices integration strategy works better. The issue is whether a company will adopt new tools and collaborative practices more efficiently if senior leadership drives the initiative or if people in low-to-mid levels develop the

*Imagine the irony in order-
ing people to collaborate!*

concept and implement it. If senior leadership insists on tool use without considering
work flow and work styles throughout the
organization, the introduction can lose
steam. Besides, imagine the irony in ordering people to collaborate!

Of course, low-level managers run into countless hurdles trying
to introduce tools and collaborative processes that can potentially
change the way an organization works, particularly when there is little interest from senior leadership. So the best strategy is usually a
combination of top-down and bottom-up. At least one senior-level
champion is essential, but so too is grass roots word of mouth and
use of tools.

Despite Ford's throw-it-out-there approach to introducing application sharing and digital white board capabilities, the company
typically uses a hybrid top-down, bottom-up strategy in introducing
new tools. The automaker has found that employees are more likely
to resist tools and changes in work styles if senior leadership imposes
the changes. Typically, Ford pilots tools with people who have the
strongest need. If employees find a tool useful, word spreads rapidly.

"You get ownership and pull from the working level, and then
you don't really get any resistance, because it helps them with their
jobs," explains Richard Parry-Jones, Ford's chief technology officer.
"The mistake you can make is when two or three people, the IT
folks or whoever has this wonderful idea on the eleventh floor of the
ivory tower decides to impose it on everybody by directing it. Then
you've got a problem."

Rather than determining in a vacuum how people should collaborate, Ford leaders establish a framework and then get input from
people who want to collaborate. Users then help design the collaboration business processes and supporting tools. The idea is to get
users' fingerprints all over the tools and processes.

Ford IT leadership realizes that everybody has a different reality
of collaboration based on their own experiences. If only two or three
people choose tools and processes surrounding those tools, then the
introduction reflects the realities of only two or three people. Ford's
approach is to let a few people formulate the strategy, but encourage
experts at basic business operations to shape and customize the tools

and processes. "It's got to have their reality built into it. Then it's going to have a much greater stability and emotional ownership," according to Parry-Jones.

A Ford senior leader sponsors or champions a new tool 60–70 percent of the time. In this way, management creates the framework, availability of resources, and strategy for the tool's use. Users create the demand and guide integration of the tool into work styles. Ford's philosophy is that the introduction of collaboration tools should involve classic change management practices. That means a clear business case and vision are essential. "There has to be clear line of site for the results and the activities you are trying to promote. If there isn't clear line of site, you get disconnected and people get confused," says Parry-Jones.

BUILDING THE BUSINESS CASE FOR COLLABORATION

Of course, it's easier to succeed with a hybrid top-down, bottom-up strategy if the idea originates with senior leadership. Then the issue is simply getting input on the tools and ensuring that process owners and experts determine how the tools fit in with work. But if your level is far below the rarified ranks, how do you initiate a new tool or collaborative approach and gain traction for broad use?

First, avoid "selling" tools and instead build a business case for enhanced collaboration. After all, tools are merely enablers. Making the most persuasive case involves putting tools in the context of value creation through collaboration. Nevertheless, tools often involve expenses that must be justified. Part of that justification requires quantifying increased revenue or decreased cost to the company that tools will provide and identifying any "soft" benefits that are difficult or impossible to quantify.

Among the most significant hard benefits is decreased cycle or product development time. Often, it's helpful to enlist somebody in finance to help with this analysis. A financial analyst can determine the value to the company of eliminating, say, ten days of cycle time for a

Among the most significant hard benefits is decreased cycle or product development time.

given product. Finance can also determine whether the hard benefits are negligible.

One manager at a Fortune 50 company believed strongly in wireless networking. He knew that the company could derive many collaboration and communication benefits from the technology, but was unsure how to quantify the expected results. He thought long and hard and ultimately realized he could link wireless to building renovation. Considering that a space was going to house fifty people, he could evaluate the cost of running copper wire to fifty workstations instead of putting in a wireless hub for fifty. He also built into his justification the cost of moving copper wire each time the company reconfigures a facility. He had his hard dollars.

Besides hard dollars, it's important to consider soft benefits. These may include increased productivity, better life/work balance, more satisfied employees, and greater collaborative synergy that will produce a higher-level of collective thinking. For instance, an engineer who specializes in chip firmware may travel frequently throughout Europe. His or her employer may need the engineer to interact with many other engineers at the Silicon Valley headquarters and still others in Asia.

One soft benefit is leveraging subject-matter expertise across the organization.

And the company may have other engineers who must collaborate with each other and with business partners but who spend significant time traveling to customer sites. Enabling notebook computers with Third Generation (3G) wireless combined with collaborative tools may increase productivity substantially. There may not be any quantifiable travel savings, but rather the benefit may be that engineers can interact with each other from airports, trains, taxis and remote locations.

In another example of soft benefits, organizations may gain opportunities to retain the best employees. Weary of long commutes, people may quit to improve their lifestyles. In some cases, they move to rural areas where living costs less, the air smells better, and life seems easier. Often, these employees have abundant skills and are invaluable to the companies they leave. They must often sacrifice a good living.

If they could gain a better life/work balance by keeping their jobs but working from their rural homes, such an arrangement could be win/win. This missing link is sometimes a more professionally intimate connection with colleagues. Introducing laptop-based personal videoconferencing and VIM can help maintain relationships and help an organization retain the best and brightest.

One soft benefit is leveraging subject-matter expertise across the organization. There may be limited numbers of company experts, say, in government relations, economics, or the sciences. Sharing their knowledge globally more quickly and more often creates obvious value for the company. However, this benefit is more soft than hard, because quantifying it is difficult. If the regulatory environment shifts in part because the government relations expert can share his or her knowledge more effectively, we know qualitatively that the enabling tools have created value, but making the case with numbers is tricky.

ENLISTING CHAMPIONS

Enlisting a senior-level champion is particularly important when faced with difficulty in quantifying the benefits. The champion can raise consciousness for tools and process improvements; and even if the item never makes it into the budget for the current fiscal year, it has a better chance of getting funded the following year.

Often the best champions are those who regularly interact with people across other companies and industries. Senior leaders who sit on multiple boards of directors are prime candidates. These executives are more likely to embrace a new tool or approach, because their scope is broader and because they may know the successes of their peers. They may also look forward to trumpeting their successes. While it might seem that introducing tools and collaborative approaches is proprietary and that executives would be unlikely to talk about strategy with external executives, the reality is that such discussion frequently occurs. Sometimes competitors even compare notes on approaches.

When Dayton Hudson's media department manager wanted to gain traction and get funding for a business television satellite network in the early 1990s, he needed a champion. Thinking about the success of J.C. Penney's satellite network, he experienced a light bulb moment. The media manager realized that his CEO was friendly with Penney's CEO. If he could get his CEO to chat about Penney's satellite network with his peer, he could possibly get his CEO to champion and fund the network. He approached his CEO face-to-face with the idea. The CEO discussed the network with his counterpart at J.C. Penney. The media manager's strategy worked, and Dayton Hudson introduced a satellite network.

Enlisting the support of business units is critical. Since the collaboration leader is typically in IT, communications, HR or some other "overhead" function, enlisting the support of business units is critical. After all, they're the revenue creators who will ultimately pay for tools. At Dow Chemical, a prospective executive champion may agree in principle with the need for a tool, but he or she will likely request more data and information. That will involve talking to business unit or manufacturing people to see if they share the view that the tool will create value. "At that point, you're going to get votes like you would in Congress," explains Chris Duncan, Dow's global leader of communications resources. "Go lobby and find out if this is really something that your taxpayers want to pay for."

In a hybrid top-down, bottom-up tools introduction, it's just as important to deputize rank- and-file champions as it is to enlist a senior leadership champion. In *The Tipping Point*, Malcolm Gladwell identifies three types of people who start "word-of-mouth epidemics." These are connectors, mavens, and salesmen. Connectors know lots of people and connect people with other people. In fact, it's sometimes unbelievable how many people connectors seem to know. "They manage to occupy many different worlds and subcultures and niches," Gladwell writes. Mavens are not only marketplace experts, but also they disseminate information by engaging people. Salespeople are, in short, persuaders.

Connectors, mavens and salesmen can be found throughout organizations at all levels. They make the best champions, because they interact with more people than anybody else. There's no need to ask these epidemic creators whether they will champion collaboration. That would complicate matters. It is more effective to help them discover collaboration practices and capabilities. Put tools in the hands of connectors, mavens and salesmen. Sit back, and let them help create a collaboration epidemic.

WHICH FUNCTION GUIDES COLLABORATION STRATEGY?

Successful integration of collaboration practices and tools into business processes and corporate culture requires a blend of skills. Since multiple business units will likely use the tools, an "overhead" function typically manages the integration. Often, this function is information technology (IT) or information services (IS). Because these tools usually run on IT's data network and may require software, hardware and network knowledge, it seems natural that IT owns collaboration initiatives.

On the other hand, corporate communications manages collaboration in some companies. The reasoning is that communicators know best how an organization interacts and exchanges information. Still, some companies let human resources manage collaboration. After all, HR "owns" employee retention, motivation, development and assessment. Collaboration touches each of these areas.

The appropriate function to guide collaboration depends on the industry, organizational culture, and the company's history of technology use. Collaboration tools are sometimes an outgrowth of distance learning and training, and human resources has historically driven those initiatives. In other cases, corporate communications has run video production and business television, and videoconferencing may have grown out of these initiatives.

The appropriate function to guide collaboration depends on the industry, organizational culture, and the company's history of technology use.

"Ownership" also may depend on the infrastructure of the data network. The more advanced the data network, the more viable the network is for collaboration, and the more likely that IT will manage those tools. If a company sends its videoconferencing traffic over a network separate from the data network, it's more likely that corporate communications or HR will manage videoconferencing.

Regardless of which function guides collaboration, effective organizations use a cross-functional approach to integrating tools into culture. Ideally, IT and corporate communications collaborate on collaboration. Ultimately, almost all collaboration and communication will occur over data networks which are rapidly evolving to handle the traffic. Therefore, IT naturally owns the collaboration infrastructure.

Effective organizations use a cross-functional approach to integrating tools into culture.

The question is whether IT, corporate communications, or HR has the expertise to integrate collaboration tools into work styles and business processes. This depends on the company. In some companies, corporate communications is primarily external relations, meaning that the department writes news releases, courts the media, schedules speakers, and provides information to industry and financial analysts. Beyond this sphere, however, the team may lack expertise.

In other companies, corporate communications has a broader role. The department develops internal communications strategy, drives content for intranet sites and focuses on how employees work and interact using the corporate network. In many companies, insight into work styles and organizational culture may reside in HR. Still, other companies may have communication expertise and cultural insight within the IT organization.

The Mayo Clinic has perhaps the largest department in the United States that manages and supports collaboration and communication tools and services. With 265 employees, the Media Support Services Division reinforces the collaborative legacy of Mayo's founders. Besides running videoconferencing and web conferencing, the division manages video production, web design, art and graphic design, and a host of other related functions. The division, which produced the first medical photograph in 1905, celebrated its centennial in 2005.

While the division's work is clearly intertwined with that of Mayo's communications team, Media Support Services is part of IT.

This organizational structure enhances the adoption of collaboration practices and tools, because there are few turf battles. Media support teams typically get needed bandwidth for collaborative applications, and network specialists work closely with tools teams in upgrading infrastructure to support new capabilities. The communications group, which develops the messages for internal and external dissemination, is an internal customer of Media Support Services.

At W.R. Grace & Co., corporate communications guides the adoption of collaborative practices and tools. As we discussed in chapter 2, Grace moved its electronic media department from HR to communications when a new VP for corporate communications realized the team's strategic potential belonged in his group. The philosophy at Grace is that electronic media combines human touch and technology.

The importance of the human element in collaboration means that communications—at least at Grace—is a more appropriate umbrella for collaboration than, say, IT. "We have a responsibility that IT doesn't have. It's the responsibility to appeal to the human aspect," observes Barry Kuhn, manager of electronic media. "The technology itself is stone cold. There's nothing warm about this technology."

Since Kuhn's background is in industrial psychology and training, he has the skills and background to nudge the corporate culture to accept new tools and approaches. He knows the value of repetition in adult learning, and he evangelizes Grace people to use techniques including repetition that can maximize collaboration and communication. Says Kuhn, "I don't know that IT has that in their frame of reference, so it seems more likely to come out of a communication function."

Kuhn acknowledges that IT has a significant role managing mission-critical systems. Because of IT's concern about security breaches and network overloads, he feels the department tends to be prescriptive, telling users what they need. In contrast, Grace's electronic media group develops strategy to make users want collaborative tools. Of course, electronic media can function more independently at Grace, because the group manages a network optimized for rich media that is separate from the IT-controlled data network.

We've discussed how IT steers collaboration at Mayo while corporate communications guides collaboration at Grace. Dow Chemical Company, in contrast, uses a cross-functional approach. While corporate communications traditionally managed videoconferencing and add-on collaborative tools when Dow used ISDN as a transport, that responsibility has shifted with the advent of IP-oriented iRooms.

Dow considers iRooms endpoints on the Information Services (IS) data network, like PC's and notebook computers, and therefore IS pays for the iRooms. However, corporate communications guides collaboration initiatives by internally marketing tools and training users. Communications also focuses on integrating collaboration tools into the organizational culture and business processes. When Dow introduces a new tool, IS and communications work closely. The relationship succeeds because of Dow's Culture of Collaboration. Communications and IS people often develop informal relationships through which brainstorming occurs. This interaction is often the genesis for new collaborative approaches.

THE COLLABORATION ROUNDTABLE

When BMW produced the X5 through telecooperation, the integration team selected a telecooperation promoter in every department. The promoters coached users, relayed feedback from users to the centralized telecooperation department, and guided telecooperation practices within their departments. Some thirty promoters formally interacted in a group called the Roundtable Telecooperation.

The roundtable met monthly in Munich with video links to BMW locations and supplier sites globally. The group shared experiences, resolved problems quickly, and decided which tools fit BMW processes and work styles. Including people from the telecommunications and information services departments in the roundtable increased efficiency in network and technology implementation.

Roundtables can help integrate collaboration into the nooks and crannies of many organizations. In contrast to organization-wide collaboration champions, promoters participating in roundtables focus on specific functions, business units and departments. The roundtable may hold scheduled meetings through videoconferencing and collaborate spontaneously using IM, web conferencing, personal videoconferencing and other tools.

PUTTING PRINCIPLES BEFORE TOOLS

" anything "

Too often organizations introduce collaboration approaches, processes and tools without linking them to organizational principles. This confuses users and stalls integration into work styles. In hierarchical, internally competitive cultures, organizational principles may run contrary to the free flow of information that collaborative

> People can accept changes in work styles more readily if they understand that those changes are based on tenets that they have already accepted.

tools often encourage. This presents a significant cultural divide. People can accept changes in work styles more readily if they understand that those changes are based on tenets that they have already accepted. We are more likely to create value through collaborative approaches and tools if we perceive that the tools reflect the collective personality of the organization.

Beliefs
Values

At Toyota, for instance, many collaborative approaches and tools fit the principle of *nemawashi* or consensus-building. Without this principle and a corresponding practice or framework, the tools would have little context. "I can't come in and say here's a white board. If you buy this, you'll be more collaborative," explains Mike Morrison, dean of the University of Toyota. "You'll be more collaborative for a day, because you'll have a brand new white board and you'll want to use it. But the tool won't drive the routinization of the practice. The tool won't drive the principle."

Because new tools and technologies could potentially compromise Toyota's principles, the company goes to great lengths in evaluating tools before implementing them. In Japan, Toyota has never warmed up to voice mail and employees can access email only from company facilities. I have called Toyota people in Japan, and the phone rings off the hook if nobody is available to answer the line. In the United States, in contrast, Toyota people use voice mail.

Avoiding voice mail would seem like a contradiction in a culture that embraces collaboration. However, voice mail is asynchronous; and asynchronous tools fall short if there is potential controversy or confusion. Because Japanese regional culture places a premium on face-to-face, there is a bias favoring real-time collaboration. In the case of email, Toyota believes that the security risks in remote access are substantial. Therefore, accessing email on the road would violate organizational principles involving security.

Procter & Gamble emphasizes principles and culture as a context for tools adoption. P&G markets 300 brands in 160 countries and has operations in over 80 countries. Almost every project within P&G involves people from across multiple functions and regions. Including the best people in processes and decision making regardless of location propels P&G's success.

At P&G, principles include promoting from within and cross-functional input and interaction. These principles foster trust on which collaboration feeds. If colleagues have grown up together within the organization, they are more comfortable with one another and more willing to collaborate regardless of function, business unit or geography. The culture also embraces innovation and change to increase market share and grow new markets.

As a collaboration proponent, Filippo Passerini is uniquely positioned to guide his company in extending a collaborative culture. Not only is he the CIO of Procter & Gamble, but also he leads multiple functions offering a smorgasbord of services to P&G business units. These include human resources, facilities and financial transactions, among others. Part of Passerini's role is to create demand for approaches, processes and tools that reduce product development time and enhance decision making.

As noted earlier in this chapter, *deployment* is a bad word at P&G. "We are moving from push to pull. We should not mandate tools, but we should let them be adopted," according to Passerini. "If you have a corporate mandate to deploy collaboration tools, that doesn't work as effectively as if you develop tools that are so good that line of business users want to adopt them for effectiveness and efficiency of their organization and for better collaboration." P&G uses a full range of collaborative tools including videoconferencing, web conferencing, IM and 3D visualization to reinforce its collaborative principles. However, the principles drive the use of tools rather than vice versa.

For Passerini, intuition is a critical success factor in the success of collaborative tools. Not only must tools be easy to use, but also they must become embedded in work processes. To this end, P&G has implemented presence-enabled tools and applications. So an HR manager seeking input on a new benefits program can locate and connect with a colleague in finance right from an application in which he or she is working. There's no need to switch applications or devices.

BUILDING AN ORGANIZATION BASED ON COLLABORATION

Start-up organizations have the opportunity to develop a Culture of Collaboration right from the start. The Myelin Repair Foundation has developed a collaborative and rather unorthodox approach to medical research. Myelin, the sheath that surrounds nerves, is damaged by multiple sclerosis. Founder Scott Johnson, who has MS, was frustrated with the competition among researchers developing cures for the disease. He found that scientists compete against one another for limited grant money and for publishing articles in top medical journals.

"There's no way they're going to give their best ideas or give out things before they have protected them or published them," according to Johnson. "To solve any significant medical problem, you need experts in several different disciplines working together as a team, and there was no way to do that in the current system."

So armed with experience founding technology start-ups, Johnson raised money and built a collaborative medical research foundation. First, he brought in Russell Bromley, another technology start-up veteran, as chief operating officer. Johnson and Bromley spent nearly five months identifying the best scientists in the world researching MS cures. Then they brought together five "principal investigators" who head labs, and they proposed a level of collaboration for curing disease that none of the scientists had ever experienced.

CULTURE + PROCESS + TOOLS = COLLABORATION AT TOYOTA

The Toyota Way, which comprises the company's key principles, evolved from the beliefs of the Toyoda family. These principles define the organization's culture. Sakichi Toyoda founded Toyoda Automatic Loom Works in 1926. An inventor and tinkerer, Sakichi involved himself in all facets of his operation. Having studied self-improvement books, Sakichi embraced the principle of *kaizen,* a Japanese word meaning continuous improvement.

Kiichiro Toyoda, Sakichi's son, founded Toyota Motor Corporation with *kaizen* in mind. The company's culture would evolve to include other key principles including *nemawashi,* which means consensus building. Though formally educated as a mechanical engineer, Kiichiro learned from his father to roll up his sleeves, reach beyond theory, and work alongside people regardless of level or function. He researched and experimented with gasoline-powered engines in the early 1930s, formally forming his automotive company in 1937.

Courtesy of Toyota Motor Corporation

Figure 6.1   Toyota's V-comm system reinforces organizational principles including *kaizen, nemawashi,* and *yokoten.*

In the 1950s, long before PC-based collaboration tools and IP networks, plant manager Taiichi Ohno developed the Toyota Production System (TPS). Inspired by U.S. supermarkets, which restocked shelves after consumers bought products, Ohno implemented a "pull system." The system produces products based on actual, rather than on anticipated, demand.

Rather than continuously cranking out products, the pull system replaces inventory at each stage as demand depletes supply. TPS and the Toyota Way ask team members at every level to think, provide input, and collaborate across functions.

Today Toyota, with fifty-one manufacturing companies in twenty-six countries, has exported its collaborative culture. "It depends on the nature of the business perhaps, but for the automotive business it's a key word, *collaboration*," says Shin Kanada, senior managing director and a member of Toyota's board. "It's an indispensable quality that you need to be successful in the market."

To closely link plants and vehicle design facilities, Toyota uses what it calls the Visual and Virtual Communication System (V-comm), developed with partners including Dassault Systemes. V-comm enables a sort of digital *kaizen* and *nemawashi*, and therefore links tools to organizational principles. Collaborators at design facilities, manufacturing plants, and at business partner locations use dedicated V-comm rooms to design vehicles and the processes supporting each vehicle program. Toyota has also implemented V-comm throughout its network of Global Production Centers (GPC), where managers share knowledge.

V-comm integrates videoconferencing with "product lifecycle management" tools and a shared knowledge database, which includes possible problems and solutions that Toyota has spent years accumulating. The system provides 3D modeling capability showing the vehicle and the assembly line. V-comm allows geographically-dispersed collaborators to visualize the entire process of designing, testing, manufacturing, and retiring a vehicle.

The system reinforces Toyota's emphasis on cross-functional interaction by involving manufacturing workers and suppliers in vehicle design. This helps eliminate production problems before they occur. In this sense, V-comm also supports Toyota's principle of *yokoten*, which means sharing knowledge across its operations.

Using V-comm, Toyota has reduced product cycle times to less than twelve months. Besides the obvious economic benefit of time savings, the company has also significantly reduced costly design changes and is phasing out test cars. Traditionally, the company built first and second-stage test cars to evaluate how parts fit and work together. Now software that is part of V-comm simulates assembly and recognizes potential problems.

During the initial face-to-face meeting in Silicon Valley, the participants all bought into the idea of a more collaborative approach to medical research. The scientists run labs at Stanford University in Palo Alto, California; The University of Chicago in Illinois; Northwestern University in Evanston, Illinois; Case Western Reserve University in Cleveland, Ohio; and McGill University in Montreal, Canada. Johnson and Bromley worked a deal with the participating universities, ensuring that their foundation would receive 50 percent of royalty revenue from any drug development. This money would fund future research.

Next Johnson and Bromley, with extensive input from the researchers, wrote a document they call the Collaborative Research Process. They refer to the document as the "rules of the road" for how the team works together. For starters, the document includes a clear goal of discovering new treatments for MS and rapidly moving discoveries to clinical trials.

The document also identifies target timeframes and dates for achieving milestones and outlines the responsibilities of the scientists, their staff and students. Rather than setting collaboration guidelines in stone, the document is dynamic and the team updates it regularly. Nevertheless, the document highlights the importance of goals, one of the Ten Cultural Elements of Collaboration discussed in chapter 1.

Johnson and Bromley were careful to address almost every aspect of the collaboration and anticipate seemingly every possible problem. The Collaborative Research Process document includes a section on maintaining a sense of urgency without sacrificing quality or integrity. Also included is a section on ensuring the collaborators have the right tools for the job and an IT infrastructure to support collaboration.

Aside from ongoing interactions among researchers, the document establishes a "monthly collaboration forum" to be held by conference call, web conference, or videoconference. The forum's purpose is to promote real-time, collaborative problem solving and foster "informal" communications between laboratories. Since each forum has an agenda, perhaps "informal" is a stretch. Nevertheless the scheduled interactions do bring all of the collaborators together regularly.

"What we're really trying to do is build community, in the vernacular of the Internet world. And there's only so much you can do to direct the development of that community," notes COO Russell Bromley. "You don't want to over engineer the technology or the need." Realizing that collaborators must see regular utility or they will recoil from any collaborative tool, Bromley chooses tools that require no training or time away from work. The collaborators use IM daily and use web conferencing and videoconferencing periodically for real-time interaction.

While a team site makes sense theoretically, in practice the scientists use the tool occasionally. Since scientists are less accustomed to sharing knowledge than, say, management consultants, their work habits often preclude depositing what they know in a team site. Typically what drives collaboration among the team is that one scientist encounters something unfamiliar and wants to tap the expertise of a colleague in a related field. Often a real-time exchange fits the bill. Bromley believes that effective use of a team site may require a "referee" or somebody to look for information that the collaborators can use. The referee would then post the material to the team site.

Part of what makes the Myelin Repair Foundation collaboration work is that the foundation selected scientists with complimentary specialties, creating a cross-functional team. "Before the project, there would have been a certain threshold of 'I don't want to bother this person. Maybe they're busy. They don't know me.' Those barriers are gone," notes Brian Popko, who runs a participating lab at The University of Chicago. "By being part of the Myelin Repair Foundation, our collective area of expertise is far greater. And so when we approach problems, we're able to think of them in a broader scope." This, in turn, accelerates efficiency and reduces the time to achieve the goal.

Effective collaboration is rarely automatic. Integrating collaboration into culture requires linking practices, processes and tools to organizational principles, getting input from multiple functions, enlisting grass roots and senior-level champions, and creating demand rather than "deploying" software and hardware.

CHAPTER 7

THE TAO OF TOOLS

Our reach is rapidly becoming longer, broader and richer because of the Culture of Collaboration and the tools that support collaborative culture. Increasingly, we can collaborate with greater impact in ways that more closely fit our work styles. Using tools within a Culture of Collaboration can dissolve the barriers of time and distance, deliver awesome results, and create value. Deriving these benefits, however, requires understanding both the potential and the limitations of tools. Because we are drowning in a sea of capabilities, we sometimes face tool confusion. So let's also consider how to match the right tools with particular situations.

> *Using tools within a Culture of Collaboration can dissolve the barriers of time and distance.*

THE COLLABORATIVE PALETTE

We can categorize collaboration and communication modes into *synchronous* and *asynchronous*. Synchronous is interactive, meaning collaborators and communicators can exchange information in real time. A phone call, for instance, is synchronous. Asynchronous means people send or store information or material without simultaneous interaction; the recipient reviews the material at his or her convenience. Email is asynchronous. Some tools work best for one-to-one interactions. Others are better for one-to-many. Still others are optimized for many-to-many interactions. Definitions of collaboration and communication tools are on pages 158 and 159.

To describe the selection of tools, I often use the analogy of a painter's palette. Just like a painter uses the range of colors in his or her palette to create a picture, a collaborator chooses—and sometimes mixes—the modes that fit particular situations. If you're more practical than artistic, you may prefer the toolbox analogy. The box is brimming with a variety of collaboration and communication tools. The trick is choosing the tool or, using the palette analogy, mixing the color that fits the situation.

During the early stages of collaboration, nothing takes the place of an in-person meeting. This is because sharing physical space expedites building trust and professional intimacy which are critical to collaboration. This connection ultimately reduces virtual distance, which we discussed in chapters 2 and 3. As tools become more robust and as cultures evolve, we may feel less of a need to meet one another in the flesh before using tools. This point inspires debate, and we will discuss it more later in this chapter and in subsequent chapters.

COMPARING COLLABORATION MODES

The collaborative palette provides many choices. How do we avoid tool confusion and choose effective collaboration modes for specific situations? Here's a discussion of how to decide between certain pairs of tools that often raise questions:

Video vs. Web Conferencing

Web conferencing offers collaborators the advantage of simplicity. All you need is a web browser and either a phone or an audio connection over IP. Many large companies have used web conferencing extensively, because it costs relatively little to implement and use.

However, much of the use traditionally has been for presentations rather than collaboration.

For instance, a VP of sales might use web conferencing to brief his or her global sales force on strategy for the upcoming quarter. The team can view his or her slides while listening to the presentation live, and the broadcast is also archived and available on demand. These web conferences are organized, scripted events rather than spontaneous interactions.

The broadcast use of web conferencing is significantly different and less collaborative than the use of the tool between an internal communications specialist and a

> *Tools offer only the potential for collaboration.*

partner working for an external investor relations firm collaborating on an annual report. In such a case, both participants share knowledge, provide input, and mutually create something of value. The point is that tools offer only the potential for collaboration; collaboration requires more than merely using a potentially collaborative tool. And how we use tools determines our level of collaboration.

Procter & Gamble has used one-to-one web conferencing internally, with business partners, and to manage its acquisition of Gillette. Because its presence-enabled web conferencing tool integrates with standard business productivity applications, P&G people can launch a web conference from a spreadsheet.

"You're able to very quickly initiate with button pushes a Live Meeting on an ad hoc basis, drop content into it, do notations, do white boarding and other kinds of things off to the side more readily just with simple button pushes rather than having these big planned out, subscribe and pay sessions," according to Laurie Heltsley, P&G's director of computers and communications services. Business unit people may begin an IM session that deals with staffing. At some point, they realize they would like input from a human resources person. They can easily see if the HR person is available and can launch either a web conference or videoconference.

The ability to share applications and annotate documents, spreadsheets, slides, drawings and other material while talking with others can save time and enhance productivity. Though some web

Collaboration and Communication Tools

CONFERENCING TOOLS

Application Sharing

Live, interactive use of software programs by two or more users on different PC's. Users can work in programs together screen-to-screen. Web conferencing often includes this capability.

Audio Conferencing

An audio connection involving three or more people each using a PC, phone, speakerphone or other device.

Document Conferencing

Live, interactive sharing of documents between two or more users. Users can edit and annotate documents simultaneously screen-to-screen. They can also engage in group writing. Web conferencing often includes this capability.

Group Videoconferencing

Live, interactive audio and video connections between people at two or more sites using systems optimized for conference rooms.

Personal Videoconferencing

Live, interactive audio and video connection involving two or more people each using a PC, notebook, stand-alone videophone, or handheld device.

Virtual Hallway or Media Space

An always-on video and audio link between two or more sites. A media space connects break rooms, hallways, lounges or other areas where people congregate. The idea is to encourage chance encounters and enhance idea generation.

Web Conferencing

Live, interactive audio plus application sharing and other features that may include document conferencing, shared digital whiteboard, shared web browsing, public and private text chat, and audience polling.

Web Presentation

Audio plus screen sharing in which the presenter shares his or her PC screen with one or more remote PC users. Only the presenter can edit or annotate material.

Whiteboarding

Live, interactive sharing of a digital whiteboard program between two or more users. Users can use digital writing and drawing tools together screen-to-screen. Web conferencing often includes this capability.

MESSAGING/MAIL TOOLS

Email

Asynchronous exchange of text with possible file attachments delivered to in-boxes of one or more recipients.

Instant Messaging (IM)

Exchange of text that appears almost immediately on screens of users.

Text /Multimedia Messaging

Exchange of text, images and multimedia among mobile phones. Text messages can also be sent to email addresses and from the service provider's web site to mobile phones. Typically, there is a character limit on text messages.

Collaboration and Communication Tools (continued)

Video Instant Messaging (VIM)
Exchange of video and audio that appears almost immediately on screens of users.

Video Mail
Exchange of video and audio messages delivered either as email attachments or as links to server-based content.

REPOSITORY TOOLS
Digital Asset Management
Systems allowing archiving and search-based retrieval of video, audio, images, text and other data.

Team Sites, Team Spaces
Intranet and Extranet-based work environments designed for groups of collaborators to exchange or post video, voice, images, documents, presentations, spreadsheets, and other material.

PUBLISHING/DISTRIBUTION TOOLS
Blog
Short for weblog, a blog is a frequent, chronological publishing of stream-of-consciousness writing with links to related information

Podcast
A method of distributing multimedia material that allows users to subscribe to a feed of new or updated content. Podcasts can be played on mobile devices and on PC's. *Podcast* refers to the multimedia content as well as to the distribution method.

Vlog
A frequent, chronological publishing on the Web of videos featuring stream-of-consciousness talk.

Wiki
A server program allowing multiple users to develop the content of a Web site. Any user can change the contributions of others or add material including text, images, hyperlinks, graphics and tables. Wikipedia, a wiki web site, is an online encyclopedia allowing broad collaboration.

BROADCASTING/ON-DEMAND TOOLS
Webcast/Streaming
Live audio and video delivered over IP networks that can be archived for later retrieval. Streaming is a more efficient approach to media delivery than simple download in that the compressed material is sent in a continuous stream and is decompressed as the user receives it. Therefore, the user can begin watching and listening to the clip before receiving all of it.

CREATION TOOLS
Animation Tools
Used with conferencing tools over IP networks, animation tools allow dispersed collaborators to jointly create animated content.

Computer Aided Design/Computer Aided Manufacturing (CAD/CAM)
Used with conferencing tools over IP networks, many CAD/CAM tools allow dispersed collaborators to jointly create and annotate 3D and 2D models.

conferencing tools support video, many people use web conferencing without video as an inadequate substitute for videoconferencing. So for each session, it helps to ask ourselves whether video would enhance or detract from collaboration and communication.

If there is any anticipated controversy, video fits the bill. Using web conferencing for negotiations falls flat. When business partners say they are unable to offer more money, we want to look them in the eye. If a leader is announcing a major shift in strategy to direct reports, video is critical. Such shifts make employees uneasy; seeing senior leaders while absorbing the information often reassures them. Bad news is easier to absorb through video than through web conferencing, because it's easier to comprehend subtext and emotions when we see facial expressions.

If holding people's attention throughout the interaction matters, videoconferencing is the better choice. A study conducted by Roper ASW and funded by Tandberg indicates that many participants in web conferences and audio conferences do unrelated work and multiple tasks. The study reports that videoconferencing significantly increases attention levels. According to the study, 23 percent of respondents gave their full attention at their last audio conference. Of the remaining respondents, 25 percent wrote email, 13 percent surfed the web, and 27 percent did other work. Videoconferencing is perhaps the best choice of tool when we need to be in the same room with people but time and distance prevent that from happening.

The better people know one another and the less controversial the interaction, the better the chances are that web conferencing will work as a one-to-one or small group collaborative tool as opposed to a presentation tool. The greater the importance of data and other work product, the greater the opportunity for a successful web conference.

If the interaction is more geared towards decision making, videoconferencing makes sense. Participants have already evaluated data and they want to have a dialogue about the relevance of the information. "Those kinds of meetings we're finding lend themselves more to videoconferencing, because now it's not so much the data that's important. It's whether somebody's body language is saying 'I'm with you on this.' It's whether they're leaning forward," says Barry Kuhn, who leads the electronic media group at W.R. Grace & Co.

Kuhn, who has a background in industrial psychology and training, guides users to choose the right tool for the situation. "Having a question or not understanding a point has that universal expression. It doesn't matter the language. It's almost an anthropological thing. Confusion looks the same almost everywhere." And without video, that confusion may go unread.

To summarize, videoconferencing is a better choice than web conferencing if:

1. An in-person meeting is desirable but seemingly impossible.
2. Controversy is likely
3. Minimizing distractions is essential
4. It's time to make a decision.

IM vs. Email

As instant messaging (IM) takes hold as a viable business collaboration tool, how do you know when to use email and when to choose IM? Email allows reflection, while IM enables reaction. Therefore, it makes sense to select email over IM if the message requires thought or research before responding.

IM works better than email to initiate a brief brainstorm or provoke an immediate response. IM offers the benefit of presence awareness. Presence, described in chapter 1, informs us whether a collaborator is available for text chat, for a phone call, for a web conference, for a videoconference or is unavailable because he or she is at lunch, on the phone or "back in 10."

The urgency of interaction or the timeframe of a decision also plays a role in the choice of IM or email. While some decisions require immediate, real-time input, others can wait. It makes more sense for an event planner on deadline to IM an available colleague regarding podium configuration. However, if the event is two months out, email is the better choice.

At Industrial Light & Magic, animators and other artists use IM to get immediate feedback from colleagues and supervisors and to instigate spontaneous design reviews. These reviews often involve sharing creative work on a digital whiteboard. Artists use email, however, to notify technical professionals about possible bugs in software. ILM people also subscribe to in-house email lists or forums in which they can participate in discussions regarding software, hardware, and other issues. At ILM, people typically use email if they can wait a minimum of a half hour for a response, but they rely on IM for creative interaction.

IM also lends itself to support and customer service functions in that representatives needing to escalate a customer call or requiring expert input can, through presence, determine who is available. This allows for faster resolution and increased customer satisfaction. While email is asynchronous, IM is a hybrid; it appears synchronous because it enables chat. However, the chat has enough delay that IM could also be classified as asynchronous. IM works best among an established team that is already collaborating. Because IM is potentially jarring, it is a poor choice for contacting people with whom we have a limited or no relationship.

IM vs. Video IM

Video IM (VIM) offers a higher-touch, more personal experience than text IM. VIM is ideal for customer support situations, because the visual element makes a customer feel like the vendor cares more about resolving his or her problem. Among collaborators, VIM breaks up the monotony of one-dimensional text interaction. It is a more effective choice in communicating emotion, because a real smile is worth a hundred emoticons. Emoticons are those expression faces that look like ☺ or ☹. If we want to display a prop such as a book, report, or a prototype, VIM works better than IM.

Videoconferencing vs. Video Mail

This is a choice between a synchronous and asynchronous tool that is similar to the choice between a phone call and a voice mail (which is often decided by the recipient depending on whether he or she answers the phone).

Video mail works for a team member updating his or her geographically-dispersed leader or colleague on project progress. The tool offers a key advantage over videoconferencing: the ability to re-

record the video until it looks right. This is particularly useful for updating those on whom we wish to make a good impression. The tool has the disadvantage, however, of providing no real-time feedback, such as facial expressions, from the remote collaborator.

Like VIM, both video mail and videoconferencing lend themselves to props. Some videoconferencing services offer video mail capability. Users can record an outgoing video greeting just like an outgoing voice mail greeting. If somebody calls a videoconferencing system and the user is unavailable, they view the outgoing greeting and leave a video mail. Depending on the system, users may receive the video mail as an email attachment, receive notification by email with a link to the video mail on a server, or receive notification and retrieve video mail through the videoconferencing application or system.

Team Sites vs. Web Conferencing

Team sites, sometimes called team spaces, provide a web-based environment through which collaboration occurs. Team sites allow dozens of people to work on the same document asynchronously. Users can set "alerts" so that they receive email if a collaborator changes a document. These sites are repositories for team documents, spreadsheets, images, schedules and other information. However, real-time collaboration on work product requires web conferencing.

Collaborators who work on longer projects derive greater benefit from team sites. For instance, a software development group may write code for months and therefore need a virtual place where collaborators

Collaborators who work on longer projects derive greater benefit from team sites.

can contribute to the project over time. Another example is a group of scientists researching a new drug for a pharmaceutical company. The team site would include voluminous test materials and clinical trial results. In contrast, media relations people writing news releases on deadline may derive greater value from web conferencing, which enables real-time group writing.

Though certain functions lend themselves to one tool over the other, the situation should determine which mode to choose. As sensitivity to time increases, web conferencing becomes more useful.

Web conferencing as a collaboration—as opposed to a presentation—tool is better suited to smaller numbers of collaborators. While fifty people might provide input on a team site document, such a large group would cause confusion in a web conference in which everybody is interacting. Work product that collaborators create in a web conference can then be pushed to a team site, so that the larger group can retrieve and review the material.

IM vs. Team Sites

Increasingly, team sites offer IM capability so these modes are becoming integrated. However, we must still choose a color in the collaborative palette. In this comparison, we are dealing with a hybrid tool and an asynchronous one. IM is a hybrid, because it is nearly real-time, though not absolutely. We have already established that people working on longer projects derive the most value from team sites. The presence awareness of IM gives us greater access to each other and enables greater efficiency, because we can determine instantly whether and how to connect with colleagues.

Transaction-oriented teams derive greater benefit from IM than from team sites.

In contrast, transaction-oriented collaborators derive greater benefit from IM and less value from team sites. For instance, technical support groups, real estate teams, and stock brokers all deal with transactions. They focus for hours, days or weeks on an incident or sale and then they move on to something else. They are less likely to update or add documents over many months. What's most important for these collaborators is immediacy and knowing how to find colleagues. IM fits their work styles more closely than team sites.

USING CROSSOVER TOOLS TO ENABLE COLLABORATIVE CULTURE

Crossover tools are communication tools that can be used to foster a Culture of Collaboration. Typically, their optimal use is for one-to-many or few-to-many dissemination of information rather than for shared creation.

Crossover tools are communication tools that can be used to foster a Culture of Collaboration.

They are crossover tools, because they bridge communication with collaboration. As we discussed in chapter 1, communication is a key element in collaboration; therefore an organization must communicate well to collaborate effectively. Let's discuss how some key crossover tools can enable collaborative culture.

Webcasting: Embracing Feedback

Webcasting gives leaders the opportunity to reach an entire global organization. Webcasts can be archived so that those who are unable to watch live, because of time zone issues or schedule conflicts can view the material later. During live webcasts, leaders

The most effective leaders embrace live feedback and encourage confrontational questions from every level and region.

can take questions by phone, through email, via IM, or from a live audience. The most effective leaders embrace live feedback and encourage confrontational questions from every level and region.

If something is bothering a facilities employee in Brazil, his or her concerns will likely reflect the thoughts of thirty other people. When leaders welcome tough questions, it sends a message that the organization values input over hierarchy. This approach contributes to a Culture of Collaboration in that people feel that there is no penalty for speaking their minds. Otherwise, the tendency might be to rubber stamp prevailing opinions rather than to develop innovative approaches to business processes, services and products.

Leaders can also leverage webcasts to make every employee feel as if he or she matters and that leadership not only welcomes the input of employees, but also expects it. Andrew Liveris, CEO of Dow Chemical, reinforces a collaborative culture by conducting "town hall meetings" via satellite at least once per quarter. I attended one such event at Dow Headquarters in Midland, Michigan about six months after Liveris had become CEO.

For this town hall, Liveris abandoned the traditional and more formal broadcast setting of the auditorium. Instead he and three other senior leaders fielded questions while sitting on stools in the cafeteria. Although he had spent more than thirty years at Dow and had most recently been the company's COO, Liveris told all of Dow's employees globally that he was receiving lots of training on being CEO and had been learning a lot. The message was: I don't have all the answers. I am open to your ideas. These kinds of messages help create a collaboration-friendly climate.

During the broadcast, Liveris reviewed key financials including day sales and inventory, which measures how much product awaits shipment from warehouses. In many companies, senior leaders and financial professionals share this type of information only with key managers. Dow educates every employee about significant financials and about how the contribution of each worker impacts the bottom line.

"Don't assume that it's not important to the person working at the depot who is putting your products on the rail cars. Don't assume that this is not important to them. It is!" insists Chris Duncan, Dow's global leader of communications resources and the company point person on collaboration.

Blogs: Invitation to Collaboration

While a blog is typically a one-to-many communication tool, it nevertheless has a collaborative quality. Blogging represents a spirit of sharing and a less hierarchical environment. The medium's inherent democracy reinforces the Culture of Collaboration. Collaborators can include blogs on team sites so that both project participants and employees throughout the organization can view their thoughts.

Leaders can use blogs to communicate more personally and informally with employees. This provides a welcome break from the often heavily-scripted executive communications that large corporations disseminate. A leader can write about his or her experiences on the road, views on the economy, the industry, products, life/work balance, or whatever moves him or her. Companies can also use blogs to establish closer customer relationships by providing tips, addressing concerns, and informing customers about how to use products.

Blogging nourishes the Culture of Collaboration, because employees sense that the company values informality, brainstorming, expressing opinions, and providing input. W.R. Grace & Co. believes blogging will help make communications less linear. Barry Kuhn, Grace's manager of electronic media, writes a blog and is encouraging senior leadership to follow suit. "The nice thing about blogs is that they are biased. It's like your personal diary. If an executive officer writes a blog that sounds heavily favorable towards Grace, that's okay. That's what blogs are supposed to be. A blog is not a news report. It's an opinion, and you're entitled to your own," Kuhn insists. "It would be interesting for some of our employees to get a sense of the personal feelings of some of our executives."

Aside from executive communication, collaborators can use blogs to keep each other updated on projects more efficiently than writing more formal emails. Because blogs are more stream of consciousness, grammar and organization take a back seat to conveying ideas and opinions. I know several frequent collaborators with great ideas who struggle with writing. For them, blogs make sense in that they can share ideas without worrying as much about constructing sentences.

Vlogs and Podcasts:
Capturing Light Bulb Moments

Like blogging, vlogging and podcasting inject informality into organizations. These tools encourage free-flowing communication and reinforce a collaborative culture. Many people within companies have access to compelling business-oriented experiences that they want to share. Such experiences might include a trip to the Paris air show, a meeting at Buckingham Palace, a visit to what is arguably the world's tallest building in Taipei, or a trade mission to Indonesia.

I remember from my days covering the Detroit auto show the stacks of media kits, thousands of hours of corporate video, and other formal communications with which car companies inundated reporters. Because of the structure and formality of these handouts, the material was somehow less compelling and less believable.

Similarly, internal corporate communications usually comes across as too corporate! Which is more likely to capture the hearts and minds of employees: a heavily-produced video on the company's participation at an event or an executive's vlog or podcast of his or her activities, discoveries and opinions during the event? The latter offers a more genuine, believable and compelling experience.

Vlogs and podcasts can infuse a company with the informality necessary for effective collaboration. Collaborators can use these tools to capture their thoughts and share them with colleagues. I know a retired food company executive whose idea bulb went off when he saw a crop duster airplane. He realized the same type of technology used to spray fields could be used to put sugar coating on cereal. Suppose he had a video camera with him when he saw the crop duster. Then he could have captured, preserved, and shared his entire light bulb moment with collaborators who were developing cereal products.

VIRTUAL HALLWAYS: UNITING TEAMS THROUGH ALWAYS-ON VIDEO

Companies can use virtual hallways or media spaces to link research labs and other groups of intense collaborators. A virtual hallway provides an always-on video and audio link between two or more sites. The idea is to preserve the informal communication or water cooler chat that makes people feel as if they work shoulder-to-shoulder. This informality is essential to forming close relationships and encouraging collaboration.

Though researchers have used media spaces to link cubicles, this tool is most effective when it connects areas where people congregate. These include break rooms, corridors or informal meeting spaces. Virtual hallways let collaborators get the buzz from remote locations and enable remote colleagues to join conversations. This approach increases spontaneous interaction among geographically-dispersed colleagues.

Parker Hannifin has used a virtual hallway in its Compumotor division to link a human-machine interface group in Milford, Ohio with a factory automation group in Rohnert Park, California. The division supplies motors and controllers that do everything from filling ketchup bottles in factories to spraying water through the fountains at the Bellagio Hotel in Las Vegas.

When Parker Hannifin acquired the Ohio group some years ago, the frenzy of merger management sparked the spontaneous video interactions that soon became commonplace. Both teams worked together at a distance while integrating financial systems, tech support, repair process management, and quality control. Rather than scheduling video meetings, collaborators could call or email their remote colleagues and ask them to rendezvous in the virtual hallway. Collaborators, though separated by three time zones, felt more connected because they could participate in on-the-fly interaction.

MANAGING DIGITAL ASSETS AND REPURPOSING CONTENT

Historical perspective gives collaborators—and society—a huge advantage. Let's say a consumer products company is launching a new household cleaning product. A team forms to develop market strategy. The team includes people with various skills from several global regions, and part of the team works for an outside marketing firm. The entire team comes together every few days for scheduled collaborative sessions, and colleagues have spontaneous interactions throughout the day. The knowledge of what worked and what failed during previous product introductions could save significant time and money.

Digital asset management systems bridge the present with the past, linking current strategy with institutional knowledge. Think of all the video of television commercials, news conferences, product launches, and executive speeches that most large organizations own. Add to that archived collaborative sessions, meetings and videoconferences. The ability to digitize that archive, index the audio, and repurpose the video gives companies a strategic edge. Asset management systems also link still images, documents, presentations and other content. With the click of a mouse, a user can bring up all content related to a key word.

While developing market strategy for the new cleaning product, team members could examine all content related to past product roll-outs. The content might also include a competitor's commercials, print ads, and other material. This ability brings perspective and insight to collaboration, because team members can more effectively leverage past successes while avoiding previous pitfalls.

How to Choose the Right Mode
for the Right Situation

With so many collaboration and communication tools, how do we know which one to use? For some people, this is an intuitive decision. Collaborators sometimes develop such an uncanny rhythm in working together that they instinctively know how to connect, brainstorm, and create incredible results without ever sweating over the choice of tools. For others, particularly those who are coping with barriers of time, distance, corporate culture, regional culture, and language, choosing tools is a big deal. In short, we may agonize over the best way to interact with each other. During a meeting I attended in Germany a few years ago, a senior manager of a large manufacturing company pounded his fist on a table in frustration saying, "I must have definitive rules when to use each tool!"

Many collaborators benefit from guidelines, and few organizations provide them.

Providing rules for using tools smacks of command-and-control leadership and runs counter to collaboration. Nevertheless, many collaborators benefit from guidelines, and few organizations provide them. With concern over security and compliance issues, many companies prefer to focus employees' attention on the content of collaboration and communication rather than on the choice of tools. Other more innovative companies fear guidelines and training might cramp the styles of collaborators and therefore avoid offering guidance.

So, how do we make the choice of tools more intuitive and relatively fast? Well, like most things, it takes practice. When you first drive a car, you wonder how you can remember to shift, steer and operate the pedals simultaneously—not to mention using turn signals, blowing the horn, and using bright headlights at appropriate times. In time, however, this skill comes naturally. The same is true of choosing tools.

When forming a collaborative relationship, it is essential to agree on tools. Discussing preferences, availability for spontaneous encounters, comfort level with modes of collaboration, and willingness to experiment with new tools will go far in choosing wisely.

When forming a collaborative relationship, it is essential to agree on tools.

Even if a choice makes sense in theory, it may be the wrong choice in practice because of culture.

While VIM might be the most efficient, high-touch way to contact the CFO and clear up a budget issue, the approach may do more harm than good in a hierarchical structure. Also, if collaborators have limited experience using a tool, it makes sense to practice in a low-impact or no-impact situation before taking the tool for a test drive on a project deadline.

In choosing collaboration and communication tools, consider these questions:

Is this interaction urgent?

Use presence aware tools such as IM or VIM. These work better than email for urgent situations. If there is complexity involved, consider personal videoconferencing.

Is this interaction complex?

Arrange a face-to-face meeting for complex interactions. If time and distance prevent pressing the flesh, choose a real-time tool. IM, though nearly real-time, is one dimensional and works better for brief brainstorming, simple chat and clarifications. Videoconferencing with application sharing provides richer interaction and will help cut through complexity.

Are there documents, drawings, slides or other material to share and discuss?

Choose web conferencing to facilitate brainstorming or resolve time-sensitive issues that involve data and materials. When urgency is less of an issue, use team sites so that everybody can contribute on his or her own schedule to documents and other work product. Team sites are also helpful when dealing with time zone differences. If there is a need to establish a better rapport or closer relationship, use videoconferencing combined with application sharing and a digital whiteboard.

Is reflection needed?

Use email or team sites. Email is often the best mode if a colleague or expert needs breathing room to consider an issue. Team sites may fit the bill if you have created a document, presentation or other material for which you are seeking reflection and eventual input from several colleagues. Wikis are also an option for collaboration that requires reflection. It is ludicrous to IM a colleague a question regarding a change in business strategy or direction. The immediacy of response that IM etiquette requires prevents reflection.

Some people get their best ideas while exercising, driving, or doing chores. I often have eureka moments while swimming laps. So, it's important to anticipate when a collaborator's reflection—rather than immediate input—will enhance the result. Real-time tools often fall short when an issue needs careful consideration. When issues requiring reflection arise during phone calls and video-conferences, the response is usually "let me think about that" or "send me an email on that." Once collaborators have reflected and are ready to make a decision, videoconferencing is a better choice.

Is there a need to update/inform or engage in dialogue/exchange ideas?

Use asynchronous tools such as team sites, blogs, vlogs, podcasts or email if the focus is on updating or informing colleagues on project status. If, however, you need to exchange ideas, choose a real-time tool like web conferencing, videoconferencing, or the nearly synchronous IM.

Are there multiple issues or a single issue?

Use email for single, simple issues. An email containing multiple concerns and questions often sits in an in-box for weeks; it works better to send a separate email for each issue. The best choice for dealing with multiple issues is real-time interaction, preferably web conferencing or videoconferencing. If collaborators interact simultaneously, they can tackle the kitchen sink, work through the problems, and reach resolution.

Is controversy likely?

Arrange a face-to-face meeting if you expect controversy. There's nothing like sharing a meal or pressing the flesh to diffuse a situation. If a meeting seems impossible, schedule a videoconference.

The ability to read body language helps considerably in clarifying positions and working through conflict.

The next choice is web conferencing or a plain old phone call. Email is perhaps the worst approach, because text can cause confusion about the emotion behind the words. Emoticons such as ☺ and ☹ help, but people often forget to use them. Also, confusion has more staying power when it remains in the in-box. Choosing team sites to post material when controversy looms delays the inevitable—and can therefore fan the flames of controversy. It's better to hash out problems in real time.

Is the interaction routine or unusual?

For brainstorming among collaborators with close relationships, favor tools allowing spontaneous interaction. Spontaneous contact also works for routine interaction regarding expense reports or calendar questions. It's better to schedule interactions involving out-of-the-ordinary subjects such as shift in direction or budget cuts …though in many companies budget cuts may be more routine than unusual. ☺

How many people/locations are involved?

While multipoint videoconferencing can often support a dozen locations, the optimal number of sites for a truly interactive experience is four. To link many locations, choose webcasting if interaction is less important. If interaction is more necessary than the high impact of video, use web conferencing.

Are time zones an issue?

Presence reduces the impact of time zones by letting us know who is "on" and available regardless of the hour. However, if time zone differences make real-time connections impractical, choose an asynchronous tool such as email, video mail, team sites, blogs, wikis, vlogs or podcasts.

TOOLS AND CULTURE

While considering the above questions helps in making the right tool choice, there are other variables to consider. Figure 7.1 provides

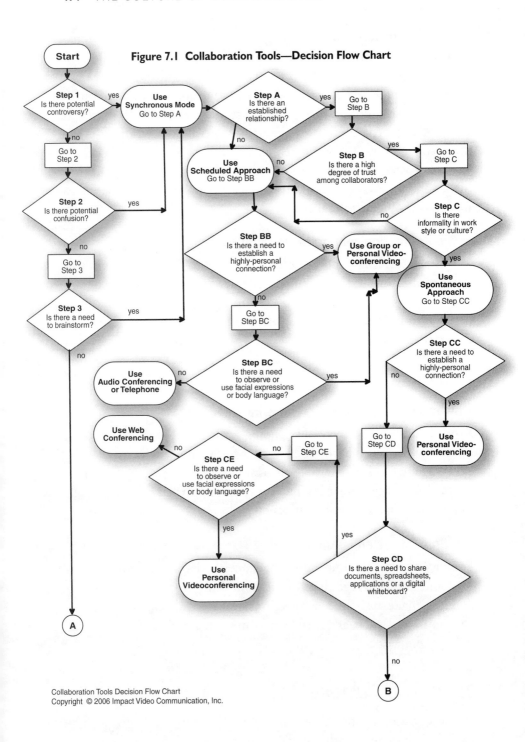

Figure 7.1 Collaboration Tools—Decision Flow Chart

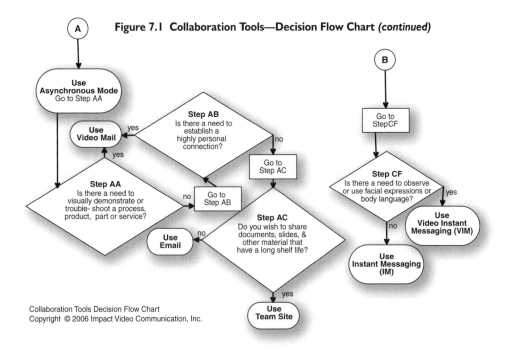

Figure 7.1 Collaboration Tools—Decision Flow Chart *(continued)*

Collaboration Tools Decision Flow Chart
Copyright © 2006 Impact Video Communication, Inc.

a decision flow chart for choosing collaborative tools. Remaining flexible and sensitive to the needs of collaborators often determines whether a tool enhances or detracts from collaboration. Tool choices, like most decisions, should never be made in a vacuum.

Culture matters. A hierarchical organization may discourage spontaneous, real-time collaboration and communication with people at higher levels, regardless of the nature of the interaction. If executive assistants or administrators typically screen the calls of senior executives, a spontaneous video call or IM may circumvent this process. If an executive is receptive, you can use the tools to shift customs or at least create exceptions, thereby nudging the culture in a new direction.

In the mid-1990s, those who had personal videoconferencing on their desktops formed a relatively small club. We often chatted with one another to experience the novelty of the tool. Therefore, we could cut across hierarchical boundaries if we collected video numbers for influential people.

Senior executives in hierarchical cultures promptly answered their video phones, abandoning the insulation of their positions.

P R O F I L E

THE DOW CHEMICAL COMPANY: iROOMS AND A COLLABORATIVE CULTURE

Global collaboration has become a way of life for the forty-three thousand employees of Dow Chemical Company. Many report to managers in other countries, and most participate in globally-distributed teams. In fact, it is the rare team that is comprised of people from a single region. Often teams begin informally through loose networks of colleagues from multiple functions, departments and business units. Brainstorming may lead to a new product or process. Clearly, the company faces the challenges of geography and time zones.

Dow is meeting those challenges by cultivating a collaborative culture. For decades, Dow has regularly rotated people around functions, businesses, and regions. This "cross-pollination" breaks down barriers, bridges regional and departmental cultures, and lays the groundwork for collaboration. And the company has provided the tools and technologies to unite its global workforce. Dow was perhaps the first major company to implement a converged network. On DowNet, video, voice and data travel over IP.

To exploit DowNet, Dow uses three hundred collaborative rooms called iRooms (see figure 2.4, page 33) which link people in forty-three countries. iRooms provide a suite of capabilities including Polycom videoconferencing, audio conferencing, shared digital whiteboard, application

Nevertheless, while democratizing the culture may be desirable, shocking the culture through the use of tools can backfire, particularly in hierarchical environments. Chatting with the CEO through IM or videoconferencing will accomplish little unless he or she is genuinely receptive. Cultural evolution is often more effective than cultural revolution.

Collaborative cultures are more likely to embrace spontaneous use of real-time tools.

Collaborative cultures are more likely to embrace spontaneous use of real-time tools. In chapter 2, we discussed the emphasis on paging at the Mayo Clinic. In a sense, paging is a crude form of IM, because it combines asynchronous and real-time functionality.

sharing, and the ability to share images from microscopes. People join collaborative sessions from iRooms or from notebook computers. The iRooms grew out of voice over IP.

With an emphasis on cross-functional collaboration, Dow avoids the degree of silo syndrome that afflicts many companies (see chapter 5). The iRooms are a joint project between information services and corporate communications, and that partnership has contributed to the successful integration of collaborative tools into workflow. While information services knows the network, corporate communications understands people and culture.

"We've had to be collaborative just to stay in business," according to Chris Duncan, Dow's global leader for communications resources. "Dow is kind of a sharing organization, because that's what is required to play in our space. The collaborative tools have enabled us to do it better and on a much broader scale than we did in the past."

Collaboration is so engrained in the Dow culture that geographically-dispersed teams think nothing of group writing news releases, marketing material and other documents screen-to-screen. While collaborating through application sharing and shared whiteboards has become standard at Dow, most videoconferencing occurs in the iRooms. As Dow equips notebook computers with cameras, more spontaneous video interactions will become possible. This will require a cultural shift that will likely be easier for Dow people, because of the company's legacy of collaboration.

Paging mirrors IM in that an immediate response is customary. Ironically, perhaps the only cultural barrier to acceptance of IM at Mayo is the preference for paging. The Mayo culture, anything but hierarchical, embraces paging among all levels of leadership.

The immediacy of the medical environment invites more collaboration perhaps than in many other industries. However, the larger influence in Mayo's case is the historical emphasis on collaboration. We can infer that the most significant factor impacting the use of tools is culture. From the user's standpoint, the need to think about tools recedes as the rhythm of collaboration takes hold.

The most significant factor impacting the use of tools is culture.

EVOLVING ROLE OF VIDEO

Culture impacts how people collaborate, and video fits some work styles more than others. Many television professionals excel at communicating through a camera but lose sleep over talking to a college class. In contrast, many teachers, who communicate daily with an in-room audience, wouldn't be caught dead in a television studio, despite the growth of distance learning.

Similarly, some leaders who thrive on face-to-face audience energy avoid delivering webcasts or satellite broadcasts. Other leaders prefer the more controlled communication of one-way video verses the comparative free-for-all of in-room audiences. And some executives use two-way video and audio as a leadership tool. I know one senior executive at a Fortune 500 company who uses a sixty-inch plasma screen mounted on his office wall to look into the eyes of his direct reports around the world. He encourages their interaction and moderates daily discussions.

Videoconferencing has historically stumbled in business because of reliability problems, ease-of-use issues, network hassles, and expense. Though engineers have made huge strides in solving these problems, the bigger, less-frequently-acknowledged barrier to videoconferencing acceptance has been culture. One of the many reasons that AT&T's Picturephone, the world's first digital video telephone, failed to take off in the 1960s was that people felt the product invaded their privacy.

That sentiment, which has short circuited innumerable videoconferencing products for three decades, is now waning. Camera phones, traffic cameras, and security cameras desensitize us to video. Reality show participants compete, decorate and even date on camera. Some even live with video throughout their homes so that the world can look into their lives. Our collective culture has accepted the invasion of video. Now when videoconferences occur, people are often less concerned about the camera than they are with the business at hand. There is increasingly less focus on the technology and more emphasis on connecting.

VIDEOCONFERENCING AND PRESENCE

Videoconferencing now manifests itself in new, more collaborative ways. The advent of IP videoconferencing means real-time video can now be integrated with data traffic and business applications rather than traveling over a separate network. The widespread implementation of voice over IP (VOIP) drives videoconferencing, because video can become an add-on to the VOIP infrastructure. Video also becomes an added feature of web conferencing, which allows application and data sharing screen-to-screen with audio.

Presence plunges videoconferencing into productivity applications. We can launch video interactions from documents, spreadsheets and 3D models. We can connect from our PC's, from mobile devices, or from video-enabled conference rooms. We can escalate an IM interaction into a video exchange. We can connect through video in the context of our work rather than stopping work to conduct a videoconference.

As presence pervades applications and devices, videoconferencing—along with web conferencing, IM, and other tools— becomes part of workflow. And integrating collaborative tools into work styles and lifestyles, which we explored in chapter 4, reinforces the Culture of Collaboration.

Integrating collaborative tools into work styles and lifestyles reinforces the Culture of Collaboration.

3G AND 4G WIRELESS

Third and fourth generation wireless systems (3G and 4G) enable handheld devices to send and receive video along with voice and data. The advent of 3G and its successor, 4G, allow people to join and initiate video calls from mobile phones, laptops and other portable or wearable devices. This means we can sit on a train, bus, or in the back of a car and see colleagues around the globe while sharing documents, spreadsheets and other programs. Presence lets colleagues find us and connect with us through video, and other modes, while we're on the go. It may not fit every work style, but mobile video and web conferencing can enhance collaboration for the most peripatetic among us.

VIDEOCONFERENCING REDUX

In this emerging world of convergence and presence, videoconferencing becomes universally available on our terms. It is no longer necessary to stop working, walk down the hall to a conference room, and conduct a pre-scheduled videoconference. This model may work under certain circumstances, but certainly not all.

We can launch a video interaction that fits our work styles—from applications that we use regularly and that run on devices we choose. We can join a video meeting in which some participants may be in a conference room while others are sitting on trains or working from home offices. In this environment, the use of videoconferencing becomes less disruptive and more integrated with how we work.

Video interaction is by no means as high-impact as sharing the same physical space, but it is often the next best thing. We can see one another and read body language, particularly facial expressions. We can tell if a colleague is confused or annoyed and can determine whether there is a meeting of the minds.

Videoconferences range from meetings at a distance to sessions in which collaborators engage in shared creation using digital whiteboards, application sharing, and document conferencing. Videoconferences bridge in-person relationships and the sort of virtual relationships that evolve among geographically-dispersed collaborators. Rather than focus on work details during videoconferences early in projects, establishing rapport accomplishes more. Sometimes it makes sense to schedule a relaxed interaction through video such as lunch or refreshments. I know of one company that has used the tool for after hours beer parties among multiple offices.

After establishing rapport, we can comfortably tackle project goals through scheduled videoconferences. Then we can more comfortably dig into details and engage in spontaneous interactions. These may include IM, VIM, audio conferencing or personal videoconferencing. Because spontaneous collaboration is potentially disruptive, success often depends on previous rapport building.

One option for videoconferences is to begin the interaction with video, set the rapport, and then minimize the video. Then the data, documents, or drawings can take center stage as collaborators engage in shared creation. At the end of the call, it's time to maximize the video, re-establish rapport, and say goodbye. "The firmer, stronger the relationship is, the more you can back off on the face to face and use the technology," notes Cindy Newman, Dow Chemical's director of corporate communications.

As we get increasingly comfortable interacting, we may have fewer qualms about meeting through video without first pressing the flesh. The pace of business at Procter & Gamble sometimes necessitates first meetings through video. After P&G's acquisition of Gillette, P&G managers found their teams expanding as former Gillette people joined their ranks. With project deadlines approaching, there was little time for travel.

Laurie Heltsley, P&G's director of computers and communications services, describes such a scenario: "I don't know you very well, but you're from Gillette and you just got added to my team. I need to get to know you. There's that immediacy thing. I need to get to know you by Wednesday, because on Wednesday we have to make a big decision together. So one way to accelerate that get-to-know process is through the use of video." Heltsley believes that video is most appropriate for personnel conversations, job interviews, get-to-know-you sessions and other interactions that require intimacy.

The main take away from this chapter is that collaboration never happens solely because of tools; collaboration happens because of culture. The tools are critical enablers in that they let us eliminate or reduce time and distance as barriers. Real-time tools help deserialize work and encourage us to brainstorm and create solutions now rather than letting problems fester.

Collaboration never happens solely because of tools; collaboration happens because of culture.

CHAPTER 8

THE BRAVE NEW WORLD OF LAW AND COMPLIANCE

Paradox governs the relationship between compliance and collaboration in that:

1. Compliance drives collaboration
2. Compliance complicates collaboration

Despite the hassles of dealing with proliferating laws and regulations, compliance encourages the move to common systems. In chapter 5, we discussed how common systems break down barriers and reduce silo syndrome in organizations. Access to the same systems and information encourages people in multiple functions, business units, and regions to interact. This, in turn, provides a fertile breeding ground for collaboration and innovation. However, compliance also inhibits collaboration because of privacy concerns and retention issues.

Of the mounting regulations and laws impacting collaboration, the Sarbanes-Oxley Act of 2002 is perhaps the most far-reaching. The United States Congress passed Sarbanes-Oxley, known as SOX, to curb financial malfeasance. After scandals at Enron, Tyco, World-Com and other companies, Congress took action forcing senior leadership to take responsibility for financial reports. In essence, CEO's and CFO's risk jail time if they certify financial statements containing knowingly false information. Among a host of other provisions, the act requires companies to provide real-time disclosures of material changes to financial conditions.

COLLABORATING TO COMPLY WITH SOX, HIPAA, AND THE PATRIOT ACT

Besides SOX, which affects all public companies, other laws and regulations are driving collaboration within specific industries. The Patriot Act, for instance, forces companies—particularly the financial services industry—to verify customer identity and maintain appropriate controls to detect money laundering. The Health Insurance Portability and Accountability Act (HIPAA) ensures that the health insurance, pharmaceutical and healthcare provider industries safeguard private information of patients and comply with standards for electronic exchange of healthcare data, among other requirements. And there are countless other laws and government regulations impacting industries ranging from chemicals to pharmaceuticals.

Compliance not only sparks the move to common systems, but also requires people across the organization to interact and share data. Therefore, compliance often drives the use of collaborative tools. Asynchronous tools such as team sites are becoming repositories for a range of compliance information as business units and functions including human resources and finance collaborate to comply. Also, companies are developing processes and applications integrated with team sites so that the right people gain timely access to relevant compliance information.

> *Compliance not only sparks the move to common systems, but also requires people across the organization to interact and share data.*

Integrating compliance applications with near synchronous tools including IM and VIM and synchronous tools including videoconferencing and web conferencing allow real-time resolution of auditing discrepancies and variations. When key people must sign compliance paperwork, they frequently want to look each other in the eye as they review quarterly financial data. Videoconferencing allows eye contact and professional intimacy when collaborators are geographically dispersed.

W.R. Grace & Co. has implemented a SOX reporting process in which some three hundred managers and "owners" of business processes such as payroll, confirm each quarter whether they are operating according to compliance procedures. The managers interact across multiple functions, business units and regions; without SOX, they would have little reason to contact one another. They use a range of collaborative tools including videoconferencing and web conferencing to resolve compliance issues and gain greater understanding of what they are confirming when they sign documents.

Also, the SOX process disrupts hierarchy by opening up a direct channel to the CEO and CFO. Before implementing the process, W.R. Grace & Company CFO Robert Tarola would regularly question a dozen direct reports about the status of compliance throughout Grace's global operations. Now three hundred managers report compliance information directly to Tarola.

"It gives them an avenue for private communication if they think something isn't as good as it could be or should be or if we truly even have a problem," explains Tarola. "The compliance factors are a net positive towards collaboration, because there has to be more collaboration among the functional areas, whether it's HR or IT or business management, to make sure that everyone knows the facts of the situation in order to deal with the reporting issues." Since compliance requires employees to accept responsibility for frank disclosure, the culture has shifted from hoarding to sharing information. This means that Grace embraces more openness in which employees not only disclose the whole truth about compliance, but also they share ideas.

RETENTION: A COLLABORATION COMPLICATION

Compliance complicates collaboration by raising new retention issues for companies using real-time and near real-time tools. If a business unit manager and financial analyst, for instance, conduct an IM session that includes information material to the company's financial health, the organization must archive the session. Dow Chemical Company is resolving retention issues before implementing IM. "Sarbanes-Oxley adds a whole other area of complexity," says Chris Duncan, Dow's global leader of communications resources. "What do we have to keep?"

Traditionally, companies have retained email, data and documents but have disposed of voice mail. Phone calls and videoconferences are often gone when they conclude. As companies implement voice and video over IP, however, archiving everything that occurs over the converged network becomes feasible. And when technology enables possibilities, possibilities quickly become expectations.

Organizations typically retain audience-oriented web conferences so that people who miss live events can review them later. It's increasingly necessary, however, to archive web conferences in which two or more participants collaborate on data and documents. The same principle applies to IP videoconferences and perhaps voice over IP conversations. Archiving videoconferences and web conferences allows people who miss sessions because of schedule conflicts or time zone differences to review interactions. And collaborators who do participate live frequently have questions. Did she say what I thought I heard? Did he look concerned about completing the project on time? Therefore, the ability to review sessions provides new insight.

Also, organizations can gain fresh perspectives from grabbing data and information on the fly from real-time encounters. These might include IM, web conferencing, and videoconferencing sessions. This information can be correlated with existing data to provide new outlooks for decision-making, thereby creating value.

On the flip side, however, people may be less open in their interactions if they know that the organization is retaining and perhaps analyzing these exchanges. There is always the danger that organizations could inhibit brainstorming and the free flow of ideas if people grow concerned that those sessions may exist forever. The next logical leap is that HR or management may use archived material in performance evaluations, which would ultimately impact

Organizations can mitigate fears by developing policies regarding access, analysis and use of archived collaborative exchanges.

raises and promotions. Organizations can mitigate concerns by developing policies regarding access, analysis and use of archived collaborative exchanges.

COLLABORATION IN A HIGHLY-REGULATED INDUSTRY

Aside from the collaborative benefits of archiving videoconferences, compliance provides another reason for retaining real-time interactions. The pharmaceutical industry must contend not only with Sarbanes-Oxley and HIPAA but also with a host of U.S. Food and Drug Administration (FDA) regulations. Also, the industry must safeguard the voluminous patient data it collects from clinical trials. The chief technical officer of a Fortune 50 pharmaceutical company and his IT risk management leader talked with me openly about compliance as I researched this book, but they requested that I withhold their names and the name of the company because of the sensitivity of the topic.

The company uses IM extensively, particularly among scientists who collaborate internally and externally in developing drugs. While the company sees no need to back up casual IM interactions, it does recognize the need to retain IM that deals with making decisions, distributing product information and other areas that touch on regulation. Of course, casual interactions sometimes become hard core business discussions.

> Intelligent systems may retain IM based on keywords and characteristics.

Ultimately, intelligent systems may retain IM based on keywords and characteristics. Meantime, the pharmaceutical company is taking few chances. "We're backing up everything, because we live in a highly-litigious society and our industry is subject to a lot of litigation from marketing practices to product liability and just in general as it relates to something you put inside somebody's body," according to the Fortune 50 CTO. "We like to keep records of how we've handled it. So we probably err on the side of being overly careful." Since the advent of videoconferencing over IP makes retention more viable, the company is considering backing up all real-time video traffic.

Another legal issue that arises in cross-organizational collaboration is intellectual property. This has particular relevance in the
highly-competitive drug discovery arena, because partners can easily
morph into competitors. So, the pharmaceutical company must balance the need to encourage collaboration with partners in developing cures with business interests and legal considerations. This
means the CTO finds himself in the awkward position of a collaboration cop.

"You might be surprised at what you find on an iPod," he says.
"You might find scientific data that's been formatted to an iTunes
format, and people use that device to carry stuff around." From an
intellectual property perspective, the CTO describes the iPod
approach as a nightmare. But, he adds, "From a collaboration point
of view, it's probably genius."

While compliance inhibits collaboration more than it encourages
it within the pharmaceutical company, compliance nevertheless has
increased cross-functional collaboration. In an effort coordinated by
the risk management leader, teams throughout the organization
have developed common processes and standardized business practices. Since compliance can add 40 percent to the cost of developing and supporting IT in new drug manufacture, the stakes are high
to eliminate redundancy and collaborate on compliance. To this
end, teams have examined regulations to find commonalities that
apply in multiple business groups and have used a unified, integrated approach.

Through collaboration, the teams have sorted out which processes add value and should be standardized and which ones are one-
off and provide little value. The pharmaceutical company has then
implemented standardized business processes that include compliance throughout functional areas, business units and regions. The
result is that business units and functions now focus on innovation
opportunities rather than getting bogged down in non-standard
business practices that previously existed only in their silos. Stan-
dardization of core processes has also allowed faster integration for
mergers and acquisitions.

While compliance has provided considerable impetus for collaboration across business unit, regional, and functional lines, the desire

to contain costs has pushed the company to approach compliance collaboratively. Shrinking margins and increased competition from generic drugs have changed the economic realities and sparked collaboration and cultural changes.

"I hate to put it this way, but if we were still making as much money hand over fist the way we used to operate, we wouldn't have the incentive," says the CTO bluntly. "The compliance issue is such a heavy burden in terms of additional overhead that it behooves you to walk across the boundaries, and many times it's what forces you to walk across the silos," notes the CTO.

The compliance approach has not only broken down barriers but also streamlined many business processes within the pharmaceutical company. These processes include software development and maintenance in the "validated" environment that the FDA requires. Validated means proof exists that an application does exactly what it was designed to do. The pharmaceutical company's compliance approach has evolved as an integral part of the execution of business processes rather than as something that is layered onto processes.

As compliance encourages cross-functional collaboration, the organizational culture evolves. Traditionally, the scientific and research units of the company have embraced a collaborative culture both

> As compliance encourages cross-functional collaboration, the organizational culture evolves.

internally and with business partners. However, the rest of the company has been more me-oriented than we-oriented. In part because of cross-functional collaboration for compliance, the collaborative culture is spreading throughout the organization. Also, the economic exigencies of the pharmaceutical industry are rendering the internally-competitive "me culture" an anachronism.

COMPLYING WITH GLOBAL PRIVACY LAWS

As saving collaborative sessions becomes standard, privacy concerns take center stage. Federal and state privacy laws may require that we inform collaborators that the videoconference or web conference is for keeps. Presence raises additional issues, because we can determine a variety of attributes about one another. These attributes may seem relatively benign. Typically they include our availability, the devices we use, and how to reach us. However, it is the potential of presence that raises the eyebrows of privacy advocates. Perhaps the biggest sticking point is location information, which we will address later in this chapter.

Presence raises privacy issues, because we can determine a variety of attributes about one another.

Organizations must determine policies regarding presence and decide whether to require that employees disclose whether, when and how they can be reached 24/7 and, particularly, their location. While technically employees can remain unavailable and therefore undisturbed, some people may feel obligated to remain available. A key question is how courts may review presence-oriented privacy concerns. Global organizations must comply with laws in multiple—sometimes dozens of—countries. In the United States, this involves Federal Communications Commission (FCC) regulations and the Privacy Act of 1974. The European Union has taken a tough stand on privacy issues, requiring member states to protect personal data.

Privacy has different connotations in different global regions.

Privacy has different connotations in different global regions. In Europe, there is a greater consciousness for governments to know information about citizens and less tolerance for companies to gather information about employees and customers. The opposite is true in the United States. Americans often equate privacy with preventing the government from knowing their business. The U.S. government's gaining knowledge of which library books a person checks out strikes most Americans as a breach of privacy, but Scandinavians have little concern about using their government-issued identifiers at libraries. While Americans are more willing to sell their personal information to companies for such trinkets as the chance to win merchandise, many Europeans would bristle at the thought.

Though often organizations consider implementation as the prime hurdle in using collaborative tools, compliance and other issues make setting up systems seem easy. "We can plug wires in any way we want to get things to do what we want them to do, but legally, can we do it? Or realistically, should we do it?" observes Dow's Chris Duncan. "The harder part is training, usability, bureaucracy, privacy, record retention, all of that stuff. That's the hard stuff."

PLAYING FOR KEEPS: POLICY ISSUES FOR ARCHIVING REAL-TIME SESSIONS

Organizations must develop policies for archiving and accessing meetings and collaborative sessions.

Organizations must develop policies for archiving and accessing meetings and collaborative sessions. Policy decisions may involve whether only the participants may access an archived session, whether a broader team may view the material, or whether the entire organization or extended enterprise has viewing rights. Other issues include whether a transcript of the interaction may be made available.

It has always been a good idea to assume a microphone or camera is live. Legend has it that microphone carelessness complicated the career of a children's radio host in the 1930s. Believing the engineer had turned his microphone off at a commercial break, the story goes, Uncle Don reportedly said "That oughta hold the little bastards." Regardless of whether the story is true, the host spent the rest of his career trying to clear his name. Many politicians and celebrities including singer Britney Spears, former British Prime Minister John Major, and U.S. President George W. Bush have sparked media frenzy by making careless remarks near open microphones at dinners and other events.

It has always been a good idea to assume a microphone or camera is live.

When I worked in television news, I always assumed that I was on the air whenever I was in the studio or waiting to do a live shot from the field. And because plenty of people monitoring the microwave signal or satellite feed can see and hear regardless of whether the material is actually on air, caution pays.

In business, we must now make the same assumption that many newscasters and politicians make. If we're near a speakerphone, a microphone, or a camera, we must assume that our words and behavior are for keeps. In an age in which security cameras are becoming connected to IP networks, we can also suppose that there is a record of our activity throughout the workplace and beyond.

Ultimately, organizations may possess—and also be able to easily search and retrieve—multimedia records that include presentations we deliver, meetings in which we participate, and collaborative sessions. These sessions may include videoconferences, web conferences, collaborative CAD, IM, and VIM. Our multimedia anthologies will also include blogs, podcasts, and wikis. Organizations will determine whether to allow use of this material for personal pages on intranets, for team sites, and even for multimedia HR records.

Organizations may possess—and also be able to easily search and retrieve—our multimedia anthologies.

In 1945, Vannevar Bush wrote in the *Atlantic Monthly* about the Memex. The Memex was a future device that would let a person store all books, records, and communications as an "enlarged intimate supplement" to memory. Gordon Bell, former head of Digital Equipment Corporation's research and development organization, is turning Bush's dream into reality. In a Microsoft lab, Bell records and scans his entire life as part of the My Life Bits project. That means archiving documents, email, phone calls, web pages viewed, music, video, images and whatever else Bell can obtain. The goal is not only to grab data but also to extract meaning from all of this material. In this same vein, organizations may soon retain face-to-face meetings.

With compliance issues and the expanding availability of video, voice and data comes a growing expectation of content availability. So if collaborators need a specific video clip or IM exchange to solve a business problem, they increasingly assume that they can put their fingers on it. Team sites allow access to whatever material collaborators push to the sites.

Also, as convergence enables organizations to create and retain collaborative sessions and compliance creates the demand for archiving, the follow-up issue becomes accessing and repurposing video, voice and data throughout the enterprise. Digital asset management systems allow storage and retrieval of rich media plus associated documents, spreadsheets and other data. Video and audio loggers, often integrated into asset management, let users search video and audio by spoken keywords.

SECURITY AND COMPLIANCE IN PARTNER COLLABORATION

As extranets proliferate for supply chain management and collaboration among business partners, a myriad of legal and intellectual property issues arises. The financial, information technology and aerospace industries have broken new ground in implementing extranets. In aerospace, Exostar provides a web environment with a "single point of connection for electronic security, commerce and collaboration."

More than sixteen thousand companies form the Exostar partner network. Exostar, as a neutral third party, safeguards intellectual property, providing access based on specific and strict guidelines determined by each partner regarding each asset. Protecting data access is critical, because of compliance issues ranging from national security to industry regulation. In chapter 10, we will discuss Exostar in greater detail.

TRUST AND MIDDLEWARE: COLLABORATING WITH CONFIDENCE

Middleware offers security capabilities that enable trust among collaborators as they interact over IP networks (See box, page 193). Middleware, software providing fundamental capabilities that many applications require, lives between the network and the applications themselves. Developing middleware is a primary focus of Internet2, a consortium of universities and corporations collaborating on advanced applications and network services. Many of these applications and services will eventually be used over the commercial Internet.

Middleware lets people and organizations interact based on trust.

Middleware lets people and organizations interact based on trust. Organizations must determine how each application fits into a trust framework. Ken Klingenstein, project

---

Functions of Core Middleware

Identification
Identification recognizes people on networks.

Authentication
Authenticators verify that users are who they say they are.

Directory
Directories are databases containing key organizational and personal data for use by many applications. Data may include email aliases, permissions to access specific data, and presence information.

Authorization
Authorization indicates the type of access to data that an authenticated identifier may gain. This function allows organizations to translate legal policies into network and data access guidelines.

Public Key Infrastructure (PKI)
PKI includes software, protocols and legal agreements to protect people, organizations and their data. The PKI may include encryption methods, digital signatures, and access controls. A Certificate Authority (CA) manages and signs certificates, while registration authorities validate users. The concept is that users have a widely distributed public key for encryption of information intended for them and an undistributed private key for decryption.

---

director for the Internet2 Middleware Initiative and chief technologist of the University of Colorado-Boulder, has identified a "continuum of trust." At one end of the continuum is *collaborative trust* and at the other end is *legal trust*.

Collaborative trust addresses such questions as whether anybody can IM with anybody else for any reason at any time, whether one person can videoconference with another person or whether somebody can post or change material on a team site. Legal trust refers to such issues as encryption and digital signatures. A legal trust issue is guaranteeing that the document a person signs is what he or she viewed and wanted to sign. Some applications can be done only at one end of the continuum, while most fit somewhere in the middle.

There are three key types of trust that impact collaborative capabilities:

1. *Global trust*—This refers to government-issued identity and identifiers and was once associated primarily with public key infrastructure. PKI has been slow to catch on in part because of its complexity.

2. *Federated enterprise-centric trust*—This applies most directly to businesses. In this model, organizations are considered realms which join into federations to conduct business. Federations include industry consortiums administering extranets that allow partners and even competitors to exchange information both asynchronously and in real time. Examples include The Automotive Network eXchange (ANX) in the auto industry and Exostar in the aerospace industry.

   In the consumer space, federated enterprise-centric trust often involves an identity service provider (IdP), an entity that brokers attributes and identity on an individual's behalf to other parties that want to know something about that individual. Identity service providers may include operating system vendors, Internet service providers, telecommunications companies, consumer product vendors and banks.

3. *Peer-to-peer trust*—This type of trust typically deals with interaction among individuals without the involvement of companies and organizations. InfoCard, a feature of Microsoft's Vista operating system, governs peer-to-peer trust. Peer-to-peer trust can protect identity but nevertheless allow interaction. This has particular relevance for online chat rooms. Collaboration is at the heart of peer-to-peer trust mechanisms, which let users determine guidelines for such interactions as sharing photos on hard drives, videoconferencing through firewalls or interacting through IM.

   A user wanting to videoconference with another user could drag an icon representing somebody's credentials over to an "allow to videoconference" box and then the firewall opens up upon seeing that person's credentials. This addresses videoconferencing trust and firewall issues in a limited way, because the approach is by no means enterprise-centric. The broader issues of trust in business-to-business interactions must be solved in the federated enterprise-centric arena.

Each of these trust models can support collaboration. The purpose of trust mechanisms and middleware is to protect privacy and ensure security. The federated model has particular ramifications for organizations striving to protect intellectual property. Because collaboration increasingly occurs among companies that are sometimes partners and at other times competitors, organizations

Because collaboration increasingly occurs among competitors, organizations must become increasingly vigilant about trust mechanisms.

must become increasingly vigilant about trust mechanisms. There are many scenarios in which companies may want researchers or engineers to collaborate externally through tools but without revealing identity. In these cases, there may be concerns regarding industrial espionage or raiding talent.

In the case of government agencies, maintaining the anonymity of collaborators may help protect national security. Ken Klingenstein of Internet2 tells the story of speaking at a conference after which two "pale gentlemen" approached him. One was from the United States Department of Defense and the other from the Department of Homeland Security. They expressed interest in tools that would allow collaboration between their departments without revealing the identity of their operatives.

What Klingenstein's community calls privacy-preserving, the government calls secrecy-preserving, but it's essentially the same use case. "We are moving from an identity-centric set of collaborative tools to an attribute-centric set of collaborative tools," explains Klingenstein. "So the issue of when do attributes reveal identity is now on the plate." In the parlance of privacy advocates, a "denial of privacy attack" is one in which a user releases a set of attributes to consummate one or more interactions, and taken together all of the attributes provides identity.

More critical than the technology in establishing trust among organizations are legal issues. An automobile company may wish to share information and collaborate with a supplier. However, the sharing company needs to verify that the supplier will use the information it receives appropriately. These contractual relationships must precede trust mechanisms driven by technology.

DYNAMIC AND STATIC PRESENCE

Presence generally refers to *dynamic presence*. Dynamic presence attributes might include the device we're using, how to reach us, our current time zone, perhaps our location, and how and whether we can be reached at a given moment. Clearly, these attributes change. Another type of presence called *static presence* involves attributes that remain constant. Trust mechanisms that protect identity while allowing collaboration might involve static presence.

Klingenstein of Internet2 and his team are working with the United States government to create an object class or entity known as U.S. Person. U.S. Person includes attributes that the government might want to use without revealing identity in an interaction or transaction. An example of such an attribute is citizenship.

On a more local level, state governments require that drinking establishments verify age. But is it necessary for bars to know a drinker's name? Perhaps not. The drinker could use a keypad to furnish age and photo to the bar through an identity service provider while protecting "privacy in drinking."

Static presence also has ramifications for collaboration within and between companies. A static presence profile could protect identity for highly-sensitive interactions while simultaneously providing enough attributes to verify that the collaborator is bona fide. Information presentation preference is a type of static presence that has particular relevance for people with disabilities or limitations. If somebody is color blind, for instance, he or she can include this attribute in a static presence profile so that any web page or application on any device he or she uses will adjust to accommodate this condition. In another example, a blind person may need text-to-voice translation regardless of device. Since laws require companies to provide equal access to job classifieds, information presentation presence is one way to level the playing field.

LOCATION INFORMATION AND PRIVACY

Presence can provide information about location, and devices such as mobile phones equipped with global positioning systems (GPS) provide specific locations. If an organization requires employees to use such tools, does the organization have the right to know location? After all, location can reveal personal information including drinking habits, sexual orientation, or the existence of an extramarital affair.

Many privacy advocates insist that requiring location information violates at least the spirit of privacy laws. Of course, mobile phone service providers can determine some degree of location without GPS. But it normally takes a subpoena, warrant or legal mechanism to reveal that information. "It's the OnStars of life that vex me a bit more, because there it's a two-way mechanism," according to Internet2's Ken Klingenstein, a child of the Sixties with strong beliefs in privacy. "People know exactly where I am down to the range of the GPS."

Compliance and collaboration make strange bedfellows. Dealing with myriad laws drives collaboration by shifting multiple functions, regions and business units to common systems. But lingering issues including retention, privacy, and trust complicate collaboration. In this brave new world, the challenge is devoting enough mindshare to laws and regulations without letting these matters impact spontaneity.

How can we feel comfortable brainstorming if the session potentially becomes part of our HR records or multimedia anthologies? The solution is clarity. Just as web sites have privacy policies regarding personal information, organizations develop guidelines about the use of archived collaborative sessions. Out of context, constructive confrontation could seem argumentative and might be used to build a case against promotion. We must guard against this tendency, which could short circuit collaboration. As we set inter and intra-organizational policies about monitoring and archiving, we will build greater value by encouraging and protecting the Culture of Collaboration.

CHAPTER 9

COLLABORATIVE LEADERSHIP

Gary Convis took a calculated risk in April, 1984 when he left behind an engineering and manufacturing management career at Ford and accepted an offer from Tatsuro Toyoda, the son of Toyota Motor Corporation's founder. The offer was to help run a new joint venture between Toyota and General Motors called New United Motor Manufacturing, Inc. (NUMMI). Shin Kanada, senior managing director and member of Toyota's board, remembers that in the joint venture "General Motors brought expertise in U.S. management and what Toyota had was a production system."

Tatsuro Toyoda was on the scene at the NUMMI plant in Fremont, California serving as the joint venture's first president. But he needed an American leader working shoulder-to-shoulder with Japanese executives and American assembly workers to help make Toyota's principles work on U.S. soil. That leader was a tall, articulate manager who majored in math at Michigan State University and cut his teeth at GM's Buick Division. From his start as plant general manager at NUMMI, Convis realized the script had changed; the culture Toyota would instill in him and in NUMMI was a world apart from that of American automobile companies in the 1980s.

There was less friction between union workers and management, less elbowing others out of the way, and greater cooperation. "If we don't accept being open, nurturing, caring about the other person and their career, if we don't have that natural feeling where people are connected to us, then the organization doesn't work so well," Convis told me at a Japan Society of Northern California dinner honoring his mentor, Tatsuro Toyoda.

USING MENTORING TO SHARE KNOWLEDGE

During a follow up conversation, Convis reflected on his transformation after moving from a more command-and-control culture to Toyota's collaborative culture. "I always thought of myself as a pretty flexible guy and a team player, but the culture within Toyota requires you to be very collaborative. The culture inside the other companies didn't necessarily nurture that, nor require it as much."

His transition into a collaborative leader occurred as his mentors, including Toyoda, kept him on track by asking questions and challenging him. While mentoring often plays a large role in collaborative cultures, mentoring relationships at Toyota are informal and, according to Convis, almost "invisible" in that mentors avoid meddling but instead guide their protégés. Convis moved up at NUMMI, as the company spent years building trust in him and developing him into the kind of leader that Toyota desires—a collaborative one.

Mentoring often plays a large role in collaborative cultures.

By April of 2001, Toyota had developed the confidence in Convis to name him President of Toyota Manufacturing, Kentucky and a managing officer of Toyota Motor Corporation. The Kentucky subsidiary is the company's largest manufacturing operation outside Japan and employs more than seven thousand people. Convis, later named chairman of the Kentucky subsidiary, is the first American to take the helm of any Toyota manufacturing plant. Therefore, it is fitting that Convis has become perhaps Toyota's most effective translator of the Toyota Way for an American audience.

DEVELOPING COLLABORATIVE LEADERS

In a collaborative culture such as Toyota's, leadership means more than perks and plush offices. "There's a level playing field," according to Convis. "I think people become leaders not because of titles but through their leadership, their natural abilities, and that is what you see at Toyota." To that end, many young managers spend long days working on the assembly line. Also, many managers gain experience selling vehicles. In Japan, this has traditionally meant door-to-door sales, giving managers an opportunity to understand customers as individuals rather than as data.

Through this approach, managers appreciate the challenges that salespeople and line workers face. "Deep respect. Deep respect. That's the point." explains Convis. "When you put in days of working on the line with your own hands building a car, what the team member does every day, that means you really connect with that team member and you have respect for what they do."

Conditioning leaders from the start to respect assembly workers and understand multiple functions reduces the role of hierarchy and prevents barriers among functions and levels from developing the way they do in many other organizations. This, in turn, fosters a collaborative culture in which everybody's input not only is welcome, but also is expected. Toyota painstakingly instills its culture in each employee and encourages leaders to evangelize the culture. However, Toyota's approach to evangelizing lacks the zeal of American corporate evangelists. The approach is more Japanese, that is to say, understated.

BUILDING CONSENSUS THROUGH NEMAWASHI

Though Gary Convis speaks little Japanese and has lived in the United States throughout his career, he embodies the essence of the Toyota Way. He speaks softly and exudes confidence but without a trace of egotism. He stresses the importance of *nemawashi* or consensus building, a key tenet of the Toyota Way, in an avuncular rather than proselytizing tone. It's as if he is your faculty advisor or coach, rather than the principal. According to Wikipedia, *nemawashi*

literally translates to "going around the roots" as in digging around the roots of a tree for awhile to prepare it for transplant.

"You just can't get your idea accepted unless you're growing roots and developing the idea with others," Convis contends. "Nemawashi fine tunes those ideas. An idea can be enhanced and improved by a lot more minds thinking about it." Essentially, his Japanese mentors taught Convis how to lead in a collaborative culture and how to perpetuate the culture.

> An idea can be enhanced when many minds think about it.

There are compelling parallels between collaborative movements in American education and the Toyota culture. As we discussed in chapter 3, the philosophy and physical design of the Stanford Center for Innovations in Learning (SCIL) reinforces the notion of "guide on the side" rather than traditional learning's "sage on the stage." The same philosophy applies to collaborative leadership. At Toyota, leaders explain direction and purpose and then guide team members towards goals. Rather than considering leaders omniscient, Toyota expects executives at all levels to constantly learn details first hand through observation, experience and discussion. There is no firing off memos or issuing directives. Instead, Toyota leaders build consensus.

An interesting manifestation of this culture is the role of the chief engineer (CE) in new vehicle development. In *The Toyota Way* (McGraw-Hill, 2004), Jeffrey K. Liker points out that the CE "epitomizes the Toyota approach to leadership." While the CE has overall responsibility for a new vehicle program, he or she has perhaps six direct reports and no authority over the thousands of engineers and others needed to design and produce the product. Functional general managers look after such areas as body, chassis and powertrain. The CE must collaborate with the general managers and others to secure resources and achieve success. Liker quotes former Toyota manager John Shook as calling this approach "responsibility without authority." This forces the CE to involve others and build consensus for ideas.

While it took many years of careful consideration before Toyota invested in the NUMMI joint venture, the move nevertheless involved calculated risk. Companies with command-and-control

Collaborative cultures embrace innovation, and collaborative leaders take calculated risks.

cultures are less likely to take even carefully-studied risks, because managers fear reprisals for rocking the boat or disturbing the status quo. This can have negative consequences, particularly during significant shifts in the business landscape or during realignments in specific industries when shifting resources in a new direction may be necessary. Collaborative cultures embrace innovation, and collaborative leaders take calculated risks.

In Monster's cross-cultural software development environment, engineers spontaneously collaborate throughout the work day and beyond. They are free to choose the tools and the approach that fits their work styles so long as they meet objectives. And Monster encourages its people to find new approaches to processes. Risk is part of that equation. "You can't take a $500 million revenue stream and drive it to zero. That's an unacceptable risk. But you've got to have some level of risk understanding and risk taking," notes Mark Conway, Monster's CTO.

Monster's approach to collaborative leadership is, for starters, to recruit the best talent regardless of geography. In the Czech Republic, the literacy rate is 99 percent and curriculum in the Czech educational system emphasizes engineering and technical skills. Those factors in part fueled Monster's decision to locate a development center in the Czech Republic. Once Monster management finds talent, leaders focus on bridging regional cultures, building trust and developing relationships. And the company provides the tools to virtually support relationships.

Sometimes it's necessary for leaders to infuse greater collaboration into the organizational culture. Economic necessity is forcing Ford's Premier Automotive Group to collaborate across its brands—Jaguar, Land Rover, Aston Martin, and Volvo. Ford PAG understands that differentiation among its brands is critical to customers, but that there are many commodity parts that have little to do with customer perception of value. In the C-Car shared technologies program, engineers and executives of Mazda (partially owned by Ford), Ford Europe and Volvo collaborated to reduce development costs for specific small car models. The result is that Ford has reduced the internal competition among brands and increased the sharing of best practices.

Ford PAG leaders are now using the C-Car example to gain traction for cooperation among brands on a wider scale. "If you have some early successes with collaboration, then it's very important to acknowledge them and to recognize them in some public way so that other people who are involved in the culture can see that this is a useful thing too and that it's valued by management and therefore it's interesting," says Ford CTO Richard Parry-Jones. To this end, Ford has featured its cross-brand collaboration in executive speeches, internal publications, and in best practice sharing sessions.

DISTRIBUTING KNOWLEDGE THROUGH YOKOTEN

Yokoten is Toyota's approach to knowledge management. Literally, the word means "taking from one place to another" and is the system through which the organization gathers and distributes knowledge. In Toyota's collaborative culture, developing an idea has limited value in and of itself. Leaders demonstrate by example and expect people at all levels to share their good ideas and ensure that they are implemented throughout the organization. A good idea either not used or used in a single location or limited way wastes resources, and Toyota frowns upon every kind of waste.

"If you found some magical idea, the next thing we look at is what you have done to tell people about it and help them understand why it's good and move it along outside of your direct control," says Gary Convis of Toyota. Therefore, a plant manager who has—with others—implemented a new process improvement has an obligation to export the idea to his peers throughout the world, rather than hoard the knowledge to make the local operation look good. The concept is to circulate good ideas and innovation around Toyota's closely-knit network of plants.

A collaborative tool that helps people share ideas may support *yokoten*, though Toyota adopts new tools slowly to ensure that tools fit its principles and production systems. To rapidly spread knowledge, Toyota has built a network of global production centers

(GPC) in Japan, Europe, and in North America. At the GPC, leaders learn best practices in manufacturing and production. They also deepen their understanding of the Toyota Way.

Besides gaining knowledge, leaders are expected to share what they know with others at the GPC and with team members at their plants. The GPC's are connected via Toyota's V-comm system, which integrates videoconferencing with computer aided design (CAD) and other tools. Each GPC has dedicated V-comm rooms, allowing managers to interact and learn how to use a system that is critical in the design and manufacturing of vehicles. We will discuss V-comm and collaboration in vehicle design in chapter 10.

Like Toyota, the Mayo Clinic relies heavily on core values and principles. And, unlike people in many other organizations, Mayo people pay more than lip service to principles. Besides teamwork, a tenet that galvanizes collaboration and collaborative leadership is "the needs of the patient." When doctors or administrators come to cross purposes, often that single principle helps guide them through the maze.

SHARING LEADERSHIP ROLES

"This is a tough place to swagger," says Dr. Glenn Forbes, CEO of the Mayo Clinic's Rochester, Minnesota campus. While arrogance runs rampant in some professions, medicine included, Mayo people quickly learn that swaggering accomplishes nothing in Mayo's collaborative culture. In fact, Mayo's founders shunned individualism when they introduced private group practice, with the emphasis on *group*, in the nineteenth century.

Doctors and others who want to soar alone grow frustrated with Mayo's brand of consensus leadership and collaboration, and sometimes they leave after a year or two. "You usually will find that people very uncomfortably or rarely use the singular word *I*. And that started with our founders," Dr. Forbes notes. Doctors Will and Charles Mayo, who helped found the clinic with their father, always talked in terms of *we* or "my brother and I." "So it's always what *we*, rather than *I*, will do, and that's really grounded right back to the idea of sharing."

Mayo's collaborative leadership model pairs a doctor with a professional administrator for each leadership role. They share responsibilities, mentor each other, and bring complementary perspectives to decisions. The doctor is obliged to advocate the patient's perspective in developing policy. "If you talk to one of our administrators they'll say, 'You know being an administrator at Mayo is a little different than being an administrator at XYZ corporation that's making widgets, because at XYZ my job is to make decisions and hire and fire people and form teams, and at Mayo my first job is I'm paired with a doc. And I have to work with this doc, and we have to make decisions together,'" according to Dr. Forbes.

Dr. Forbes notes that during his more than thirty-year career at Mayo, he has had about a dozen administrative partnerships. In some cases, he has mentored younger administrators. And in other cases, he has played more of a protégé role. "But in any case, we've shared the decision making and we've brought different aspects of healthcare delivery to the decision-making process."

Leadership role sharing, coupled with a collaborative culture, encourages doctors and administrators who lead Mayo to make decisions together rather than on their own or in a vacuum. Mayo practices consensus leadership which in Mayo's culture means infusing decisions with collective wisdom through collaboration and communication. This leads to a common ownership of the decision and the results. "In our environment, we spend a little bit more time with the engagement and ownership, so that when a decision is made, it's not your decision or my decision. It's our decision," Dr. Forbes explains. "And if you stumble, I'm stumbling. And if I stumble, I know you're going to be there to help me."

REMAINING IN THE TRENCHES

Unlike other teaching hospitals where doctors might spend a decade or two as chiefs of surgery, Mayo rotates leaders every five to eight years. This contributes to a more democratic, less hierarchical, and ultimately more collaborative type of leadership. We have discussed how Toyota expects many leaders to have gained experience producing and selling cars. In a sense, Mayo goes a step further.

The doctors who run the organization must continue practicing as they lead.

Despite his role as CEO of Mayo's Rochester organization, Dr. Forbes works as a neuroradiologist. When he switched from a job running one of Mayo's health systems and assumed the CEO post, Dr. Forbes approached the neuroradiology division chief, somebody he trained more than a decade ago.

"I go to that person and I say, 'Administratively you may report to me, but clinically I report to you. So you tell me what are you going to do with me? I'm your toughest doc on your staff, because I'm going to hardly be around very much, and I'm not going to be in all of the different areas of procedures and research,'" explains Dr. Forbes. He then requests a clinical work assignment in a narrow area that his colleagues like the least. This helps justify his existence as an irregular team member. Also, it's easier for a part-time clinician to remain on the leading edge of a narrower discipline.

BALANCING CONSENSUS WITH EXPEDIENCY

One challenge in any culture that encourages collaborative leadership is expediency. Such cultures run the risk that people will discuss, rethink, and revisit every decision ad nauseam. Mayo guards against this tendency by balancing its focus on collaboration and consensus with a concurrent emphasis on process and decision efficiency. One example of this efficiency is MAGIC, discussed in chapter 5. MAGIC involves merging all key administrative functions throughout Mayo campuses and integrating the processes and systems that support those functions.

As W.R. Grace & Company's culture evolves into a collaborative one, leaders must adjust. Problem solving now includes many perspectives, and dictating decisions and policies no longer fits the culture. However, leaders must also balance the need for consensus with the reality of deadlines. "You can't let the collaborative process take over without results or deliverables," notes Robert Tarola, CFO of Grace. Leading functions, notably finance, that involve deadlines and deliverables, requires a delicate balancing act. On the one hand, leaders want to build consensus and collaborate across functions.

On the other hand, sometimes deadlines force leaders to end debate abruptly. "It's a lot easier to dictate a decision," says Tarola. "It's a lot harder to get a collaborative consensus, but sometimes you just need to make a decision."

LEADERSHIP IN HYBRID CULTURES

On the spectrum between collaborative and command-and-control cultures is the hybrid culture. This is one in which a collaborative culture pervades particular functional areas, regions, or business units, while other areas tend towards a "me" rather than a "we" culture. This scenario often occurs in companies that have extensive scientific or research and development operations. A prime example is the pharmaceutical industry. In the case of the unnamed Fortune 50 pharmaceutical company discussed in chapter 8, the organization experiences cultural schizophrenia in that its scientific community embraces collaboration far more than other areas of the company. However, economic exigencies are forcing the broader organization to adopt a culture that mirrors that of the scientific units.

Hybrid and transitional cultures present leadership challenges and provide insight into the disconnection between people accustomed to traditional verses collaborative approaches. Leaders in the scientific arena sometimes focus more on debate, discussion and achieving consensus. When conditions change, those leaders are quick to revisit decisions. However, this approach seems like indecisiveness to leaders in finance, IT, manufacturing and other areas of the company. According to the Fortune 50 pharmaceutical CTO, "For most of the rest of the business, we need to make decisions and get on with life. Otherwise you're paralyzed by the continuous revisiting, so the leadership in the purely scientific area is much more iterative."

On the flip side, leaders of the pharmaceutical giant have learned that command-and-control styles encourage teams and leaders to focus on their piece of the puzzle without learning or caring about the entire process. When managers give instructions

When managers give instructions without inviting input, team members are less likely to think, contribute, and consider the big picture.

without inviting input, team members are less likely to think, contribute, and consider the big picture. This is why the pharmaceutical company's dominant culture is adopting the more collaborative culture that thrives among its scientists.

INCENTING PEOPLE TO COLLABORATE

In a collaborative culture, the only way to gain consensus for ideas and proposals is to collaborate. In short, collaboration is the only way to get anything done. But few organizations have purely collaborative cultures. Some still embrace command-and-control approaches, and many others have cultures that are somewhere along the spectrum between command-and-control and collaborative. In such companies, frequently there are fertile collaborative pockets—particular people or groups that work across functions, business units, and regions to chalk up impressive results. Often, leaders hope to leverage these successes so that these collaborative pockets will spread throughout the organization.

Since people in partially-collaborative cultures often perceive they can achieve targets and goals without collaborating, how do we as leaders motivate people to engage in shared creation? The question has particular relevance in environments in which sales teams and business units compete for bonuses and other rewards. 3D/I, the design and construction firm based in Texas with fourteen offices across the United States, faces this dilemma. Company leadership places a premium on collaboration, because shared creation among company personnel and business partners is part-and-parcel of building hospitals, colleges, prisons and other major projects. Leaders work to instill a barrier-busting, hierarchy-hopping mind-set. The company expects front-line employees to provide input into business processes and expects leaders to listen.

Despite committing to collaboration, an organization can stop short of adopting the Culture of Collaboration because of the recognition and reward system. If the system forces functions, regions and business units to compete rather than cooperate, *collaboration* may become a buzzword rather than a culture. 3D/I has organized its offices into profit centers, encouraging the leader of each to make better numbers than his or her peers. This approach would seem to boost revenue and encourage healthy competition. However, particular 3D/I offices and practices have talent and resources that could more efficiently handle specific projects or parts of projects.

Despite the opportunity to involve other groups, practice leaders and their teams may avoid collaborating for fear of losing business to internal competitors. "We have not found a way to set up an accounting system to correct that problem," according to Chuck Thomsen, chairman of 3D/I. "We've struggled with a million different ways to do so, like setting up little bonus tools to reward people based on the amount of revenue they're able to push to other parts of the organization…stuff like that, none of which works." Preaching the benefits of collaborating, which Thomsen and other leaders do extensively, helps remind 3D/I people that they can achieve greater results by involving broad talent throughout the organization in specific projects. Evangelizing takes a leader only so far, however, if the reward system runs contrary to the message.

> *Evangelizing takes a leader only so far if the reward system runs contrary to the message.*

Toyota incents people to collaborate by using collaboration as a yardstick in raises and promotions. A team member or manager may develop great ideas, implement innovative approaches, and exceed all targets. While the company will recognize these achievements, Toyota will refrain from promoting the person if he or she fails to collaborate effectively. This is because collaboration is a key tenet of the Toyota Way.

At some companies, "high potential" managers may give people at lower levels short shrift. We've all seen this problem in action. It's the store manager who ignores a stocker's ideas about inventory. Or it's the marketing director who rebuffs a PR specialist when he or she proposes a media interview. Or it's the sales manager who treats an administrative assistant like an indentured servant. This behavior is anything but collaborative, and such approaches at Toyota can prevent advancement.

When a mentor notices non-collaborative behavior in a protégé, he or she works to correct the problem and to transform the protégé into a collaborative leader. Gary Convis told me about a high potential manager working at the manufacturing subsidiary he runs in Georgetown, Kentucky. The manager has achieved tremendous successes but lacks collaborative qualities. Convis, who constantly interacts with people at all levels of his operation, has heard from administrative people that the manager fails to recognize their value or seek their input.

Because Convis knows that promoting the manager will benefit the company, he is committed to transforming his protégé into a collaborative leader. Also, Convis recognizes in the manager similar command-and-control behavior that Convis overcame during his transformation and maturation at Toyota. So, he brings examples to the manager's attention of how his protégé can be more collaborative in certain situations.

"A lot of us who try to get things done don't spend enough time thinking about who's impacted, who needs to be on board, what's my plan to communicate to them, how do I need to get them together to see the vision, to understand the background, because we're doers. We've got to make things happen and things are moving on," according to Convis. "Honestly, nobody's smart enough to know all the right answers. This collaborative management style in Toyota, it's real and it's important."

COMPETING IN COLLABORATIVE CULTURES

Are collaboration and competition mutually exclusive? The short answer is no. The long answer is more complicated. Healthy businesses need to compete in the marketplace, but the myopic focus on destroying competitors leads to unhealthful business habits that ultimately compromise profits. One such habit is repeating empty, bravado-baked phrases designed to convince employees, customers, investors, and the media that company X is the best in its industry.

A relative of mine was a salesperson for AT&T some years ago, and she shook her head one day in 1994 when she returned from vacation. A seemingly-possessed manager, eyes bulging, caught her by the arm and said, "Have you heard? We're at war with MCI!" Clearly these were tough times in telecommunications, and many professionals in the field felt under the gun. Nevertheless, the comment did little to motivate my relative or her colleagues, several of whom left the company shortly thereafter.

Executives often seek my help in becoming more credible. Besides getting caught in outright lies, almost nothing compromises credibility more than empty superlatives. Yet executives—many CEO's, in fact—insist on claiming "Our products are best in breed." or "We will become the envy of the industry" or "Our solution is by far the best" or "We will clean their clocks" or "Nobody can do what we can do."

Do we believe these superlatives? We barely get to decide, because we're so used to hearing comments like this that we glaze over and tune out. Given the opportunity, our BS meters would tell us that it takes more than words to demonstrate quality and value. Superlative syndrome is a disease rooted in bravado, and this ailment plagues American business. In the male-dominated technology industry, this disease has metastasized. When executives use superlatives during coaching sessions, I challenge them to prove these proclamations.

Superlative syndrome is a manifestation of what the Greeks called *hubris*, meaning excessive pride. It can ruin a business by destroying the trust of employees, partners, customers and others. Also, superlative syndrome often masks process, product, financial and other defects. Unhealthful competition, the all-consuming focus on destroying the reputation and bottom line of competitors, allows executives to talk tough without focusing the organization on what really matters—things like developing sound principles and processes, innovation, and earning the trust and confidence of business partners and customers. These, all requiring collaboration, deliver sustaining value to employees, shareholders, and communities. Therefore, collaboration lets companies compete. Competition becomes a byproduct of healthful business practices rather than of a maniacal emphasis on crushing the enemy.

When managers develop a myopic focus on competing, they often lose the rudder. They focus less on innovation, less on developing better processes and more on reacting to the competition. This can lead to price cuts, lower revenue and reduced market share.

Instilling a Culture of Collaboration

There are certain approaches that a leader can use to instill a Culture of Collaboration. These include:

ESTABLISH MENTORING SYSTEM

Companies that typically embrace collaboration also value mentoring. When people at all levels of the organization look to mentors for guidance, they realize that making decisions and doing their best work requires constant input from others.

INVITE CONSTRUCTIVE CONFRONTATION

"What do you really think?" People in collaborative organizations must get the sense that their colleagues and leaders expect answers to this question. If people fear expressing their candid views, they will have difficulty collaborating. This is because collaboration involves trust, sharing, open information flow, and constructive confrontation.

INTEGRATE COLLABORATIVE TOOLS INTO WORK STYLES

Implement tools that enhance collaboration. Think about how every person in the organization works and how to involve him or her in process improvement. Offer broad functionality including synchronous and asynchronous approaches involving video, voice and data. Ensure that people can find each other and connect through a variety of devices.

FACILITATE CROSS-FUNCTIONAL BRAINSTORMING

Provide physical environments that reject formality and encourage ideas to fly. Facilitate process improvement by including people from various functions and levels of the organization to brainstorm new approaches. Provide tools in these environments allowing people in other regions to participate.

REWARD PEOPLE FOR GAINING BROAD INPUT

Consider implementing process improvements and new approaches only if the proponents have gained input from multiple functions, business units and regions. Ask "What input have you received from sales?" or "How has facilities helped shape this proposal?" Remind people that broader input creates greater value. Evaluate people based on their track record of seeking advice, input, and additional perspectives.

REWARD PEOPLE FOR SHARING INFORMATION

Articulate the message that sharing information creates long-term value for the organization and that hoarding information compromises efficiency, chokes off innovation and hurts the bottom line. To highlight the message that sharing information saves time, give people some of that saved time to use as they wish. For example, work with HR to provide an extra day off or a bonus for creating effective team sites.

INCENT PEOPLE TO INNOVATE

Provide bonuses to people who form and participate in ad hoc teams that innovate. This will encourage cross-functional collaboration, because innovation requires input from multiple departments. Since ad hoc teams come together for a particular purpose and then disband, cliques are less likely to form. Instead, people who receive rewards for innovation on one team will then form other teams with other people and continue innovating.

PROMOTE COLLABORATORS

In identifying "high potential" managers, look for collaborative characteristics. Does the manager seek input or does the prospective leader try to shove ideas down people's throats? If it's the latter, guide the manager to become more collaborative. Promote him or her only if they mature and they come to understand why considering multiple perspectives leads to better decisions.

PRACTICE COLLABORATIVE LEADERSHIP = *Senior Team Must Model!!*

Lead more with your eyes and ears than with your mouth. Engage people at all levels of the organization and seek their input. Ask questions, and listen. Gain wisdom from mentors, while guiding and coaching protégés. Make your ideas and initiatives stronger by building consensus.

USE COLLABORATIVE VOICE TONE

Our voice tone often telegraphs more to team members than words. When some managers talk, the message is "It's my way or the highway." Speaking with unnecessary authority inhibits input, sharing and collaboration. Using the voice tone you might use with a friend often produces better results than trying to sound like a manager.

AVOID THE INTERNAL COMPETITION TRAP

When aligning the recognition and reward system around collaboration, a tempting trap is to pit teams against one another. In its zeal to spark collaboration, an organization might offer rewards to the most collaborative team. This approach runs counter to instilling collaborative values, because the organization is essentially rewarding internal competition rather than collaboration.

Meantime, managers continue using superlatives all day long wherever they go. It's as if they existed in an alternate reality. Ultimately, the credibility gap becomes so wide that managers lose trust among employees, and the organization takes its licks from customers, investors and the media.

In *Only the Paranoid Survive* (Currency, 1996), Andy Grove defines strategic dissonance as the divergence between actions and statements during a strategic inflection point, the time at which a company's fundamentals are about to change. There also exists what we might term *competitive dissonance,* a divergence between the company's ability to create value and the often superlative claims of management.

> Healthful competition requires innovation, building relationships, improving processes, and delivering value.

Healthful competition exists in the global collaborative enterprise. However, the most effective way to compete is by focusing on innovation, building relationships, improving processes, and delivering value. Aside from competition in the marketplace, many organizations—collaborative or otherwise—wrestle with internal competition. Many cultures pit people against each other, because management believes this approach delivers superior results. There is also some feeling, rarely articulated, that internal competition creates more carnivorous employees who will then be primed to devour competitors. Missing from this approach is broad organizational input gained from collaboration that leads to awesome innovation.

In *No Contest: The Case Against Competiton* (Houghton Mifflin, 1992), Alfie Kohn argues that "competition also precludes the more efficient use of resources that cooperation allows." His point is that competition typically involves duplicating efforts. The aerospace industry has identified ways that competitors can avoid redundancy and can collaborate to reduce costs. The Exostar consortium provides the industry with a common Web interface for transactions and interaction with business partners.

More murky is the notion of whether internal competition should play any role in a collaborative culture. Several business units of a single company with an overlapping customer base may compete for sales. Besides redundant efforts, another problem is that customers may tire of multiple contacts from the same company and perceive disorganization. Collaborating on an integrated sales approach may deliver greater value. Ford's Premier Automotive Group has reduced internal competition along with costs by using some common components across its brands.

Toyota, with its collaborative culture, places a premium on sharing ideas and approaches across plants. So it may seem like a contradiction that plants compete. "We compare ourselves to each other all the time in many different ways, and we recognize achievements in different ways also," according to Gary Convis of Toyota. "There is a competitive environment. There's no question that we're all trying to do our best."

LEADING IN A NEWLY-COLLABORATIVE CULTURE

The Myelin Repair Foundation is breaking new ground in medical research in part by changing the culture from competitive to collaborative. While scientists may have a natural inclination to collaborate and may say that they share data and work with colleagues, the system often prevents effective interaction. As we discussed in chapter 6, scientists developing new disease cures compete for limited grant money and for publishing articles in top medical journals. This impedes collaboration and therefore slows the development of cures.

Scott Johnson and Russell Bromley, start-up company veterans who run the foundation, have challenged the status quo by creating a medical research consortium based on collaboration. Scientists who run labs at five leading universities share their research with the goal of developing treatments for multiple sclerosis. The specific objective is to begin clinical trials within five years. Before the collaboration began, the scientists estimated it would take three or four times longer to develop a way to repair myelin, the sheaths or coating surrounding nerves. Multiple sclerosis damages myelin, leaving scar tissue in its place.

A major reason the collaboration is working is the collaborative leadership of Johnson and Bromley and the research model they've developed (see figure 9.1). They realized that to dramatically reduce the cycle time of curing MS, the key element was a shift from com-

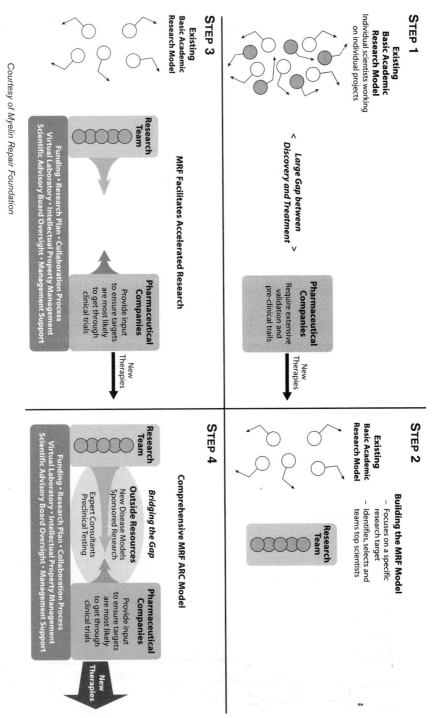

Courtesy of Myelin Repair Foundation

Figure 9.1   The Myelin Repair Foundation's Accelerated Research Collaboration Model

The Reason to have So in teamly Sessions 3

petitive to collaborative culture. To understand the nature of competition in medical research, think about the reward system and, in particular, the ultimate reward.

"How many teams have won the Nobel Prize? It's almost always individuals, and certainly those are the names you remember," says COO Bromley. And the National Institutes of Health typically makes grants to individual principal investigators. Of course, each scientist has a team of post-doctoral and graduate students, but the focus is on the top dog. "Knowledge is the coin of the realm, and it's closely held until things come to publication since the reward system is based on how many papers did you publish and how prestigious were the journals. And so it's sort of the antithesis of a truly, open collaborative environment," notes Bromley.

Changing a culture from competitive to collaborative requires collaborative leadership. A key element is recruiting the best global talent, ideally people who are frustrated enough with the status quo and have

> Changing a culture from competitive to collaborative requires collaborative leadership.

an inkling of how collaboration can create value for them and for the community. Johnson and Bromley considered 120 scientists before choosing five. Each of the chosen knew each other by reputation and respected one another's work. This gave the collaborators a leg up on trust.

Must Model

For naturally skeptical scientists to trust foundation leadership, however, has taken more time. A critical success factor is that Johnson and Bromley invite regular input on the Collaborative Research Process, the dynamic document that serves as the "rules of the road" for collaboration. Also, they refrain from assigning tasks to scientists and labs. Instead, they remind the collaborators about potential accomplishments and let them assign tasks to themselves. The philosophy is hire the best people, provide needed resources, get out of the way, and collaborators will overachieve.

After recruiting the right people, the next step is to create a reward system that includes both short-term and long-term incentives to collaborate. In the Myelin Repair Foundation model, the short-term reward is that scientists and their labs receive continued funding based on their level of collaboration. The scientific collaborators plus foundation leadership comprise a steering committee that reviews collaborative input before allocating annual funding. The long-term incentive is that once the collaborators find a cure for multiple sclerosis, this will enhance the foundation's fund raising and the level at which it funds the scientists and their labs.

In devising a reward system, Johnson and Bromley realized that scientists often specialize in narrow areas and rarely get recognized outside of those areas. Aside from the funding, they offered another incentive: the scientists as collaborators would receive broader recognition for curing multiple sclerosis rather just solving a piece of the puzzle. The incentive has no down side, because the scientists can continue receiving their usual recognition as individuals.

Many attempts at collaboration fail because a shortsighted manager puts several people in a room and expects them to "go collaborate."

Leading in a newly-collaborative culture requires facilitation. Many attempts at collaboration fail because a shortsighted manager puts several people in a room and expects them to "go collaborate" or provides tools to geographically-dispersed teams with the expectation that technology will facilitate collaboration. Six months later when the collaboration has clearly failed, the manager wonders why. Often, he or she has failed to facilitate the right chemistry among collaborators and the right environment.

"It does not evolve spontaneously. It has to be cultivated. It has to be facilitated. It has to be nurtured," says Bromley. As Johnson and Bromley have guided the scientists along the collaboration path, they have watched an intellectual interest evolve into an emotional desire to collaborate and accomplish goals that can be achieved only through trust, interaction, and shared creation. "It has not been a linear function and it has not been completely smooth along the way," Bromley adds.

CONSISTENCY IN LEADERSHIP

While competition coexists with collaboration at Toyota, so too does consistency of leadership. The word consistency, particularly in start-up cultures, conjures up images of resisting change. This would seem

Leading in a collaborative culture

- Use ears and eyes more than mouth
- Ask questions
- Earn respect by walking in the shoes of others
- Invite team members to think like leaders
- Coach and guide rather than insist
- Take calculated risks
- Build demand for collaborative tools and approaches
- Ensure grass roots buy-in
- Master collaborative tools for distance leadership
- Reward people for sharing, rather than for hoarding, information
- Align recognition and reward system around collaboration
- Perpetuate collaborative culture by instilling it in others
- Be consistent in attitude while embracing innovation

to run against the grain of innovation. However, consistency of leadership at Toyota means a continuing commitment to principles and to the Toyota production system. This means constantly recognizing opportunities for change and improvement, understanding the value of innovation, and comprehending methods of reducing waste.

For Gary Convis, leadership consistency also refers to personality and focus. Before joining Toyota, he encountered more mercurial managers who allowed their moods to drive their management approaches. In the United States, we often use the phrase *management style*. This suggests personality-driven and perhaps shoot-from-the-hip leadership without much input or consensus. This contributes to command-and-control management in which team members often need to assess the boss's mood before approaching him or her. Collaborative leadership is less about individual moods and styles and more about guiding team members, listening to their concerns, and welcoming input.

ENCOURAGING STRATEGIC THOUGHT

Asking people to think about the big picture helps them turn on their brains.

Collaborative leaders encourage team members to think like they are responsible for the department, the plant, the campus or the company. Asking people to think about the big picture helps them turn on their brains, develop innovative ideas, and share those ideas with others. Command-and-control leaders often insist that team members think like underlings and do as they're told. Sadly, this approach stifles the personal development and professional evolution of team members, squanders opportunities for innovation, and chases away good people.

In contrast, collaborative leaders seize opportunities to empower team members. Sales people must feel that leaders trust their judgment about customers. Manufacturing people must feel that leaders have confidence in their knowledge of the

Collaborative leadership requires walking in the shoes of others and inviting others to walk in your shoes.

assembly line. Collaborative leaders welcome strategic thought and input from everybody, because such input is critical to the company's success. Creating value involves asking people at all levels of the company to develop a vision and share it with others. In short, collaborative leadership requires walking in the shoes of others and inviting others to walk in your shoes.

Must do all in the context of a strategic impact perspective — If your not improving / enabling strategy and creating customer value (value-in-the-doing) your not of value to your company / org !!!.

CHAPTER 10

THE GLOBAL COLLABORATIVE ENTERPRISE

G*lobal* is one of many buzz words companies love to embrace. The word suggests that the organization has muscle. The word also connotes having a broad view and perhaps sensitivity to regional cultures. In fact, many companies who open one or two sales offices abroad consider themselves global. But what constitutes the real deal?

UNDERSTANDING THE GLOBAL COLLABORATIVE ENTERPRISE (GCE)

True global companies go well beyond marketing, selling and supporting their wares worldwide. They design, assemble, and produce products and services concurrently around the world. This book's definition of *global collaborative enterprise* (GCE) is a collection of interdependent companies that engage in shared creation of value, often in real time. These companies are suppliers and customers of one another or, using the current parlance, business partners.

In this model, one interdependent company—usually the largest—leads, integrates and facilitates the GCE. Often the leading company takes responsibility for quality and markets the products. However, rather than pounding its chest and perhaps bullying suppliers, the leading company realizes and recognizes its interdependency with business partners.

> One interdependent company—often the largest—leads, integrates and facilitates the Global Collaborative Enterprise.

The GCE leverages multiple regional and organizational cultures and utilizes the best talent regardless of location. Rather than passing work back and forth in a relay-race fashion, the GCE embraces the deserialization of work. Also, the GCE exploits time zones and may leverage *mirror zones* and global work sharing to design, assemble and produce products and services twenty-four hours a day. Mirror zones are time zones that are either opposite or nearly opposite. They provide an opportunity for work sharing between zones to create a round-the-clock work environment.

> Mirror zones are time zones that are either opposite or nearly opposite.

In such scenarios, collaborators in different time zones share jobs and functions. When night falls in one part of the world and people are completing their work day, the sun rises in the mirror zone where people with identical or similar functions begin work. They may collaborate in real time during the workday overlap and asynchronously while their mirror zone colleagues sleep. Within their own or similar time zones, people collaborate in real time while engaging in concurrent design or production of products and services. Only a handful of companies, including Boeing and Toyota, fit our definition of a global collaborative enterprise. However, the efficiency of this approach means that many other companies are following suit.

BOEING: FROM LINEAR TO CONCURRENT DESIGN

Boeing has reinvented itself as a global enterprise, and this book calls the company a *global collaborative enterprise*. The enterprise, as

Boeing sees it, includes the supply chain, customers, and customers' customers which include airline passengers. Boeing considers itself both a technology company and a large-scale systems integrator which is mov-

> Boeing considers itself both a technology company and a large-scale systems integrator

ing away from designing and manufacturing products by itself. The company has divested one of its major manufacturing facilities in Wichita, Kansas, and that facility has become a Boeing design partner. In the old days, Boeing designed and built airplanes itself. On the company's newest airplane project, the 787, Boeing retains ultimate authority for the design, safety and certification of the entire airplane. However, Boeing's global design partners are designing and manufacturing much of the airplane.

What makes this business shift viable is a major change in the way the Boeing enterprise designs parts and assemblies. The change is from *linear design* to *concurrent design*. To understand this shift, let's examine the history. During World War II, an elaborate mechanism developed for the way aerospace engineers worked on drawings. The hub of their design work was a big, steel file cabinet called the vault. The vault contained just one copy of each drawing, and only one person at a time could work on a drawing. Whenever the engineer wanted to work, he or she had to see a clerk and sign out the drawing. Then colleagues knew, by checking with the clerk, that the drawing was in the hands of a particular engineer. Engineers used colored pencils on the drawings: red to delete, green to add, blue to comment.

Now think about eight people in Moscow taking one drawing out and everybody marking in red at the same time and being able to see what all eight people are doing in color on their document. Think about those eight people describing to eight other people in Everett, Washington the changes they have made, describing their blue comments in detail, discussing potential constraints, and referencing other drawings on which other teams are collaborating. This is the nature of concurrent design, a phrase that many companies use but few companies really do.

Through the 1980s, aerospace companies designed all parts individually, made wood representations of each part, and assembled them three times with three levels of detail. Boeing called these class one, class two, and class three mockups. The B-2 bomber was one of the first airplanes designed "in a box," meaning designers eliminated mockups and used computers. The 777 was the first commercial "digital" airplane. Designers used CAD/CAM tools not only to design but also to assemble parts for the 777, developing a digital model. Boeing created visualization software which lets users virtually fly through the plane and examine parts, wire bundles and hydraulic lines.

As engineers interacted and used these tools, they had moved well beyond the old vault days. However, their approach to design remained linear, which limited collaboration. One engineer built and designed each part by computer. Once each part was finished, engineers assembled those parts. Often partners traveled to Boeing facilities for design reviews.

> *For the 787, Boeing has moved beyond* linear design *to* concurrent design.

For the 787, Boeing has moved beyond linear design to concurrent design in which engineers design parts and assemblies, which are groups of parts that fit together, at the same time (see figure 10.1). This

Figure 10.1 The Boeing 787 Dreamliner. For this airplane, Boeing and its global partners engage in concurrent design, which is inherently more collaborative than linear design.

approach is inherently more collaborative and radically reduces product cycle time. This means that people working for some forty-five companies—all part of the Boeing global enterprise—in multiple time zones, representing many regional cultures concurrently design the four million parts of the 787. It is, in short, an extraordinary effort.

Using "product lifecycle management" tools from Dassault Systemes including Catia, version 5 CAD/CAM, a Boeing engineer designing a bracket that attaches to an assembly can collaborate with an engineer who's designing the assembly. In contrast, linear design would require designing the bracket first and then fitting it into the assembly. Besides creating the 3D geometry together screen-to-screen, the engineers interact via video and, at times, through audio-only connections.

BOEING'S ENGINEERING CENTER: A COLLABORATION HUB

Boeing's engineering center, built for the 777 project and now used for the 787, sits on Puget Sound in the city of Everett, Washington about twenty miles north of Seattle. Dubbed the "twin towers," the white, nearly square buildings 40-87 and 40-88—connected by a walkway—are more wide than they are tall. It was here that nearly all of the design work for the 777 occurred. At the time, all of Boeing's partners for the 777—primarily Japanese heavy industrial companies commonly called "heavies"—were colocated in the twin towers. When the design was complete, they returned to Japan to build the parts. That was before what CIO Scott Griffin terms "high-level" collaboration. We will compare the different levels of Boeing collaboration later in this chapter.

For the 787, many of the partners spend time in Everett as the collaboration begins. They get acquainted, learn to use common tools, and establish professional intimacy. Then they return to their home countries to design the airplane. From eleven multimedia rooms in the twin towers, Boeing engineers collaborate with more than thirty global design partners on the 787. There is at least one multimedia room at each partner location. Design partners include

Kawasaki, Fuji and Mitsubishi in Japan as well as other partners in Italy, the UK, Australia, and Russia, among other locations. Many partners also collaborate on updating and supporting the company's other commercial airplanes.

Global Collaboration Center is the name Boeing gives to its largest multimedia room in Everett. Boeing designed the center specifically for the 787 (see figure 10.2 on page 231). The GCC is reminiscent of NASA's Mission Control with several rows of chairs and tables. In front are two large, high-definition plasma screens on which engineers can videoconference, web conference, and share 3D CAD/CAM. Bandwidth capability runs up to 1.5 megabits per second (mbps) over IP and 384 kbps over ISDN delivering thirty frames-per-second.

John La Porta and Bill Wilson of Boeing's airplane services integration team ensure the design partners effectively collaborate and communicate using the capabilities of the multimedia rooms. La Porta, who has worked in production and tooling, grew up in an Air Force family and lived in France and Germany as a child. Wilson, a mechanical engineer who worked with the team who designed the Boeing visualization tool, has lived in South America and in Mexico. They both grasp the potential of collaborative tools, but more importantly they understand multiple regional cultures and how to bridge them. In short, they have a global perspective.

"You're working together instantaneously, real-time and you're going to save that time and money because you're right here doing it right now," according to La Porta. As an Everett engineer examines the landing gear on his notebook computer, the same fly-around motion appears on the large plasma screen at the front of the room. And, with almost no lag time, the same motion appears on the partners' screens often a continent away. An electrical power line appears in blue. One partner is responsible for the line, while another partner creates the landing gear structure.

Since the landing gear folds up into the airplane, that particular motion involves incredible complexity. Therefore, the routing for the blue cabling is critical. "It requires an immense amount of interaction to get it right. And it's got to be right or the airplane can't fly," says Wilson as he demonstrates the visualization tool in the

Global Collaboration Center. Using the tool, teams can look around the nooks and crannies of the airplane, examining parts and searching for potential problems. They can also click on any part and learn which partner "owns" the part and get contact information for the people involved.

The visualization tool runs on any PC with at least a DSL connection to the Internet. This allows people to participate in design reviews with an audio-only connection from their desks. Through high-level collaboration, the cabling team and landing gear structures team can change the design using CAD/CAM tools, which run on workstations. Before concurrent design, the landing gear structures team would have completed most of its work before the cabling team got involved. When problems arose, it could take weeks or even months to resolve them. The current economics of aerospace, however, requires compressed product cycle times. Through concurrent design, every team gets involved and collaborates on design simultaneously.

Through concurrent design, every team gets involved and collaborates on design simultaneously.

GLOBAL WORK SHARING: TAKING COLLABORATION TO NEW HEIGHTS

Every morning at 7:00 a.m. Pacific time, engineers in Everett, Washington, in Moscow and in other locations gather virtually for a collaborative session. Engineers beginning their day in the United States greet their global colleagues via videoconference on one screen and on another screen view, annotate, and discuss work that their counterparts have been tackling. The cross-cultural team uses CAD/CAM and visualization tools to examine aircraft assemblies in 3D and make needed changes.

Aside from leveraging aerospace tradition and engineering talent regardless of geography, global collaboration also lets Boeing exploit mirror zones. Moscow, for instance, is almost exactly on the other side of the world from Everett with a time difference of eleven hours. So when Everett is sleeping, Moscow works. This allows the potential of a twenty-four-hour day without geographical boundaries. Both sides could work two and a half shifts per day with overlap. So rather than an engineer designing a part individually, he or she could work on the part in the morning and design the part concurrently with a geographically-separated colleague in the afternoon.

Before they go home, designers in Moscow connect with their counterparts in Everett who are arriving for work. During the session, engineers engage in a show-and-tell. For each part they're working on, they bring their colleagues up to speed on their progress, describe potential problems, relay information regarding which geometry they have stored and which people are working on specific versions. "It's just like turning over a shift on a battleship where you ask permission to come to the bridge and a captain debriefs you and says here are the challenges I found overnight. Here's what I think's going to happen. Here's what I did during the day," explains Boeing CIO Scott Griffin.

Collaborative sessions among Boeing design partners typically occur via videoconferencing. Video unites the geographically-separated team, providing professional intimacy and helping maintain trust. This, in turn, helps bridge regional cultures. Engineers share CAD/CAM and other applications while interacting through video face-to-face or sometimes through an audio-only connection. Besides participating in geographically-dispersed teams, engineers also engage in concurrent design screen-to-screen with colleagues in the same room.

THE THREE LEVELS OF COLLABORATION AT BOEING

Boeing CIO Scott Griffin has classified collaboration into three levels: low, mid, and high. These levels are as much about the purpose and complexity of collaboration as about the tools. Some tools, such as videoconferencing, may be used in multiple levels.

Low-level collaboration involves exchanging information through threaded text discussions and working together on documents, spreadsheets and other material through team sites. Low-level collaboration also involves synchronous exchanges through videoconferencing and web conferencing.

Mid-level collaboration enables Boeing to collaborate via the Web with companies that may be partners on some projects and competitors on others. An aerospace industry consortium called Exostar, of which Boeing is a founding member, provides a web-based, mid-level collaboration toolset.

High-level collaboration involves designing parts, plans, tools, and processes concurrently among global partners. For high-level collaboration, Boeing uses advanced CAD/CAM tools to create 3D geometry while also using audio and videoconferencing. "High level collaboration is rarified air. There are not many people doing it," notes Griffin.

> High-level collaboration involves designing parts, plans, tools, and processes concurrently among global partners.

Griffin has delineated these different collaboration tiers so that Boeing people can better understand which tools and approaches make sense for specific activities. For instance, advanced CAD/CAM tools are inappropriate for geographically-distributed accounting people interested in sharing a payroll application or presentation slides in real time. The best solution for this type of collaboration, which is low-level, is web conferencing. Team sites work well for storing slides and documents, but for Boeing the database size falls short for engineers who need to create and store 3D geometry in high-level collaboration. That activity requires the high-end CAD/CAM system.

Griffin uses low-level collaboration in leading the thousands of people who work in Boeing's IT organization. To reach all of those people at once, Griffin uses webcasting. Before Monday leadership team meetings, Griffin and his direct reports use team sites to post, change, and edit presentations. He also uses web conferencing from planes, hotel rooms, airports and Boeing facilities to conduct leadership meetings and participate in many other interactions with colleagues. Griffin uses a personal videoconferencing system in his office primarily to interact with customers and suppliers, because maintaining professional intimacy in such situations is critical. However, he finds video overkill for most internal interactions. Since data generally drives those conferences, web and audio conferencing are adequate.

HOW BOEING'S MOSCOW DESIGN CENTER COLLABORATES TO CREATE AIRPLANES

Tucked away in the McDonald's building two blocks from the Kremlin, designers engage in advanced collaboration. At Boeing's Moscow Design Center, engineers collaborate with counterparts in Everett, Washington in designing airplanes including sections of the 787 Dreamliner. The effort breaks new ground in the aerospace industry, because Boeing is using concurrent design.

The approach helps reduce development-to-delivery time by a year as compared with the development schedule for the 777, Boeing's previous commercial airplane program. Efficiency defines not only the 787 design process, but also defines the airplane itself. The 787 uses 20 percent less fuel than other airplanes of comparable size.

Sergey Kravchenko, the president of Boeing Russia, has developed a maverick's reputation. He often ignores the confines of convention, pushing past countless barriers to achieve his objectives. So when another Boeing visionary, CIO Scott Griffin, invited him to a lab in Bellevue, Washington in the late 1990s to view a prototype multimedia conference room for "high-level" collaboration, Kravchenko quickly realized the potential and seized the opportunity.

The rooms provide two high-definition, plasma screens, one displaying a videoconference (see figure 10.2). The other screen allows engineers on both sides of the ocean to use CAD/CAM tools and work together in 3D models. Kravchenko and Griffin realized that Boeing could tap Russia's rich aerospace heritage and contract engineering talent to create a rich, collaborative global design operation.

"I dreamed that it would become a way of life, and it actually did," says Kravchenko. "We've done a lot of very interesting things that nobody else did before. I don't believe that there was ever a global work sharing project in aerospace engineering on the scale that we have here." Kravchenko began the operation with five engineers that Boeing sent to Seattle for training and orientation.

Now Boeing's Moscow Design Center employs over a thousand engineers plus managers and support personnel. Boeing has bridged regional cultures and developed considerable trust among Russian and American colleagues. This, in turn, has fueled collaboration, turning the Russian engineers into real-time design partners.

The time difference between Moscow and Everett, Washington means that as the work day winds down in Moscow, engineers interact with their Everett counterparts who are beginning their day. The approach compresses the product design schedule and boosts efficiency. Also, Boeing can tap Russian aerospace talent, which is particularly adept at simplifying design approaches.

Boeing now includes multimedia conference rooms as standard operating procedure in each new facility it opens in other regions. "The global collaborative environment that we work in is an absolutely critical element in the success of Boeing mobilization," Kravchenko insists. "We just do things so much faster and we are way more efficient than before."

©Boeing™. Used under license.

**Figure 10.2   Boeing's Global Collaboration Center in Everett, Washington.
From here, engineers collaborate with Boeing's Moscow Design Center and
many global business partners.**

COLLABORATING WITH COMPETITORS

To understand mid-level collaboration at Boeing, let's rewind to the year 2000. Boeing was using twenty-one different purchasing systems, and the company conducted twelve million procurement transactions. Clearly, an opportunity existed to streamline the process. Paul Pasquier, then director of Boeing's eBuy procurement program, used the financial industry as a model. He looked at moving purchasing transactions to the Web. Because in the aerospace industry competitors often partner, Boeing teamed with four of its largest competitors—BAE Systems, Lockheed Martin, Raytheon and Rolls Royce—plus suppliers to create the Exostar consortium. The consortium would offer a "shared, controlled working environment." The goal was to reduce costs by bringing commonality to purchasing throughout the industry.

The concept was that some processes deliver no competitive advantage, and therefore Boeing and its competitors could all become more efficient by adopting the same approach to those processes. Besides providing paperless purchasing and electronic sourcing, Exostar also focused on collaboration. Team sites called "virtual team rooms" allow consortium members to collaborate on certain projects while competing on others. Exostar, which offers an unusually secure level of encryption, provides a neutral space where competitors store their data. Each company determines rules regarding access to the data it stores with Exostar.

Exostar lets competitor/partners and suppliers share data not only asynchronously through team "rooms" but also synchronously through integrated web conferencing. Before this collaborative consortium existed, Boeing had to send drawings for parts it needed to suppliers. There was little interaction, let alone collaboration. The supplier would send back a bid, Boeing would approve it, and then a machinist might begin fashioning aluminum into a fastener or bracket.

Exostar's team rooms allow the machinist working for the supplier to view a document while discussing the bid with the Boeing designer. The machinist can get a better understanding of what the designer wants to accomplish and which specifications can be changed so that the part can be produced more economically. The machinist might tell the designer that if he or she can modify the plan, the supplier can trim half the cost.

Exostar also provides the capability to view—but not to create—3D modeling. So on a regular PC over the web, collaborators can view the geometry that engineers have created using high-end work-stations. In the past, Boeing had to send videotapes of 3D models to suppliers who lacked not only workstations but also the skills and experience of manipulating the geometry. Using Exostar, viewing the geometry is easy.

"It's not the official design, but it sure shows where you have, let's say, gaps, overlaps, where you have parts that won't fit, those types of things, so that really starts facilitating your discussions," according to Boeing's Paul Pasquier. "We're figuring out how to work with our partners, knowing what their limitations are, their training levels and their equipment." Exostar has allowed Boeing and its competitor/partners to move beyond a U.S.-centric aero-space industry culture. Says Pasquier, "Long story short, we've learned some great things from our British partners on this and it's starting to break down all sorts of barriers."

MIGRATING TO "HIGH-LEVEL" COLLABORATION

At times, partners begin using mid-level collaboration and then migrate to high-level tools. The sweet spot for Exostar is at the beginning of a project when interaction among teams is limited. For instance, a propulsion group early in a project may focus more on collaborating within the group and interact with other teams on occasion. As the project progresses, the propulsion group may need to regularly collaborate with teams in other engineering disciplines.

As multiple teams start interacting with work flow and begin approving one another's designs, they may use Exostar less and use what the industry calls product data management (PDM) tools more often. These tools include CAD/CAM applications that pro-duce 3D models. Engineers use these tools to create the configura-tion control drawings that govern the design of the airplane. The process of shared creation using these tools among partners is what Boeing considers high-level collaboration.

In high-level collaboration, Boeing's global partners work together seamlessly as though there were no geographical boundaries.

In high-level collaboration, Boeing's global partners work together seamlessly as though there were no geographical boundaries. This level of collaboration requires an incredible amount of trust, because once Boeing has worked with the partner to perfect a part, the risk is that the partner will build the same part for a Boeing competitor. Design partners share the same database that stores 3D models and use the same high-end work stations and identical configuration control drawings.

These tools allow global concurrent design of parts, plans, tools and processes for airplanes potentially round-the-clock. Someone builds the components while somebody else designs the assembly while someone else figures out how to make the assembly while someone else decides how to put assemblies together into subassemblies that will fit into the airplane.

As engineers design the 787 on one screen, they either videoconference on a second screen or use an audio-only connection. Because the work product is proprietary, only designated partners in the Boeing enterprise may participate in high-level collaboration.

The CAD/CAM tools Boeing uses have allowed the company to develop in 3D the entire process of designing, assembling, delivering and maintaining the 787. Using the toolset, manufacturing engineers design robotics and the production line while designers conceive the airplane. So, the manufacturing people and designers access and use the same data. If somebody moves a door six inches to the left, the change automatically occurs in everybody's data and everybody receives an email notification.

This concurrent design and manufacturing approach helps break down silos that often develop among product design, manufacturing, and maintenance. Barriers melt away, as collaboration occurs among these functions. Using the tools, geographically-dispersed engineers conduct reviews that show in 3D whether wires are too hot or whether rotors could clip another part. They can then revise the design and manu-

The concurrent design and manufacturing approach helps break down silos that often develop among product design, manufacturing, and maintenance.

facturing process with a few mouse clicks. Also, engineers use the toolset to conduct stress tests. The CAD/CAM and collaboration tools combined with the concurrent design approach allow Boeing and its partners to design and build larger, more integrated sections of the 787. Boeing expects this will contribute to its goal of reducing the time each airplane spends in final assembly from the standard twelve to fifteen days for other wide bodies to three days for the 787.

TOYOTA'S BRAND OF "HIGH-LEVEL" COLLABORATION

While Boeing is perhaps in a class by itself when it comes to high-level collaboration, another company that is setting the standard for global collaborative enterprises is Toyota. Toyota uses the same CAD/CAM tools as Boeing does, though Toyota has highly customized the tools to fit its development process. Toyota product designers, manufacturing specialists, and business partners connect globally through its Visual and Virtual Communication system (V-comm). V-comm integrates videoconferencing with advanced CAD/CAM and a shared knowledge base allowing the simultaneous design of cars and the manufacturing processes that support production.

Designers build virtual vehicles, build virtual production lines, and develop and test quality assurance systems. Globally-dispersed designers and manufacturing specialists use V-comm to simulate the contact and position of parts, simulate assembly procedures for line workers, and visualize and test the viability of the finished product. This allows them to detect potential problems before assembly begins.

Plants, design centers, and partner sites then feed the data back to R&D operations, which then shares the data with plants around the world. The system reduces cycle time, enhances product quality and boosts production efficiency. Because of the visual nature of V-comm, the system reduces language barriers. This, in turn, helps bridge regional cultures and enhances shared creation.

While Toyota engineers previously had to do considerable rework in resolving issues, this higher level of collaboration lets Toyota people across many functions test and visualize the design

Courtesy of Toyota Motor Corporation

Figure 10.3   Through high-level collaboration, Toyota tests and visualizes design and production processes up front.

and production process up front (see figure 10.3). Jeffrey K. Liker notes in *The Toyota Way* that Toyota's business and manufacturing processes combined with advanced CAD/CAM tools have reduced product development time from forty-eight months when Toyota began using CAD in the 1980s to less than twelve months.

As we have discussed, implementing collaborative tools falls short without the culture to support collaboration. Similarly, introducing collaborative design technology in hopes of fixing a broken production process would produce limited results. According to Liker, Toyota "took a finely tuned development process, based on exceptionally well-trained engineers and excellent technical leadership, and surgically inserted information technologies to enhance it." Clearly, Toyota's collaborative culture also paved the way for the introduction of high-level collaboration tools. We have already discussed the role of *nemawashi* or making decision slowly by consensus, which is a key tenet of the Toyota Way.

Consensus clearly has contributed to a collaborative culture at Toyota (see figure 10.4). Other factors include the shift from an export-oriented company to an enterprise that manufactures abroad. In 1984, Toyota began manufacturing outside Japan by forming New United Motor Manufacturing, Inc. (NUMMI) in Fremont, California. NUMMI is a joint venture with General

Courtesy of Toyota Motor Corporation

Figure 10.4   The principle of *nemawashi*, which means making decisions slowly by consensus, contributes to Toyota's Culture of Collaboration.

Motors. Toyota now manufactures vehicles at over fifty sites in twenty-six countries and must bridge many regional cultures as engineers and others collaborate.

"We realized that we can't get the job done by ourselves," according to an American manager who works at Toyota headquarters in Tokyo. To infuse each foreign plant with its collaborative culture, quality manufacturing processes and the Toyota Way, Toyota assigns a "mother plant" to each foreign plant. A dozen plants in Japan serve as mother plants to two or more plants in other countries.

> To infuse each foreign plant with its collaborative culture, quality manufacturing processes and the Toyota Way, Toyota assigns a "mother plant" to each foreign plant.

Let's say a plant in Vietnam encounters a mechanical problem with machinery. Engineers at the mother plant can establish a videoconference or, in some cases, an audio link with engineers in Vietnam. Together they can view images or video of the broken switch or damaged part, view maintenance videos and animation and use the same tools at each location to simulate solutions until they solve the problem.

The approach is reminiscent of collaboration between astronauts and mission controllers during the Apollo 13 flight on April 14, 1970. Gene Kranz in his book *Failure is Not an Option* (Simon and

Schuster, 2000) details the mission, which was also the subject of a 1995 film directed by Ron Howard. Nearly fifty-six hours into the Apollo 13 launch, an oxygen tank exploded, compromising the spacecraft and threatening the lives of astronauts.

With fuel, water and oxygen running out, astronauts and mission controllers brainstorm against the clock. On the ground and in the spacecraft, they cut, tape, and assemble a maintenance solution to prevent the crew's breathing from poisoning the cabin atmosphere with carbon dioxide. They use cardboard, a plastic bag, a sock and a hose. Ultimately, the astronauts beat the odds and return safely to Earth. In both *Apollo 13* and Toyota's mother plant system, a team with a maintenance problem collaborates with a team many miles away, using the same tools, to create a solution.

The Global Production Center applies the Toyota Way principle of kaizen, *which means continuous improvement, to the mother plant system.*

Toyota has enhanced its mother plant system by inaugurating a Global Production Center (GPC) in Toyota City, Aichi Prefecture, Japan. The company is also building branches of the GPC in Kentucky and in Belgium. The GPC applies the Toyota Way principle of *kaizen*, which means continuous improvement, to the mother plant system. The GPC standardizes methods across mother plants and prepares plant managers and shop floor supervisors to launch new vehicle models. Each GPC provides three V-comm rooms, allowing experts to collaborate on assembly procedures at a distance, and reducing preparation time for new model rollouts.

SHIFTING TO CONCURRENT PRODUCTION AT INDUSTRIAL LIGHT & MAGIC

Industrial Light & Magic is shattering traditional notions of film industry post production and special effects by moving from linear to concurrent production and sewing the seeds of a global collaborative enterprise. In chapter 5 we discussed how ILM's move to an integrated systems framework has ensured that its artists, regardless of specialty, work in the same system environment and have access to the same data. Each can reach out beyond his or her specialty to perform some tasks that traditionally belonged to a specific discipline or function.

The next phase of ILM's collaborative evolution involves allowing multiple people, regardless of physical location, to work concurrently on scenes and shots. They can reach into shots simultaneously and collaborate screen-to-screen while seeing and talking to one another through videoconferencing. Sound familiar? It's a parallel trend to what Boeing and Toyota are doing in their industries. ILM is abandoning a linear pipeline in which specialists work independently and toss the result to another function. In place of the linear pipeline is a star-shaped approach. "You can think of the scene in the middle of a room and artists coming at it from all sides, some of them painting, some of them building more models, some of them setting up lights…and it's by definition, collaborative," according to Steve Sullivan, ILM's director of R&D.

Industrial Light & Magic is abandoning a linear pipeline in which specialists work independently and toss the result to another function.

Engineers in manufacturing environments tend to collaborate more methodically, asking questions like "Who owns that part?" or "Let's look at the last version." With artists, however, the creative juice often pumps so fast that protocols must evolve for what's considered polite. As ILM shifts to a new way of working and considers culture in collaboration, the company is tackling etiquette questions. Should collaborators talk at the same time? Can anybody grab a mouse and start changing anybody else's creation?

Because collaboration involves collaborative chaos, artists *should* talk at the same time unless technology constraints impose a voice delay. That's the way people interact face-to-face. In the most effective brainstorming, people must feel free to jump into the discussion. Of course, in a split second, one person takes the floor. However, changing somebody else's creation requires judgment. Ideally, collaborating artists consider their creations shared, rather than individual, works. If, however, an individual has begun creating the work solo and then others join the process, collaborators should ask if it's alright to change the work before clicking the mouse.

ILM often models its collaborative culture on that of movie sets. In such environments, many specialists—wardrobe, camera, lighting—interact to shoot a film. The difference in the virtual environment is that it offers a less sensory experience. Rather than working in a crowd on a set where smell, touch, and peripheral vision all help in collaborating, the virtual environment offers a more sterile workspace. "You can imagine social problems being magnified by an order of magnitude when you have multiple people able to change or edit the same sequence," Sullivan notes.

ILM's collaborative model is reminiscent of multiplayer video games in which geographically-distributed players engage each other in a common, virtual space. Rather than competing as gamers do, ILM artists collaborate without the barriers of separate systems. A server holds the master scene, and geographically-dispersed collaborators log into that scene and make changes concurrently. The director and a visual effects supervisor may join the collaborative session from Los Angeles. The producer could participate from another location. So that artists can remember the director's reaction, the director can annotate or mark up the shots and attach audio or video notes for reference. But more importantly, the artists can work in real time together.

Part of ILM's collaborative approach involves utilizing global talent. As the company launches an animation division in Singapore, animators on both sides of the Pacific can share work. This will likely mean leveraging the work day in both time zones so that ILM can complete projects more efficiently. Since outsourcing is becoming common in post production, an opportunity exists for ILM to join with business partners and form a global collaborative enterprise (GCE). ILM can deserialize the process by providing access for partners to the company's systems. "Instead of having the finished result sent back and forth," says Sullivan. "We can look very early on in the process and say, 'Yeah. This is the right track. Keep going.' Or 'Correct it,' if it's not."

HOW COMPANIES IN OTHER INDUSTRIES CAN LEVERAGE THE GCE

We have discussed concurrent design as enabling the global collaborative enterprise. Boeing and Toyota are setting the standard in the aerospace and automobile industries, respectively. Industrial Light & Magic has set the stage for migration to a GCE. While manufacturing airplanes and cars requires a degree of complexity perhaps unique to those industries, we can nevertheless apply the model of the global collaborative enterprise more broadly. Consider these industries:

Architecture and Construction

Building airports, subways, semiconductor plants and other large-scale projects involves huge budgets and plenty of complexity. Architects, structural engineers, mechanical engineers, and others collaborate to create projects. These teams often form for the project and disband when the job is done. Applying the global collaborative enterprise model to the design, building, and maintenance of these projects could reduce project time and boost efficiency by eliminating false starts and anticipating potential problems, saving perhaps tens of millions of dollars per project.

Applying the model could also help break down barriers between construction companies and their clients. The architecture and construction industry has been using collaborative tools for years. San Francisco-based Bechtel Corporation, for example, has used video-conferencing to link construction sites with engineering teams. The company has also used 3D modeling plus audio links to connect architects, engineers, and others in multiple continents.

3D/I, a design and construction company with a dozen locations in the United States, has instilled a collaborative culture throughout its operations. Besides talking the talk by including collaboration as a core value and encouraging team members to skip levels by bringing concerns directly to senior leaders, 3D/I walks the walk by giving everybody access to the same project data and information. This short circuits the traditional tendency to hand down and hand up information through a hierarchy.

The company has developed its own web-based tool to accomplish information democracy. The tool also interfaces with web conferencing so that geographically-distributed team members can view and discuss 4D modeling and simulation applications. 4D adds the fourth dimension of time, according to 3 D/I. Specifically, 4D combines 3D simulation with a Gantt chart showing a graphical illustration of a project schedule.

Imagine applying the level of collaboration that Boeing uses in aerospace to architecture and construction. Teams employed by multiple partners—all part of the same global collaborative enterprise—can visualize the entire process of designing, building, and maintaining an airport before laying the first brick. With concurrent design, work that normally happens sequentially could occur simultaneously. As the architect designs a section, engineers can view the design and put the plans into action.

Large-scale construction companies can exploit mirror zones by implementing global work sharing in the engineering and design processes. A team in San Francisco, California could collaborate with counterparts in Bangalore, India using videoconferencing combined with advanced CAD for real-time interactions. When one team goes to sleep, collaboration could continue using such asynchronous tools as video mail.

Consumer Goods

Consumer goods companies frequently reformulate products, retool production processes, and redesign packaging. By forming global collaborative enterprises, these companies can utilize the best talent regardless of location. Partners in one time zone can share design work with counterparts in another time zone. Take, for example, the launch of a new packaged cookie. Collaboration for such a project involves flavor professionals, package designers, manufacturing people, marketing teams, and many others. With a Culture of Collaboration and the right tools, these professionals can be physically located in almost any location.

Package designers can connect via video to production planners or manufacturing managers. They view and change the packaging together using 3D modeling so that if the production planners believe the box dimensions are too large, the planners and the designers adjust the size accordingly. However, this approach requires professional intimacy among multiple functions. For this to occur, the company must discourage barriers from developing among departments by encouraging cross-functional interaction and fostering a collaborative culture.

Procter & Gamble is rapidly becoming a global collaborative enterprise. The company uses visualization to simulate the entire product process from concept to delivery. Using 3D CAD, the company tests how existing production lines can handle a new package design. P&G can determine how a new bottle works with conveyor belts and how well packaging will stand up to shipping.

Also, 3D visualization lets P&G determine how products will look on store shelves, how products will perform during normal use, and how different consumers will react to different products. People in product development, manufacturing, and sales and distribution collaborate using visualization tools. The approach eliminates the need to create physical models for consumer testing, and reduces time-to-market by an order of magnitude.

Healthcare

In healthcare, the global collaborative enterprise lets people access the best medical expertise regardless of geography and time. If a hospital patient in Sacramento, California develops symptoms at 2:00 a.m., the nurse or resident documents the problem and a specialist typically gets involved hours later. If a Moscow hospital were part of the enterprise, however, a cardiologist working at 1:00 p.m. Moscow time could view echocardiograms or other images in real time while interviewing and examining the patient through telemedicine. When night falls in Moscow, the doctor's counterpart in Sacramento could take over for both hospitals. During the shift overlap, the two physicians could collaborate through video and simultaneously examine patient charts and medical images.

Because, in this example, two regional cultures are partnering in treating the same patients, the dynamic dimension of cross-cultural collaboration creates solutions that include a broader perspective. Just as they do in aerospace, the Russians have a rich tradition in diagnosis and treatment of disease. However, they are likely to approach medicine a little differently. The same is true of physicians in Japan and China. A healthcare GCE creates 24/7 diagnosis and treatment in which hospitals can break the distance barrier and access the best talent regardless of geography.

Television and Film Production

In the television and film business, production typically occurs in stages. The writer produces a script. Other writers rewrite the script. The producer lines up financing and hires a director. A casting company finds actors for each part. After the director determines a shooting schedule, production begins. The cast and crew often travel to the shooting location, and film or videotape the raw product. Often weeks later, editors and post-production teams create the final product.

Clearly, the entertainment industry involves more collaboration than many other industries. The question is whether a higher level of collaboration would increase efficiency, produce a better product in less time, and eliminate percentage points from astronomical budgets. In a GCE, post-production people in one time zone share work with counterparts in another time zone. In such an enterprise, there is greater collaboration among functions that would otherwise interact less.

Also, sequential processes become simultaneous. Traditionally, post-production teams are limited to using whatever material the crew has shot. The shooting schedule is complete, and re-shooting scenes is out of the question. But suppose post-production people got involved much earlier? They could collaborate with the director, director of photography, production designers and others by viewing and changing 3D models of the production process long before shooting begins. Since editors and post-production people play a huge role in determining how the finished product looks, including more of their input earlier makes more sense than simply dumping material in their laps later in the process.

Advertising

This industry shelters countless creative people whose work benefits from collaboration. Advertising is particularly time-sensitive, because the introduction of products must coincide with the production of commercials and print ads. In the political realm, a candidate responds to another candidate ASAP, particularly during the last few weeks before an election. This means advertising professionals must sometimes turn around ads in a day.

Applying the GCE to advertising enables geographically-dispersed copywriters to "group write" print ads and scripts for commercials screen-to-screen while connecting through audio or video. In contrast to developing advertising campaigns in sequential steps, concurrent design and production brings more functions together earlier in the process. In this way, a director of photography views storyboards in real time with the team developing the concept so that his or her input gets reflected almost immediately. This reduces changes that typically occur—at greater cost—after production begins. Also, global work sharing of such functions as layout and design could reduce turnaround time by several hours a day, creating particular value during political season.

The Global Collaborative Enterprise

- Recruits the best talent regardless of location
- Develops products and services in real time
- Leverages mirror zones
- Exploits global work and job sharing
- Capitalizes on input from multiple regional cultures
- Capitalizes on input from multiple organizational cultures
- Recognizes interdependency among business partners
- Provides dedicated collaborative spaces
- Integrates collaborative tools and capabilities into work styles
- Uses visualization

COMMON ATTRIBUTES OF GLOBAL COLLABORATIVE ENTERPRISES

The Global Collaborative Enterprise deserializes work through real-time collaboration.

Global collaborative enterprises share common attributes. Some of these attributes also apply to highly-collaborative companies that may ultimately participate in GCE's. The GCE deserializes work through real-time collaboration. Accomplishing this requires visualization, which combines 3D modeling with videoconferencing. Visualization not only allows geographically-dispersed collaborators to view each others' efforts but also can enable people to work concurrently while developing a product or service. The ability for collaborators to see and hear one another while engaged in shared creation becomes the GCE's glue, because we are able to overcome many hurdles of time and space while creating a virtual production environment.

The GCE and highly-collaborative organizations also leverage physical and virtual spaces specifically designed for collaboration. Such spaces are no substitute for integrating collaboration into work styles. We must have access to collaborative capabilities from desktops and mobile devices. However, there are many situations in which a dedicated collaborative space helps us create value.

Toyota uses the Visual and Virtual Communications System (V-comm). To link geographically-dispersed collaborators, Dow uses iRooms. So that animators can work together regardless of location, DreamWorks uses Virtual Studio Collaboration (VSC). At the Mayo Clinic, cross-functional teams develop services in the SPARC unit. And in designing airplanes, Boeing people use the Global Collaboration Center.

So despite presence-enabled tools and the ability to work with colleagues from anywhere, dedicated collaborative spaces can extend the Culture of Collaboration.

CHAPTER 11

THE NEW SCRIPT

As the Culture of Collaboration permeates work styles and life-styles, our habits are changing faster than we may realize. Indeed, the script has changed. Wallace Stevens, describing the impact of modernism on poetry, put it this way: "The scene was set; it repeated what was in the script. Then the theatre was changed to something else. Its past was a souvenir."

REINVENTING BUSINESS MODELS

The new script is the deserialization of work.

The Culture of Collaboration is having a similar impact on business models and the nature of work. We can no longer act on the same old stage and read the same old lines. Performing our part and then passing the work product along to another function or level is the old script that is no longer relevant. The new script is the deserialization of work. While asynchronous interaction has its place, collaboration is increasingly rich, real-time and spontaneous.

Remember how in acquiring Gillette, Procter & Gamble required immediacy in integrating two organizations? Often there's no time to wait for answers or for input into decisions. Through presence-enabled tools, as we've learned, people from multiple functions come together spontaneously to develop solutions. The Boeing 787 Dreamliner is the culmination of Boeing's shift to concurrent design. Rather than designing parts, plans, tools and processes sequentially, the Boeing global collaborative enterprise designs all of these simultaneously. Add to this the use of mirror zones, which let GCE's exploit time, talent and tools round-the-clock.

The result is a phenomenal reinvention which slashes product cycle time and lets Boeing remain competitive amid the changing economics of the aerospace industry. And, as we've learned, countless other industries face similar economic pressures. The realities of the entertainment industry are encouraging Industrial Light & Magic to curb silo syndrome by moving to common systems and tools so that any artist can engage in shared creation with any other artist, regardless of specialty.

EMPOWERMENT FOR IMPROVEMENT

The Culture of Collaboration is about dollars and cents. But it's also about empowering us to enrich our work and improve our lives.

The Culture of Collaboration is about dollars and cents. But it's also about empowering us to enrich our work and improve our lives. The Mayo brothers, at the turn of the last century, realized that medicine was a cooperative science. Today anybody, whether he or she builds examination rooms or performs surgery, may collaborate in developing healthcare delivery services at the Mayo Clinic. The SPARC unit enables cross-functional innovation and brainstorming and extends Mayo's Culture of Collaboration. It's certainly more satisfying to collaborate in developing services and products than to receive instructions and pass them along to somebody else.

Similarly, Toyota expects input into key decisions from every function, region, and level. Because of that input and because management trainees may spend time on the assembly line, leaders develop deep respect for those who physically assemble cars. Team members who think, contribute, and collaborate accomplish more for themselves and for the organization. And remember how the Myelin Repair Foundation has rewritten the rules in medical research? The impetus was the frustration of its founders with the status quo. By discouraging competition among researchers and building a consortium with a collaborative culture, Scott Johnson and Russell Bromley can conceivably help develop a cure for multiple sclerosis in less than a third of the time it might otherwise take.

There are signs that the Culture of Collaboration is spreading to other areas of medical research. In funding AIDS vaccine grants, The Bill and Melinda Gates Foundation requires researchers to share data and results. Over two decades of competition among researchers has failed to produce an AIDS vaccine. Like their counterparts investigating multiple sclerosis cures, AIDS researchers traditionally guard results until a prestigious medical journal publishes their articles. Frustrated with the status quo, Microsoft Chairman Bill Gates and his wife, Melinda, are committing $287 million for five-year grants to scientists willing to pool results. For researchers, it's a radical shift in the nature of their work.

THE EVOLUTION OF CULTURE

We used to think of larger organizations as embracing bureaucracy. Decisions took seemingly forever, often because decision makers preferred to play it safe. In such a climate, making no decision was better than risking a bad one.

But the in-box culture is dead.

Increasingly, business rejects bureaucracy as wasteful and costly. Innovative companies have already determined that linear, serial approaches—which are inherently bureaucratic—create red tape and red ink. In contrast, we create greater value when we engage one another in real time;

Innovative companies have already determined that linear, serial approaches—which are inherently bureaucratic—create red tape and red ink.

design products and processes concurrently; and collaborate across functional, business unit, corporate and regional boundaries.

And we've also learned that four key trends—technological, economic, cultural and regulatory—drive the desire for spontaneous collaboration. The convergence of video, voice and data over Internet Protocol (IP) enables organizations to extend collaborative culture. Consider how Dow Chemical Company provides collaborative spaces called iRooms, linking colleagues in forty-three countries. And for those unable to reach an iRoom, convergence allows them to easily participate from airports, hotels, homes, and practically anywhere.

The economic trend is exploiting the best talent at the best price regardless of geography. The 787 Dreamliner is the physical manifestation of this trend. We've examined Boeing's approach to tapping global talent through a network of business partners comprising the global collaborative enterprise (GCE). And we've discovered that the input of multiple regional cultures provides complimentary perspectives that can get the job done more efficiently. Utilizing the Moscow Design Center, Boeing capitalizes on the Russian aerospace tradition. And through mirror zones, the company substantially reduces time-to-market by creating a nearly twenty-four-hour design and production environment.

The cultural trend involving the expectation of immediacy clearly drives spontaneous collaboration and the deserialization of work. Let's again consider P&G's Gillette acquisition. Colleagues expected one another to roll up their sleeves, hash out problems, and resolve differences between two organizations. There was no patience for letting requests for input pile up in in-boxes. The desire for immediate feedback drove the use of presence-enabled tools including IM and web conferencing. Because of the cultural expectation of immediacy, anything short of spontaneity would have increased frustration and could have short circuited the integration.

The regulatory trend of compliance with federal, state and local laws encourages organizations to adopt common platforms, systems and reporting processes. For W.R. Grace & Co., compliance with Sarbanes-Oxley has leveled hierarchies by encouraging communication and collaboration among three hundred managers and "owners" of business processes and between those managers and senior leadership. And we discussed the Fortune 50 pharmaceutical company in which people across functions and business units have collaborated to identify commonalities in regulations that apply in multiple organizational areas. Collaborating to comply not only keeps the organization on the right side of laws, but also extends the Culture of Collaboration.

REVISITING THE TEN CULTURAL ELEMENTS OF COLLABORATION

Some organizations like Toyota, the Mayo Clinic and the Myelin Repair Foundation were designed with collaboration in mind. But we've discovered that others like Ford Motor Company's Premier Automotive Group and W.R. Grace & Co. are adopting the Culture of Collaboration. Regardless of the path, the Ten Cultural Elements of Collaboration are present when collaboration works.

As Boeing engineers in Everett, Washington and at the Moscow Design Center design and produce the 787, what is the role of **trust**? Substantial. When Toyota people develop great ideas and better processes, does **sharing** matter? You bet. As Monster encourages collaboration between development centers in the Czech Republic and the United States, do **goals** play a role? Of course. In reducing specialization and moving to common systems at Industrial Light & Magic, is **innovation** a factor? Certainly. As nurses, marketing people, facilities specialists, doctors and others brainstorm to develop healthcare services at the Mayo Clinic, does **environment** matter? Absolutely.

As researchers affiliated with the Myelin Repair Foundation develop a cure for multiple sclerosis in a fraction of the anticipated time, does their work involve **collaborative chaos**? Indeed. As Ford Motor Company's Premier Automotive Group bridges cultures across silos and brands, does **constructive confrontation** make a difference? Sure. When DreamWorks Animation artists collaborate in a global production environment, how important is **communication**? Essential. In transitioning from the appointment model to real-time collaboration around the globe, what is the significance of **community** to The World Bank? Fundamental. And within each organization that collaborates, what does **value** represent? Everything.

NEW NOTIONS OF COLLABORATION

And what about the evolution of tools? Well, those that we use for fun become integrated into work styles and organizational culture more readily than tools we use only for work. Many teenagers and adults spend countless hours gaming, for which 3D is increasingly the medium of choice. Enjoying that 3D experience as a pastime raises the ante for work-oriented applications.

Just as exchanging IM with friends has prepared us to use IM for work, gaming conditions us to expect 3D for a range of business-oriented applications and collaborative tools. And as we get more desensitized to the presence of cameras—at intersections, in conference rooms, on desktops and elsewhere—video plays an increasingly greater role. In fact, collaborative organizations realize that real-time, interactive video is essential to collaboration.

Today we struggle to collaborate as effectively at a distance as we do in the same room. Tomorrow the challenge becomes the reverse. As we get more accustomed to collaborating at a distance, creating value while sharing the same physical space falls short. So meeting in the same room may seem awkward, while engaging in shared creation from anywhere with colleagues in planes, trains, automobiles, homes and offices globally may feel more natural.

> *Today we struggle to collaborate as effectively at a distance as we do in the same room. Tomorrow the challenge becomes the reverse.*

Often what we call collaboration in shared physical space is nothing more than a meeting, because we may produce no work product and arguably create little value. So as collaboration at a distance becomes the norm, collaboration in the same room may require reengineering. The better collaboration at a distance gets, the more the bar is raised for collaboration in the same room.

People will tolerate greater technology challenges in tools used for virtual collaboration, because these tools help establish professional intimacy and curb the need to travel. Such benefits are absent when people share physical space. Therefore, it's a greater challenge to pry us away from standard meeting environments so that we can collaborate face-to-face. But it's happening. The Stanford Center for

Innovations in Learning (SCIL) and the Mayo Clinic's SPARC unit have chalked up early successes in this arena. Also, intelligent meeting systems let us capture, browse and search meetings based on key words in the audio and key events in the video. We can get a panoramic view plus a close-up of each participant. These emerging capabilities take knowledge sharing and organizational memory to new levels.

THE CHALLENGE OF CULTURE

Despite compelling tools and environments on the horizon, tools can only extend or enhance—rather than create—the Culture of Collaboration. Our biggest challenge involves organizational evolution. While

Tools can only extend or enhance—rather than create—the Culture of Collaboration.

some organizations embrace collaboration, many others endorse the word rather than its meaning. Some companies reject both the concept and the word, *collaboration.* Often promoting hierarchy and control, these organizations remain suspicious of anything that threatens the status quo. One such company, a bank in Britain, has told vendors its objective is to stifle communication and collaboration among all but a small, elite group of employees.

The bank blocks Internet access and restricts functionality of tools. The reasoning is that only five percent of employees are so-called information workers. These are the people who develop marketing campaigns, produce products, create strategy and supposedly think for a living. Management's view is that these are the only workers whose opinion counts. The bank considers the other 95 percent of employees "costs to be optimized." In other words, they are paid to do rather than to think. The more these workers collaborate and share information, the bank believes, the lower their output.

And doesn't the bank have a point? Tellers should be processing deposits and loan payments rather than thinking about how to make products better. Banks have marketing and strategy people at headquarters to develop services. If tellers collaborate with people in other functions, they will be less productive. For certain positions, companies just need people to do what they're told. Right? Wrong!

We have learned from Toyota, Boeing, Dow, Mayo and other organizations that good decisions include perspectives of people throughout the organization at every level. We have also discussed how better decisions often reflect input from many regional cultures and from multiple business partners. Therefore, tellers at the British bank undoubtedly have ideas that will contribute to better products, better customer service, and more effective business models. Sadly, their ideas are lost. The culture of control leaves knowledge, ideas and value untapped. Curbing collaboration crushes innovation.

So a struggle continues between the control paradigm and the Culture of Collaboration. These extremes, rooted in human nature, clash in many organizations. However, the necessity of maximizing time, talent and tools in the global economy gives the Culture of Collaboration an edge. The quest to innovate and create greater value drives the desire to collaborate as organizations embrace the global collaborative enterprise.

A struggle continues between the control paradigm and the Culture of Collaboration.

For more on collaboration including my blog, visit:
www.thecultureofcollaboration.com

NOTES

Preface:

p. ix, "Before the X5...": Evan Rosen, "BMW Uses Telecooperation to Design the first SAV," *Teleconference*, September/October, 1999, p. 20.

Chapter 1: Climate Shift: A Ripe Time for Rich, Real-Time Collaboration

p. 1. "We were running relay races…": Franklin Becker and Fritz Steele, *Workplace by Design* (San Francisco: Josey-Bass Publishers, 1995), p. 70. Becker and Steele contrast the relay-race and rugby models of work.

p. 8. "According to Wikipedia…": Wikipedia, http://en.wikipedia.org/wiki/Collaboration, viewed August 3, 2006.

p. 8. "The Oxford English Dictionary…": *The Oxford English Dictionary* online, www.oed.com, viewed August 17, 2006.

p. 8. "In *No More Teams*...": Michael Schrage, *No More Teams!: Mastering the Dynamics of Creative Collaboration* (New York: Currency, 1995), p. 32.

p.11. "Sometimes there is a disconnection…": Franklin Becker and Fritz Steele, *Workplace by Design* (San Francisco: Josey-Bass Publishers, 1995), p. 39.

p. 12. "Antibiotics, for example…": Alexander Fleming, Nobel Lecture, December 11, 1945 from *Nobel Lectures: Physiology or Medicine* (Amsterdam: Elsevier Publishing Company, 1964).

p. 12. "The Hirzel Canning Company…": Michael Barbaro, "Dawn of the New Can: To Survive Container Wars, It's Taking Surprising Forms," *The Washington Post*, October 17, 2004.

p. 13. "Researchers at Tate & Lyle…": Genevieve Frank, "Sucralose: An Overview," *Undergraduate Research Journal for the Human Sciences*, Kappa Omicron Nu honor society web site: http://www.kon.org/urc/frank.html, viewed March 5, 2006.

p. 13. "In 1953, a group headed by 3M's…": 3M Company web site, "Patsy Sherman and the Discovery of the Scotchgard Fabric Protector," http://www.3m.com/about3m/pioneers/sherman.jhtml, viewed May 4, 2006.

p. 14. "Former Intel CEO…": Andrew S. Grove, *Only the Paranoid Survive: How to Exploit the Crisis Points that Challenge Every Company and Career* (New York: Currency, 1996), p. 116.

p. 17. "And by 2010…": Jack Nilles. "Telework Forecast." JALA International, Inc. web site: http://www.jala.com/ustcforecast.php, viewed May 7, 2006.

p. 17. "It turns out that presenteeism…": Paul Hemp, "Presenteeism: At Work— But Out of It," *The Harvard Business Review*, October 1, 2004, p. 53.

p. 22. "Merriam-Webster Dictionary definition…": Merriam-Webster Online, www.m-w.com, viewed September 3, 2006.

Chapter 2: The Culture of Collaboration

p. 23. "As the brothers…" Helen Clapesattle, *The Doctors Mayo* (Minneapolis: The University of Minnesota Press, 1954), p. 131.

p. 23. "With thirty-seven people dead…" National Weather Service Forecast Office, La Crosse, Wisconsin, "The Rochester, MN Tornado of 1883," http://www.crh.noaa.gov/arx/events/rst_tor1883.php, viewed January 4, 2006.

p. 24. "It has become necessary…" Mayo Clinic, Rochester, Minnesota "History" http://www.mayoclinic.org/about/history.html. Viewed March 3, 2006.

p. 27. "Early in the last century…" Claude S. Fischer, *America Calling: A Social History of the Telephone to 1940* (Berkeley: University of California Press, 1994), p. 1.

p. 27. "In a 1916 public relations…" Claude S. Fischer, *America Calling: A Social History of the Telephone to 1940* (Berkeley: University of California Press, 1994), p. 2.

p. 31. "In their book…" Ed Michaels, Helen Handfield-Jones and Beth Axelrod, *The War for Talent* (Cambridge: Harvard Business School Press, 2001), p. 101.

p. 31. "Malcolm Gladwell, writing…" Malcolm Gladwell, "The Talent Myth," *The New Yorker*. July 22, 2002.

p. 38. "Groves writes…" Andrew S. Grove, *Only the Paranoid Survive: How to Exploit the Crisis Points that Challenge Every Company and Career* (New York: Currency, 1996), p. 122.

p. 38. "One such guideline…" Tom Kelley, *The Art of Innovation: Lessons in Creativity from IDEO, America's Leading Design Firm* (New York: Currency, 2001), p. 61.

p. 42. "Johnson, considered the best…" Ben R. Rich and Leo Janos, *Skunk Works: A Personal Memoir of My Years at Lockheed* (New York: Back Bay Books, 1996), p. 7

p. 42. "In *Skunk Works*…" Ben R. Rich and Leo Janos, *Skunk Works: A Personal Memoir of My Years at Lockheed* (New York: Back Bay Books, 1996), p. 108.

p. 47. "When there are higher levels…": Joe Mullich, "Ending the Emotional Friction of Virtual Teams." *Ziff Davis CIO Insight* (June 12, 2005).

p. 49. "BMW achieved its goal…" Evan Rosen, "BMW Uses Telecooperation to Design the First SAV," *Teleconference,* September/October, 1999, p. 20.

Chapter 3: The Collaborative Environment

p. 54. "At a San Antonio bar…" *International Directory of Business Biographies*, "Herb Kelleher," http://www.referenceforbusiness.com/biography/F-L/Kelleher-Herb-1931.html, viewed December 3, 2005.

p. 54. "In December of 1981…": Joe Wilcox, "The Compaq Portable: The Machine that Forever Altered the Computer Industry Landscape." *Computer Reseller News* "Special Supplement," http://www.crn.com/sections/special/supplement/816/816p61_hof.jhtml, viewed January 9, 2006.

p. 59. "Some workplace designers…": Robert J. Grossman, "Offices vs. Open Space: Deciding Whether to Tear Down the Walls or Build Them Up Isn't Always and Open-and-Shut Decision." *HR Magazine*, September, 2002.

p. 60. "The history of the cubicle…": Haworth web site, "The History of Haworth," http://www.haworth.com/Brix?pageID=152, viewed August 18, 2006.

p. 60. "We can start with the premise…" Robert Propst, *The Office: a Facility Based on Change* (Zeeland, Michigan: Herman Miller, 1977), p. 42.

p. 64. "There is a correlation…" David Packard, *The HP Way: How Bill Hewlett and I Built Our Company*, (New York: Harper Business, 1995), page 157.

p. 74. "Allen also discovered…" Franklin Becker and Fritz Steele, *Workplace by Design*, (San Francisco: Jossey-Bass Publishers, 1995), page 72.

p. 74. "In *Workplace by Design*…" Franklin Becker and Fritz Steele, *Workplace by Design*, (San Francisco: Jossey-Bass Publishers, 1995), page 70.

p. 86. "Karen Sobel Lojeski…" Karen Sobel Lojeski, Richard Reilly and Peter Dominick, "The Role of Virtual Distance in Innovation and Success," *Proceedings of the 39th Hawaii International Conference on System Sciences*. 2006.

p. 87. "Nevertheless, Microsoft is considering…" Barr, Adam. "Proudly Serving My Corporate Masters." blog about Microsoft's workplace, http://www.proudlyserving.com/archives/2006/04/microsofts_work.html. April 16, 2006.

Barr, a former Microsoft engineer, describes the company's new Workplace Advantage Plan that would reconfigure workspace to accommodate different types of workers. The idea is that private offices match the needs of some, but not all, Microsoft people.

Chapter 4: Lifestyles and Work Styles

p. 96. "When A.G. Lafley…" Julie Schlosser, "Another Space Race," *Fortune* (June 12, 2006), p. 120.

p. 95. "Taiichi Ohno…" Toyota Motor Corporation, "The Thinking Production System," Special Report from Public Affairs Division, October 8, 2003.

p. 95. "An environment where people…" Toyota Motor Corporation, "The Thinking Production System," Special Report from Public Affairs Division, October 8, 2003.

Chapter 5: Breaking Down Barriers

p. 120. "An overall Six Sigma process...": Wikipedia, http://en.wikipedia.org/wiki/Six_Sigma, viewed August 20, 2006.

p.128. "Boeing has implemented a program…" Bill Seil, "Design Anywhere, Build Anywhere, Work Anywhere," *Boeing Frontiers*, June, 2005.

Chapter 6: Integrating Collaborative Tools into Culture

p. 142. "These are Connectors, Mavens and Salesmen…" Malcolm Gladwell, *The Tipping Point: How Little Things Can Make a Big Difference* (New York: Little, Brown and Company, 2000), p. 34.

p. 150. "An inventor and tinkerer…" Jeffrey K. Liker, *The Toyota Way: 14 Management Principles from the World's Greatest Manufacturer* (New York: McGraw-Hill, 2004), p. 16

p. 150. "Inspired by U.S. supermarkets…" Jeffrey K. Liker, *The Toyota Way: 14 Management Principles from the World's Greatest Manufacturer* (New York: McGraw-Hill, 2004), p. 23.

Chapter 7: The Tao of Tools

p. 160. "A study conducted by…" Tandberg, "RoperASW and Tandberg International Survey: Results Overview." November, 2003.

p. 168. "Parker Hannifin, for example…" Evan Rosen, "No Time for Face Time," *NetworkWorld*, February 11, 2002, p. 34.

p. 169. "Think of all the video…": Evan Rosen, "Videos with Value: Companies Turn Idle Video into Digital Media Assets with New Management Tools," *InformationWeek*, October 4, 1999, p. 112.

p. 178. "One of the many reasons…": Evan Rosen, *Personal Videoconferencing* (Greenwich: Manning/Prentice Hall, 1996), p. 46.

Chapter 8: The Brave New World of Law and Compliance

p. 191. "In 1945, Vannevar Bush wrote…" Vannevar Bush, "As We May Think," *Atlantic Monthly*, July, 1945.

Chapter 9: Collaborative Leadership

p. 201. "In The Toyota Way…" Jeffrey K. Liker, *The Toyota Way: 14 Management Principles from the World's Greatest Manufacturer* (New York: McGraw-Hill, 2004), p. 178.

p. 214. "Andy Grove defines…" Andrew S. Grove, *Only the Paranoid Survive: How to Exploit the Crisis Points that Challenge Every Company and Career* (New York: Currency, 1996), p. 128.

p. 214. "Alfie Kohn argues…" Alfie Kohn, No *Contest: The Case Against Competition* (New York: Houghton Mifflin, 1992), p. 61.

Chapter 10: The Global Collaborative Enterprise

p. 237. "The approach is reminiscent..." Gene Kranz. *Failure is Not an Option: Mission Control from Mercury to Apollo 13 and Beyond* (New York: Simon & Schuster, 2000).

p. 238. "Toyota has enhanced..." Toyota Motor Corporation, "Toyota Global Production Center," Special Report from Public Affairs Division, October 8, 2004.

Chapter 11: The New Script

p. 247. "The scene was set..." Wallace Stevens, "Of Modern Poetry," *Parts of a World* (New York: Alfred A. Knopf, 1942).

p. 249. "There are signs that..." Marilyn Chase," Gates Won't Funds AIDS Researchers Unless They Pool Data," *The Wall Street Journal* (July 20, 2006)

SELECTED
BIBLIOGRAPHY

Barbaro, Michael. "Dawn of the New Can: To Survive Container Wars, It's Taking Surprising Forms." *The Washington Post* (October 17, 2004).

Bauer, Kent. "The Power of Metrics: CPM and Six Sigma—Common Themes, Part 2." *DMReview* (February, 2004).

Becker, Franklin and Fritz Steele. *Workplace by Design*. San Francisco: Jossey-Bass Publishers, 1995.

Besser, Terry L. *Team Toyota: Transplanting the Toyota Culture to the Camry Plant in Kentucky*. Albany: State University of New York Press, 1996.

Brandt, E.N. Growth Company: *Dow Chemical's First Century*. East Lansing: Michigan State University Press, 1997.

Bush, Vannevar. "As We May Think." *Atlantic Monthly* (July, 1945).

Cairncross, Frances. *The Company of the Future: How the Communications Revolution is Changing Management*. Boston: Harvard Business School Press, 2002.

Chase, Marilyn. "Gates Won't Fund AIDS Researchers Unless They Pool Data." *The Wall Street Journal* (July 20, 2006).

Clapesattle, Helen. *The Doctors Mayo*. Minneapolis: University of Minnesota Press, 1954.

Cutler, Ross et al. "Distributed Meetings: A Meeting Capture and Broadcasting System." *ACM Multimedia* (December, 2002).

Davenport, Thomas H. "Why Office Design Matters." Harvard Business School web site. (September 12, 2005).

Frank, Genevieve. "Sucralose: An Overview." *Undergraduate Research Journal for the Human Sciences* Kappa Omicron Nu honor society web site: http://www.kon.org/urc/frank.html, viewed March 5, 2006.

Fischer, Claude S. *America Calling: A Social History of the Telephone to 1940.* Berkeley: University of California Press, 1992.

Fleming, Alexander. Nobel Lecture, December 11, 1945 from *Nobel Lectures: Physiology or Medicine.* Amsterdam: Elsevier Publishing Company, 1964.

Gladwell, Malcolm. "The Talent Myth." *The New Yorker.* (July 22, 2002).

_____. *The Tipping Point: How Little Things Can Make a Big Difference.* New York: Little, Brown and Company, 2000.

Grove, Andrew S. *Only the Paranoid Survive: How to Exploit the Crisis Points that Challenge Every Company and Career.* New York: Currency, 1996.

Hemp, Paul. "Presenteeism: At Work—But Out of It." *The Harvard Business Review* (Oct. 1, 2004).

Huyck, Tom. "Innovation Incubator: SPARC Innovation Program Aims to Push Clinical Innovation in Pursuit of the Ideal Patient Experience." *Mayo Today.* (August/September, 2004).

Jouppi, Norman P, Subu Iyer, Stan Thomas, and April Slayden. "BiReality: Mutually-Immersive Telepresence." in the Proceedings of ACM Multimedia 2004 (New York, 2004).

Jouppi, Norman P. and Subu Iyer. "Telescopic Spatial Radio." *Journal of the Audio Engineering Society* (2004).

Jouppi, Norman P., Subu Iyer, and April Slayden. "A Headphone-Free Head-Tracked Audio Telepresence System." in the Proceedings of the 117th Audio Engineering Society Convention (San Francisco, 2004)

Kelley, Tom. Interview with Michael Krasny. *Forum.* KQED-FM, San Francisco. (October 13, 2005) .

_____. *The Art of Innovation: Lessons in Creativity from IDEO, America's Leading Design Firm.* New York: Currency, 2001.

Kohn, Alfie. *No Contest: The Case Against Competition.* New York: Houghton Mifflin, 1992.

Kranz, Gene. *Failure is Not an Option: Mission Control from Mercury to Apollo 13 and Beyond.* New York: Simon & Schuster, 2000.

Liker, Jeffrey K, Durward K. Sobek II, and Allen C. Ward. "Another Look at how Toyota Integrates Product Development." *Harvard Business Review* (July-August, 1998).

Liker, Jeffrey K. *The Toyota Way: 14 Management Principles from the World's Greatest Manufacturer.* New York: McGraw-Hill, 2004.

Lojeski, Karen Sobel, Richard Reilly, and Peter Dominick. "The Role of Virtual Distance in Innovation and Success." *Proceedings of the 39th Hawaii International Conference on System Sciences.* 2006.

Mayo Clinic web site: http://www.mayoclinic.org/about/history.html, viewed September 15, 2005.

McElroy, John (Producer). (2005). A Car is Born. [Video]. Livonia, Michigan: Blue Sky Productions, Inc.

Michaels, Ed, Helen Handfield-Jones and Beth Axelrod. *The War for Talent.* Cambridge: Harvard Business School Press, 2001.

Mullich, Joe. "Make Your Team Stronger By Bridging Virtual Distance." *Ziff Davis CIO Insight* (June 16, 2005).

———. "Four Ways to Make Virtual Teams Work." *Ziff Davis CIO Insight* (June 24, 2005).

———. "Ending the Emotional Friction of Virtual Teams." *Ziff Davis CIO Insight* (June 12, 2005).

Nilles, Jack. "Telework Forecast." JALA International, Inc. web site: http://www.jala.com/ustcforecast.php, viewed May 7, 2006.

Normile, Dennis. "Toyota Takes Auto Assembly Digital" *Design News* (February 5, 2001).

Packard, David. *The HP Way: How Bill Hewlett and I Built Our Company.* New York: Harper Business, 1995.

Propst, Robert. *The Office: A Facility Based on Change.* Zeeland, Michigan: Herman Miller, 1977.

Queenan, Joe. "The Cocktail Napkin as Magna Carta." *Chief Executive* (October 1, 1999).

Reingold, Edwin M. *Toyota: People, Ideas and the Challenge of the New.* London: Penguin Books, 1999.

Rich, Ben R. and Leo Janos. *Skunk Works: A Personal Memoir of My Years at Lockheed*. New York: Back Bay Books, 1996.

Robinson, Alan G. and Sam Stern. *Corporate Creativity: How Innovation and Improvement Actually Happen*. San Francisco: Berrett-Koehler Publishers, 1998.

Robotics Industries Association. "Digital Tools Provide Solution to High-Quality, Low Cost Manufacturing Demands." *Robotics Online* (October 1, 2002).

"RoperASW and Tandberg International Survey: Results Overview." *Tandberg* (November, 2003)..

Rosen, Evan. "BMW Uses Telecooperation to Design the First SAV." *Teleconference* (September/October, 1999).

———. "Extreme Videoconferencing." *InformationWeek.com.* (April 16, 2001).

———. "No Time for Face Time." *NetworkWorld* (February 11, 2002).

———. *Personal Videoconferencing*. Greenwich, Connecticut: Manning/Prentice Hall, 1996.

———. "The Videoconferencing Adventures of Rocky & Bullwinkle." *Teleconference* (June, 2000).

———. "VOW Power: Video Over Wireless is Just Around the Corner." *NetworkWorld* (October 23, 2000).

———. "Videos with Value: Companies Turn Idle Video into Digital Media Assets with New Management Tools." *InformationWeek* (October 4, 1999).

Sabbagh, Karl. *21ˢᵗ Century Jet*. New York: Scribner, 1996.

Schlosser, Julie. "Another Space Race." *Fortune* (June 12, 2006).

Schrage, Michael. *No More Teams!: Mastering the Dynamics of Creative Collaboration*. New York: Currency, 1995.

———. *Serious Play: How the World's Best Companies Simulate to Innovate*. Cambridge: Harvard Business School Press, 1999.

———. *Shared Minds: The New Technologies of Collaboration*. New York: Random House, 1990.

Seil, Bill. "Design Anywhere, Build Anywhere, Work Anywhere." *Boeing Frontiers* (June, 2005).

Schlosser, Julie. "The Great Escape: Forty Million American Employees Toil in Soulless Cubicles. How Did They Get There—and Can Business Ever Break Out of the Box?" *Fortune* (March 20, 2006).

Stevens, Wallace. "Of Modern Poetry." *Parts of a World*. New York: Alfred A. Knopf, 1942.

Stodder, Gayle Sato. "How to Build a Million Dollar Business." *Entrepreneur* (September, 1997).

Thomke, Stefan. "R&D Comes to Services: Bank of America's Pathbreaking Experiments." *Harvard Business Review* (April, 2003).

3M Company web site. "Patsy Sherman and the Discovery of the Scotchgard Fabric Protector." http://www.3m.com/about3m/pioneers/sherman.jhtml, viewed May 4, 2006.

Toyota Motor Corporation. "The Thinking Production System." Special Report from Public Affairs Division. (October 8, 2003).

———. "Toyota Global Production Center." Special Report from Public Affairs Division. (October 8, 2004).

Valenti, Michael. "Detroit, We Are Here!" *Mechanical Engineering* (March, 2001).

Webber, Alan M. "Reverse Brain Drain Threatens U.S. Economy." *USA Today.* (February 23, 2004).

Wellner, Pierre, Mike Flynn and Maël Guillemot. "Browsing Recorded Meetings with Ferret." IDIAP Research Institute (Martigny, Switzerland, 2004).

Wilcox, Joe. "The Compaq Portable: The Machine that Forever Altered the Computer Industry Landscape." *Computer Reseller News* "Special Supplement," http://www.crn.com/sections/special/supplement/816/816p61_hof.jhtml, Viewed January 9, 2006.

ACKNOWLEDGMENTS

It's not brain surgery or aircraft design, but writing a book is more collaborative than it appears. Or, at least, it should be. Many collaborators with considerable schedule demands and responsibilities have graciously contributed time, ideas, and material for this book. The author wishes to acknowledge these people and organizations for their contributions:

3 D/I: Yashpal Mehta, Ron Schappaugh, and Chuck Thompsen; The Alden B. Dow Archives: Daria Potts; Blue Sky Productions, Inc.: Dan Dancer, Chip Drake, John McElroy, and Denise Scioli; Boeing: Scott Griffin, Mary Kane, Sergey Kravchenko, Paul Pasquier, Brian Nelson, Tom Koehler, John La Porta, and Bill Wilson; Broad PR: Tracy Wemett; The Communications Media Management Association: Richard Van Deusen; Dassault Systèmes: Derek Lane; The Dow Chemical Company: Chris Duncan, Romeo Kreinberg, Andrew Liveris, Bob Long, Cindy Newman, and Mike Rehberg; DreamWorks: Patty Bonfilio, Manny Francisco, and Ed Leonard; Ford Motor Company: Sarah Adkins, Marisa Bradley, John Gardiner, Kay Lowry, Ursula Naber, Richard Parry-Jones, Jon Pepper, George Surdu, Kevin Timms, Rodger Will, and Jennifer Zanoni; Glance Networks: Rich Baker and Taylor Kew; GlowPoint: Michael Brandofino, Stuart Gold, and David Trachtenberg; Herman Miller: Linda Baron, Bruce Buursma, Cecelia Lyra, and Joe Schwartz; Hewlett Packard: Ken Crangle, Norman Jouppi, Anna Mancini, April Slayden Mitchell, Kristann Orton, Emma Wischhusen and

Susie Wee; Hill & Knowlton: Medalla Bautista; IBM: Seena Peck; Industrial Light & Magic: Tim Alexander, Megan Corbet, Miles Perkins, Suzy Starke, and Steve Sullivan; Internet2: Ken Klingenstein, Sharon Moskwiak, Lauren Rotman and Douglas Van Houweling; Intuit: Scott Cook, Noelani Luke; The Japan Society of Northern California: Lisa Kitayama; Johns Hopkins: Alex Nason; Mayo Clinic: Lee Aase, Ryan Armbruster, Laura Bates, Glenn Forbes, Warren Harmon, Deborah Holbein, Jeff Kane, Terri Knudson, Karen Koka, Phil McAteer, Mark McGlinch, Marvin Mitchell, John Murphy and Ann Woslager; Microsoft: Kurt DelBene, Jeff Raikes, John Richards, Erik Ryan, Yancey Smith, and Jeff Teper; Monster: Mark Conway; Myelin Repair Foundation: Russell Bromley, Carol Menaker, and Scott Johnson; Polycom: Jessica Kersey, Kimberly Klawuhn, Hans Schwartz, and Kevin Young; Procter & Gamble: Laurie Heltsley, Lisa Popyk, and Filippo Passerini; San Francisco Public Library: John Nelson; Stanford Center for Innovations in Learning: Eric Grant and Robert Emery Smith; TalkSwitch: Chris Brennan; Toyota: Bruce Brownlee, Gary Convis, Rick Hesterberg, Shin Kanada, Charlotte Lassos, Denise Morrissey, Mike Morrison, Paul Nolasco and Tatsuro Toyoda; The University of Chicago Hospitals: Brian Popko; The University of Illinois at Chicago: Tom DeFanti, Robert Kooima, and Dan Sandin; Weber Shandwick Worldwide: Carrie Riley; Waggener Edstrom: Aubrey Donnelson, Melissa Havel, Carrie Hoople, Erica Harbison, Erica Mortensen, Austin Stewart and Julie Woodbury; Wikipedia: Jimmy Wales; W.R. Grace & Co.: Bill Corcoran, Barry Kuhn, Bridget Sarikas, and Bob Tarola; The World Bank: Hajrudin Beca.

An extra mention goes to GlowPoint for providing access to its IP videoconferencing network during book research.

Also thanks to Marilyn Babb, Eduardo Bonsi, Audrey Caliguiri, Alexandra Cefalo, Elizabeth David, Keith David, Tony Debo, Laura Ehlert, Minako Hisamatsu, Richard Imbro, Lemuel Johnson, Linda Joyce, Allen Kessler, Dave Kirby, Yoko Kondo, Eugene F. "Gene"

Kranz, Jeanette Kretz, Ron Lehrman, Barbara Linderman, Gerald F. Linderman, Eugene Lisansky, Glen Mazzone, Marny Midkiff, Richard Midkiff, Alan Morris, Sue Morris, Milton Munke, Jim Parker, Hedley Rainnie, Tempe Reichardt, Russ Riesinger, Julia Roberts, Brenda Ropoulos, David Rubel, Julia Rubel, Catherine Saunders, Carol Simkin, Tom Whitaker, Mary Lou White, Richard White, Jody Weiner and Gilbert R. Whitaker, Jr.

⊰ ⊱

And extra thanks goes to Dottie Marsico for her incredible attention to detail and magnificent work in designing the book, her second effort with this author. Also, extra thanks goes to Calvin Chu for his skill in translating concepts into a compelling book cover, to the amazing artist Nancy Calef for logo design, to Michael John Parker for designing the book's superb web site, to David N. Ragan for a keen eye in editing, and to the staffs of Red Ape Publishing and Impact Video Communication, Inc. for collaborating on this project.

Special Thank you

The author wishes to extend a heartfelt, special thank you to Katherine Hirzel for her valuable insight, for coordinating research and images, and for her considerable input into the manuscript.

INDEX

ABOUT THE AUTHOR

Internationally-recognized communication and collaboration strategist EVAN ROSEN consults to Fortune 500, mid-sized, and start-up companies. A sought-after speaker and seminar leader, he has written numerous articles for business and technology magazines. He has also reported on Silicon Valley and the automobile industry for television stations, and his work has aired on CBS News and CNN. Rosen is Chief Strategist of Impact Video Communication, Inc. in San Francisco. This is his second book. He can be reached at erosen@impactvid.com.